Monika Sosnowska Tower

HATJE CANTZ

HAUSER & WIRTH

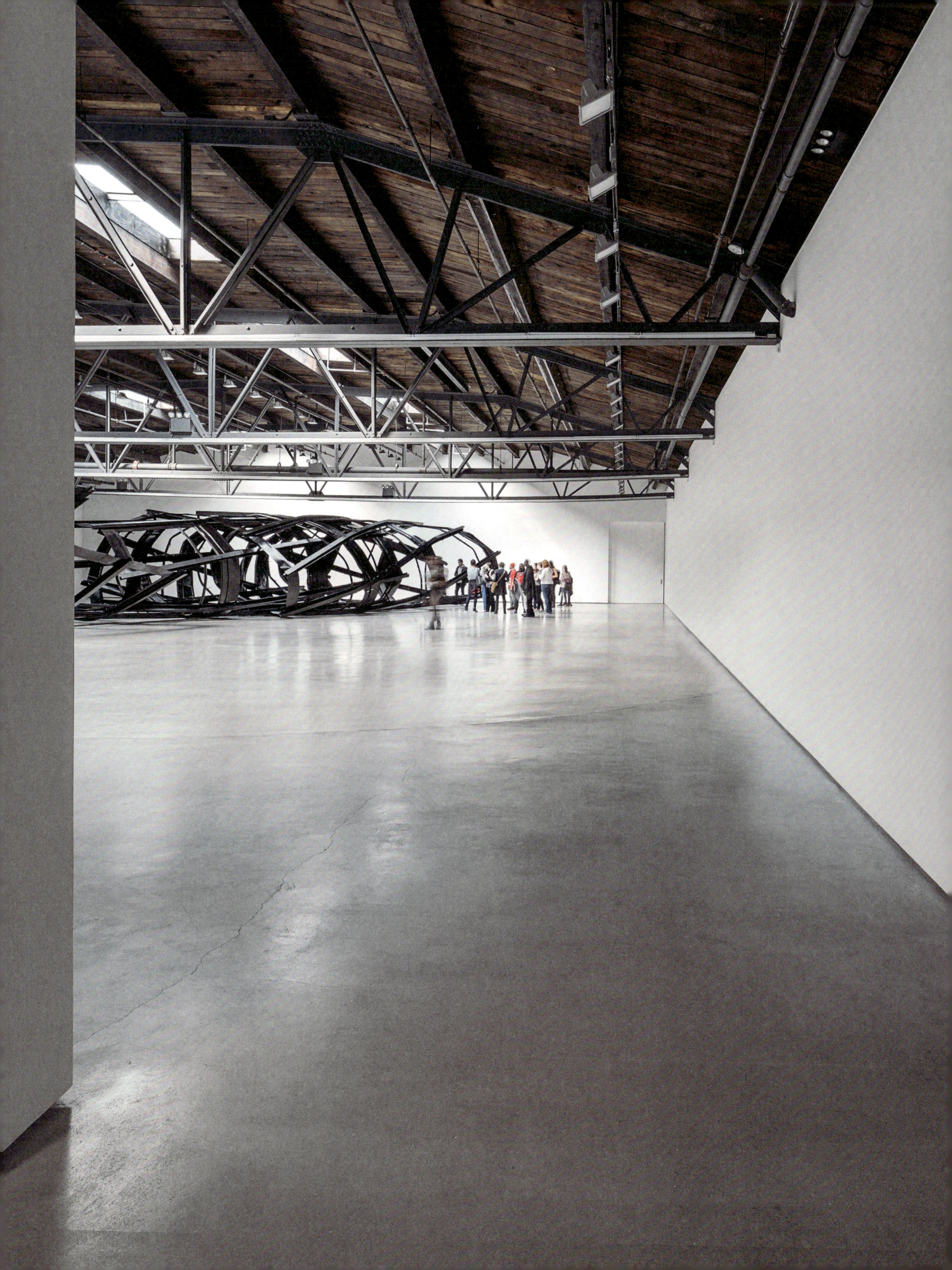

Contents

Tower

Poland, Spring/Summer 2014
Photographs by Juliusz Sokołowski

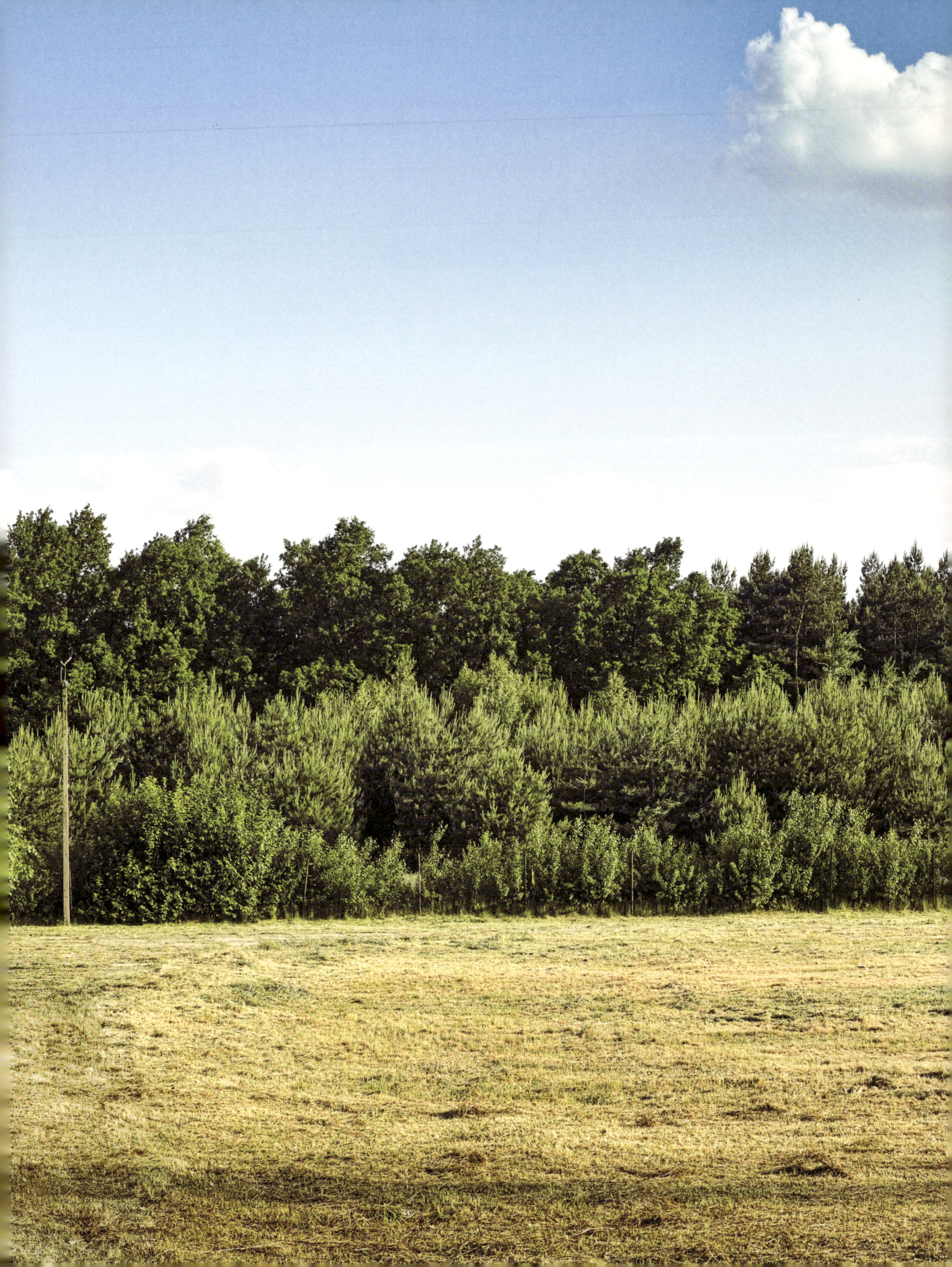

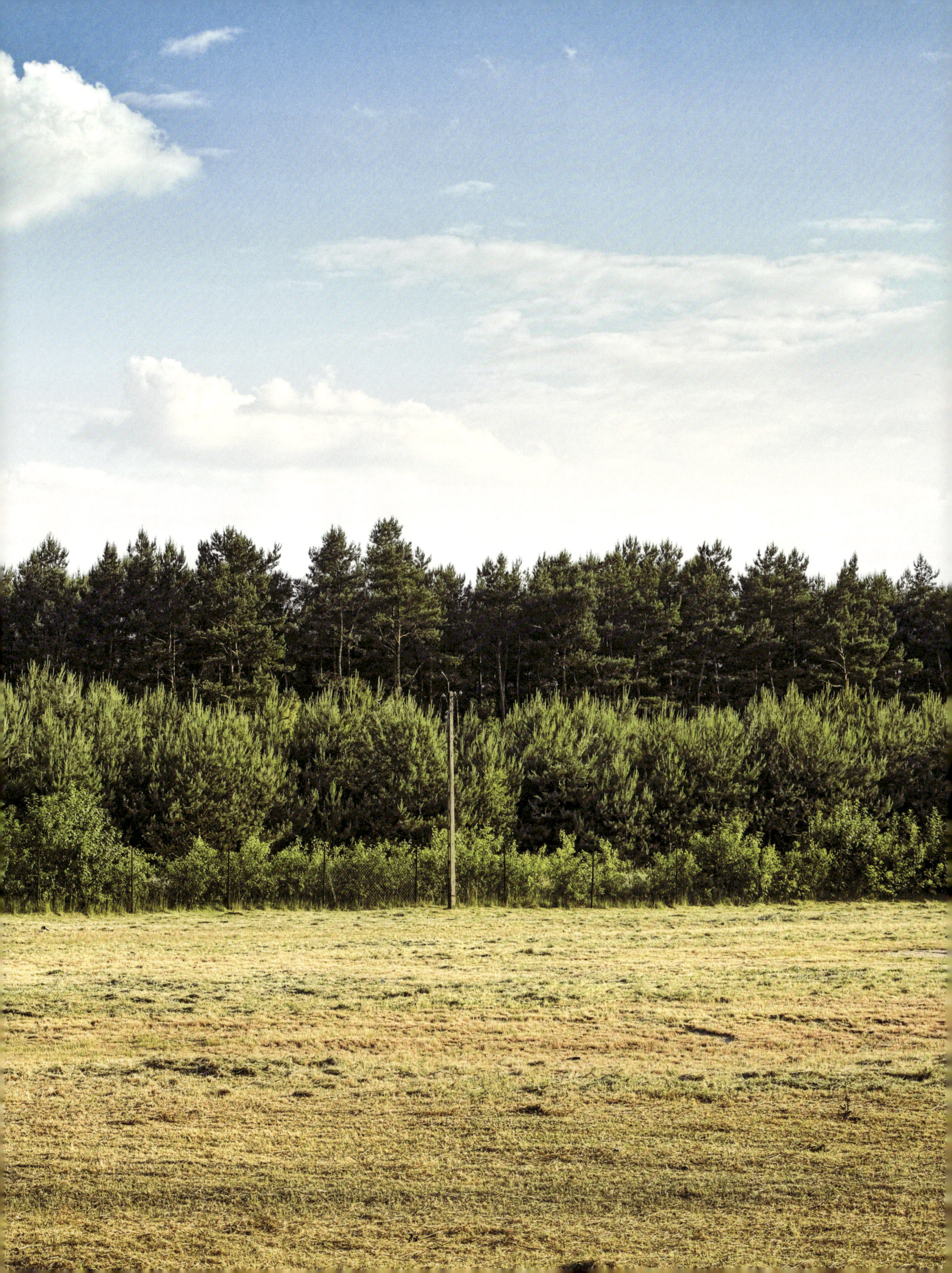

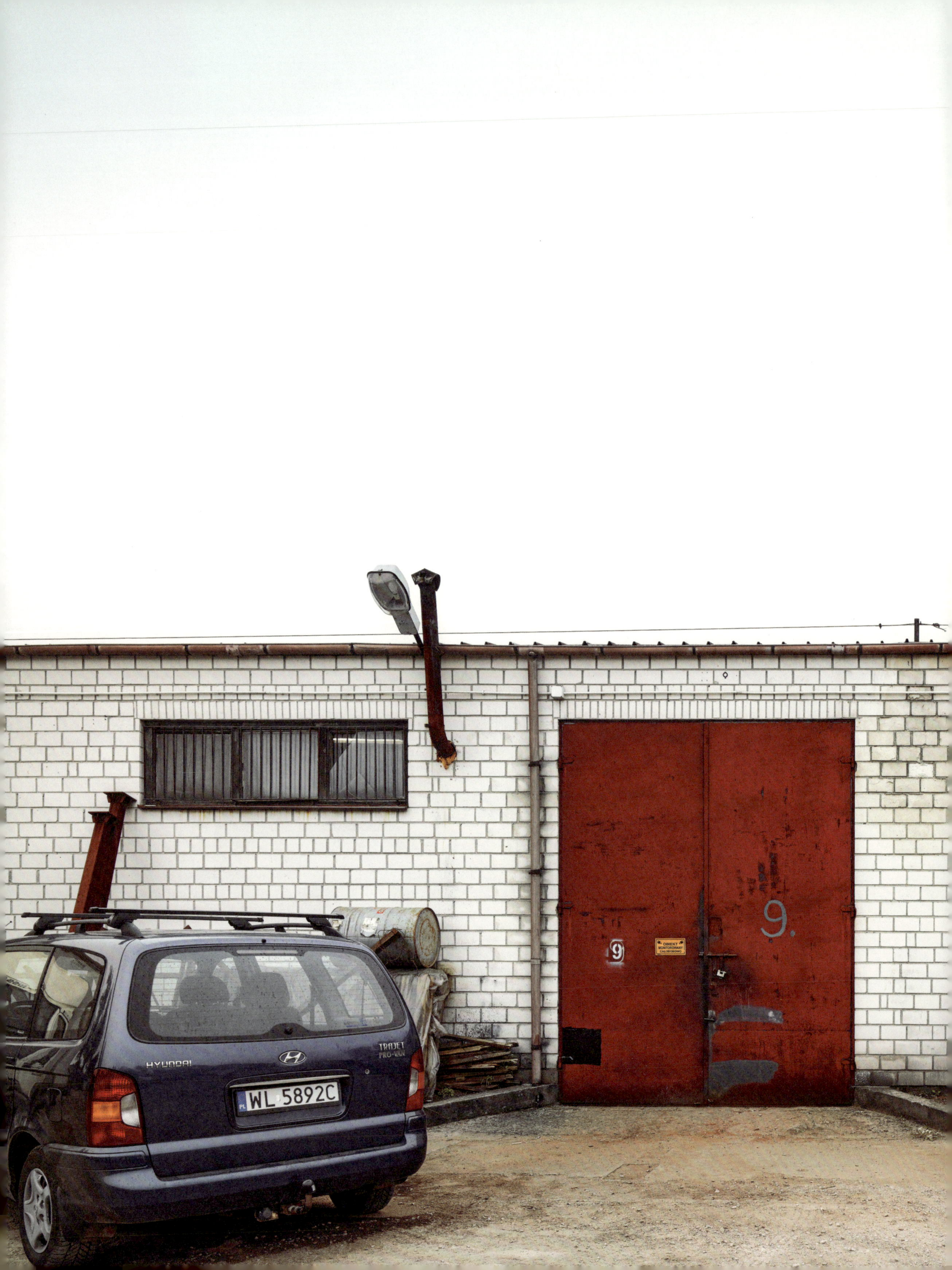
9
9.
TRAJET
PRO-VAN
HYUNDAI
WL 5892C

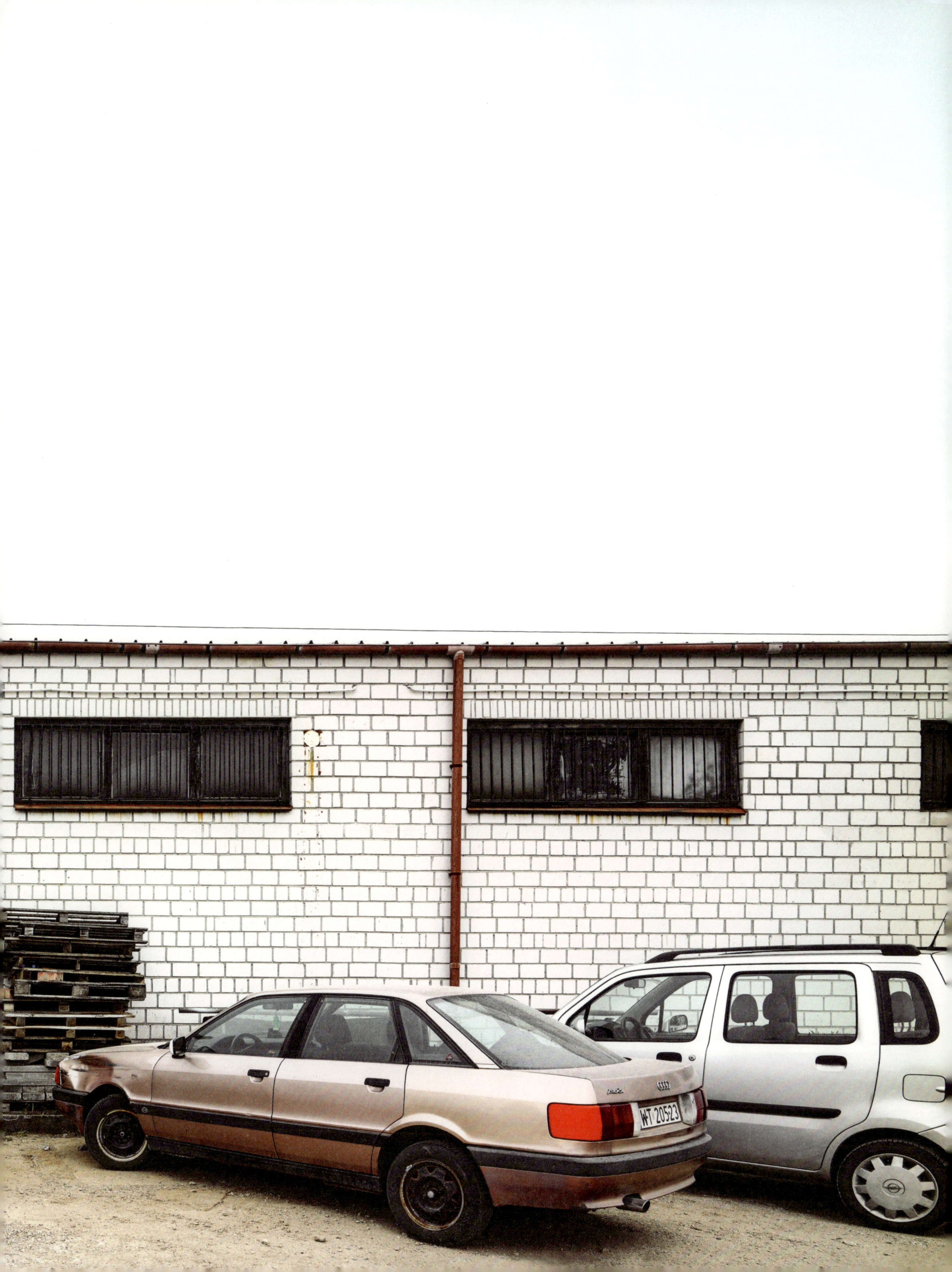
WT 20523

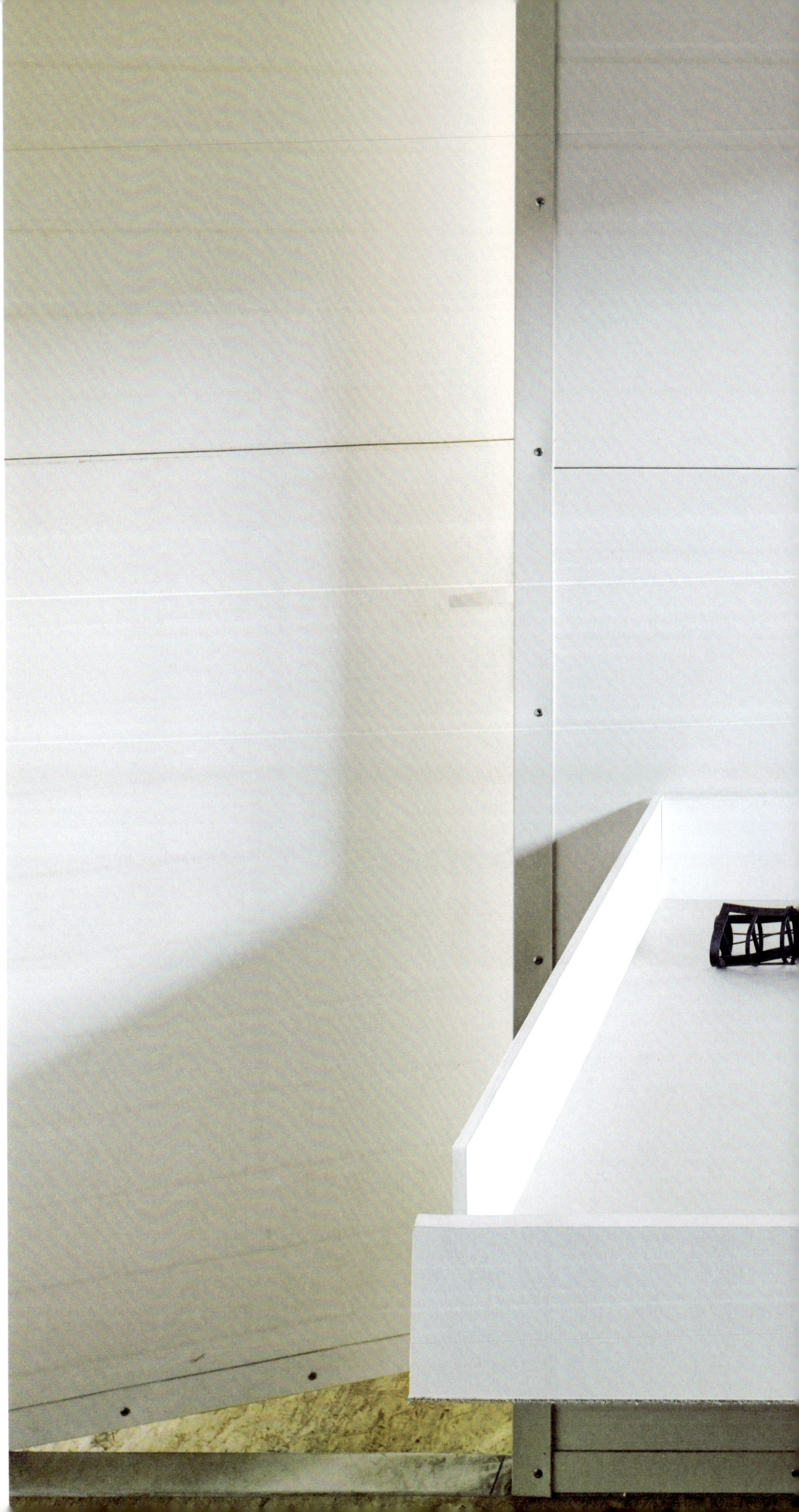

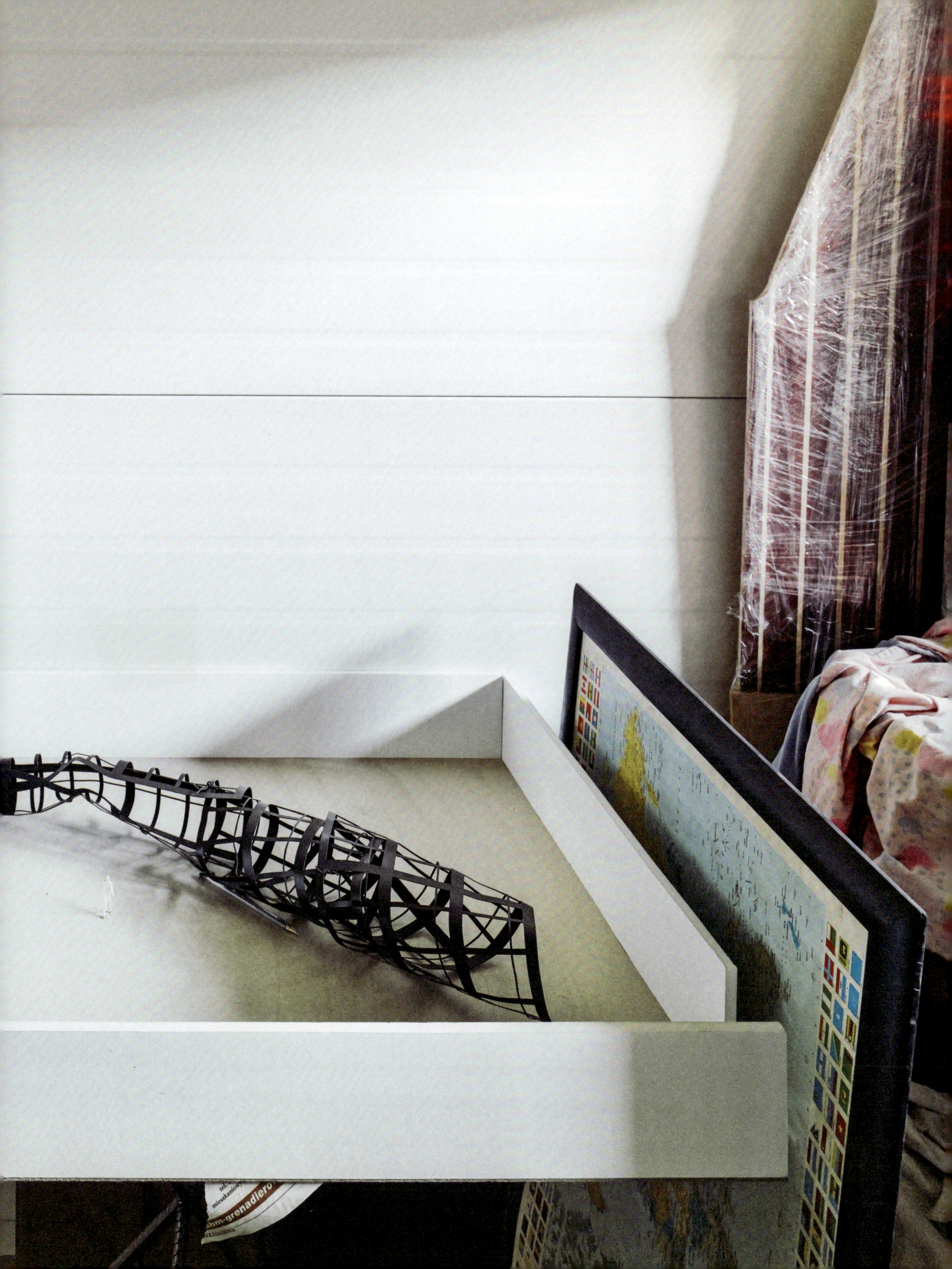

480mb 80szt

68 mb 11 szt
68 mb 11 szt.

609 mb 102 szt.

68 mb 11 szt.
61 mb 11 szt.

129 mb 22 szt.
135 mb 23 szt.
122 mb 20 szt.

257 mb 43 szt.

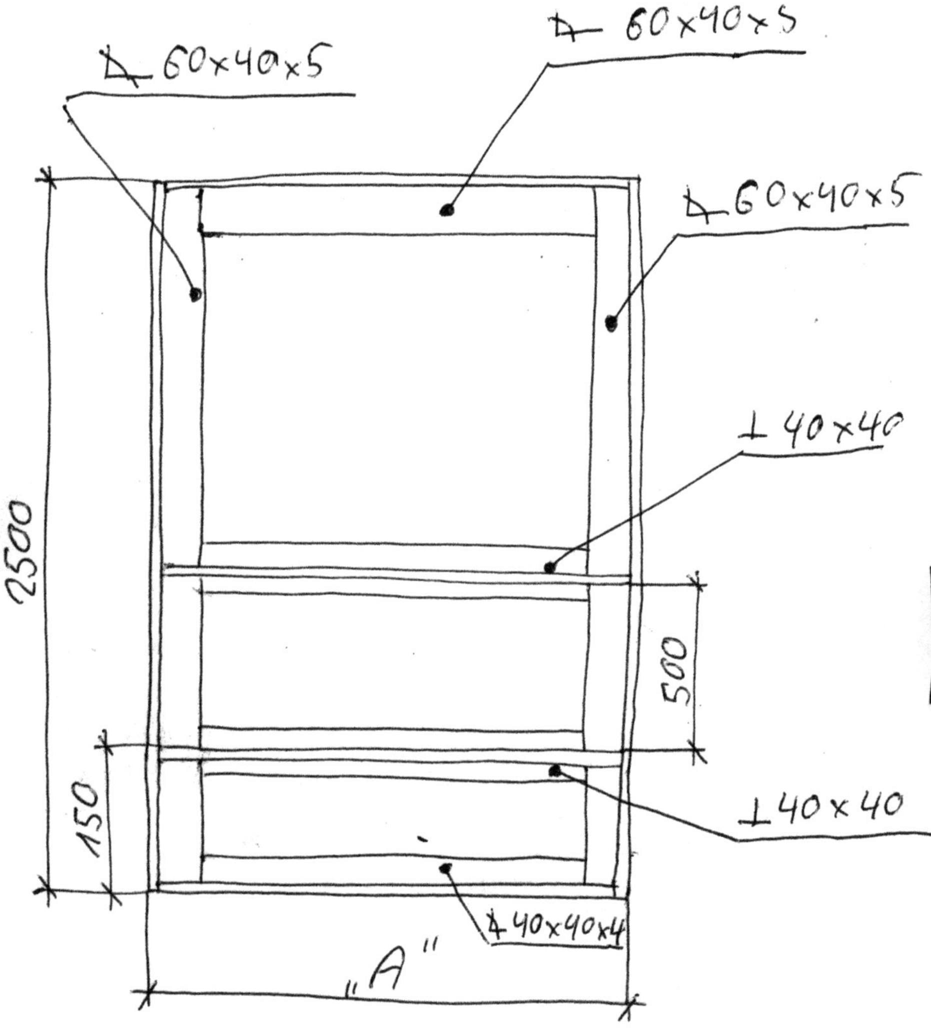

wymiar „A"

L-1420 48 ram

L-1280 48 ram

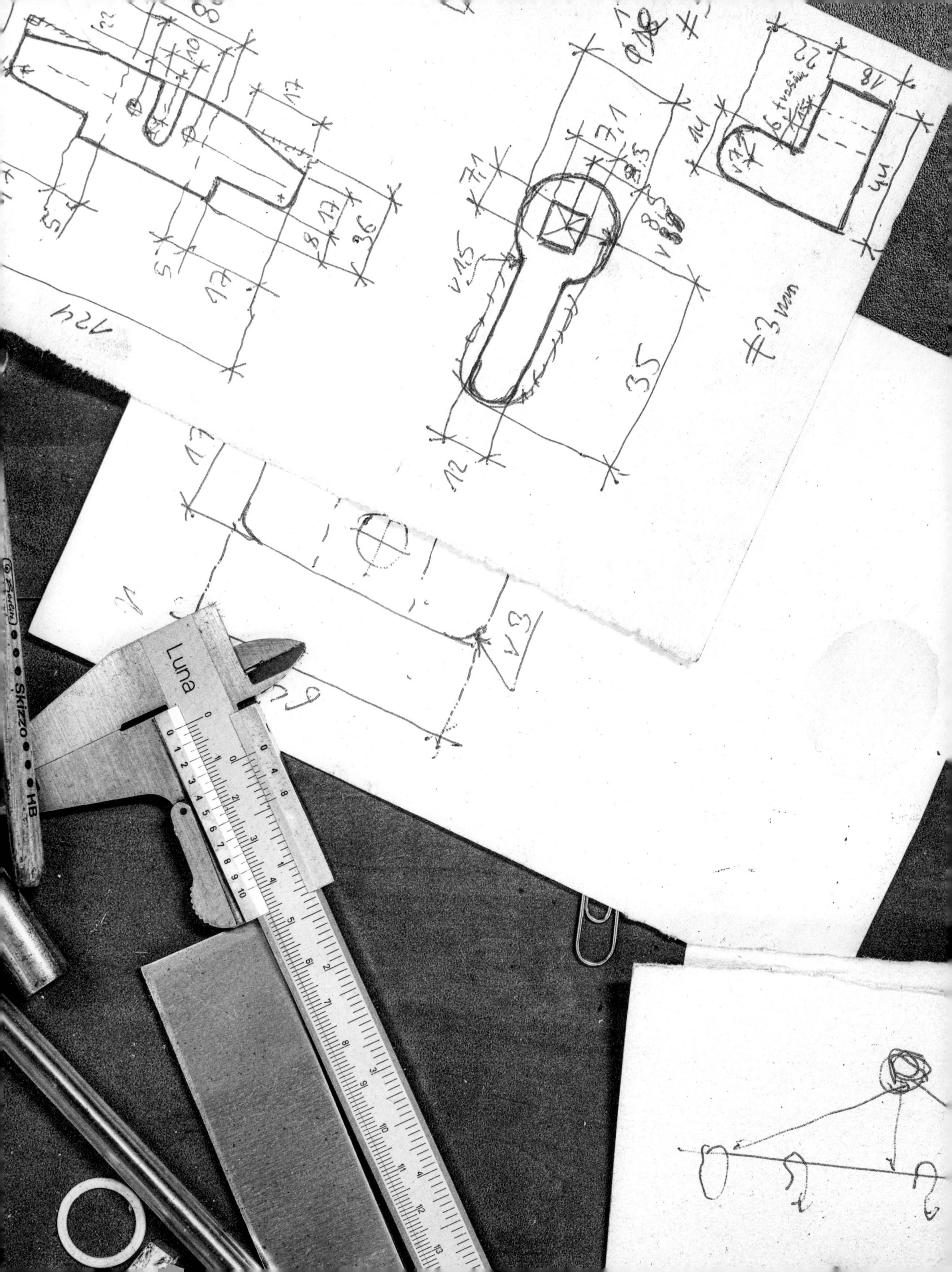
Luna
Skizzo HB

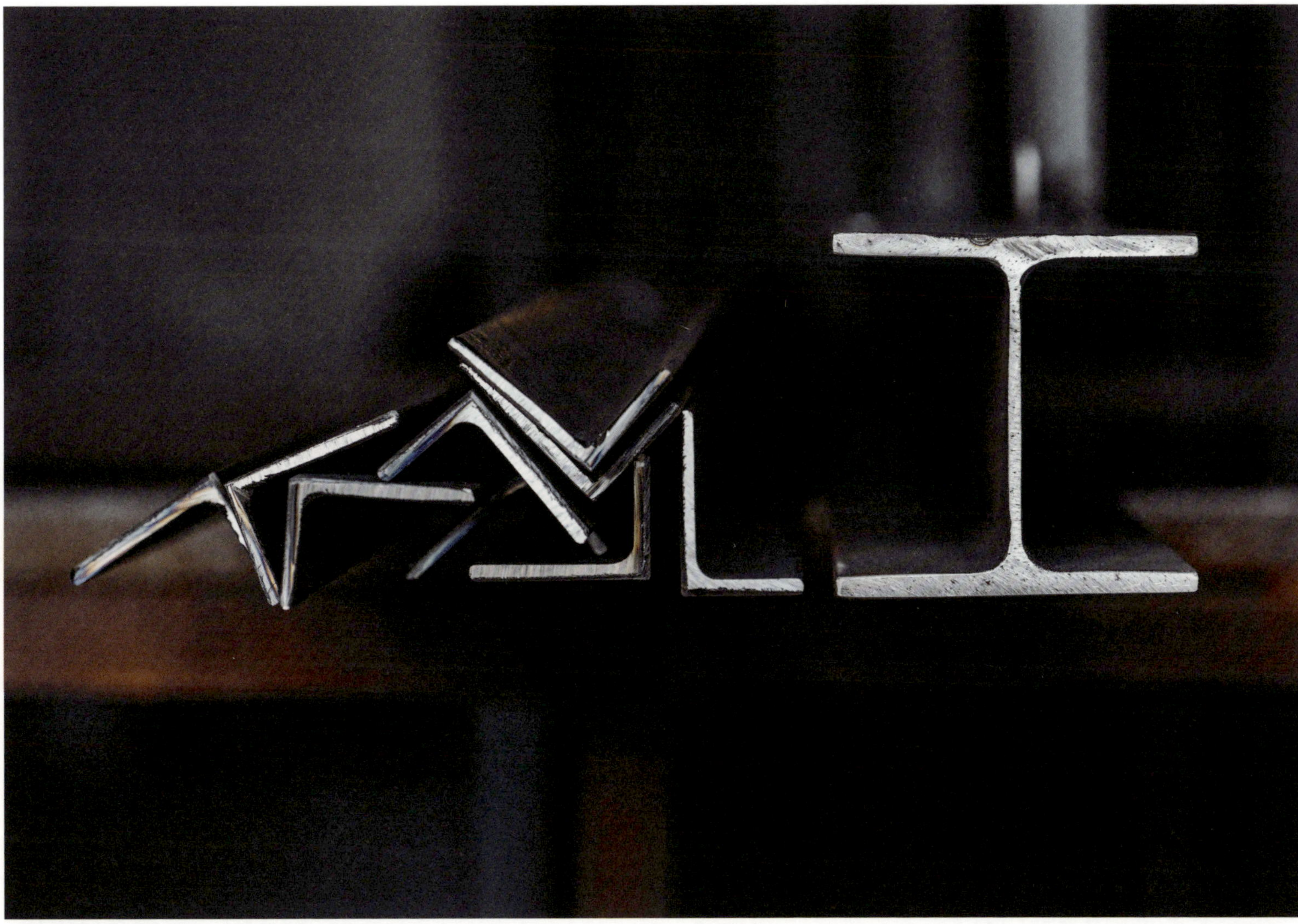

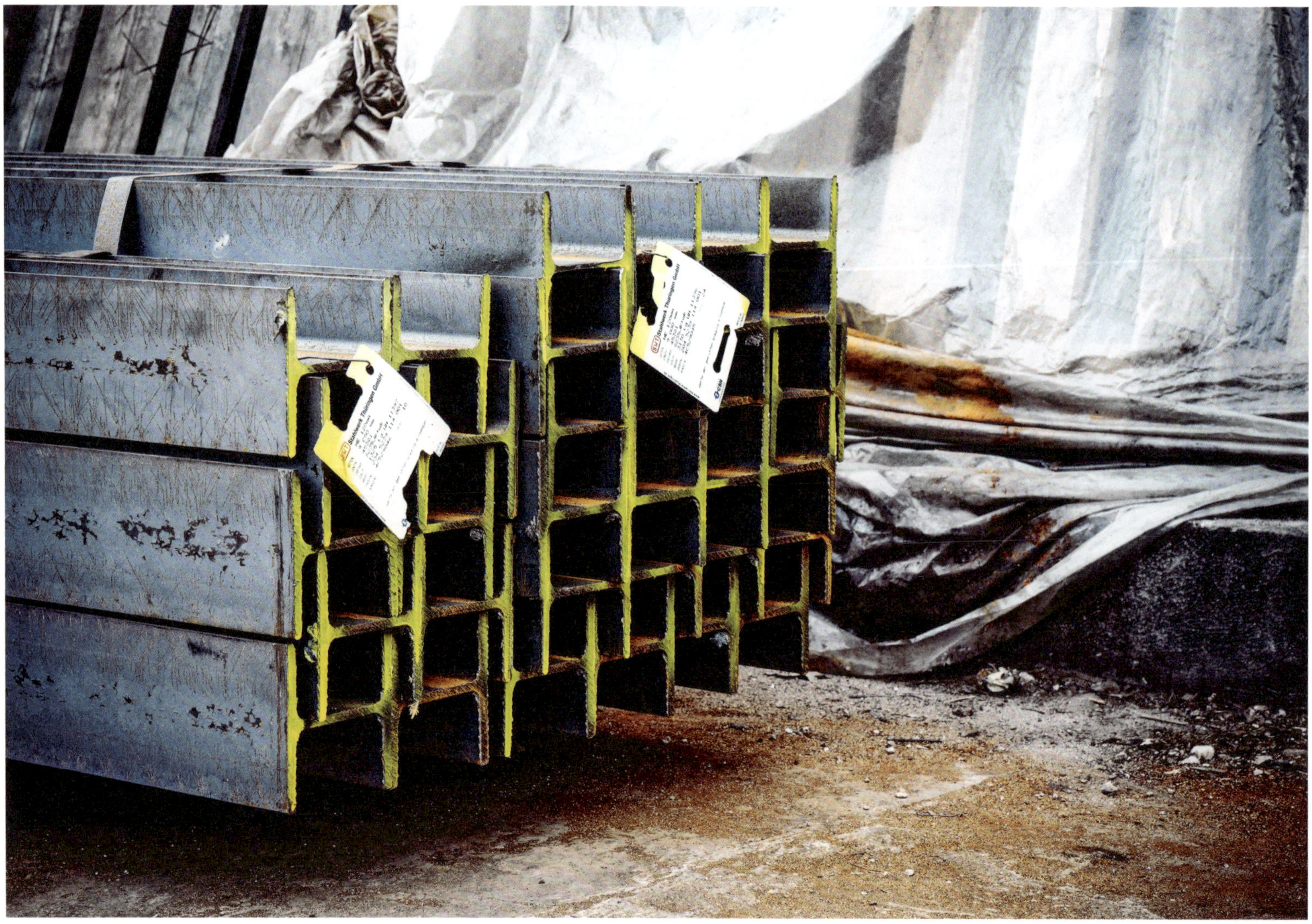

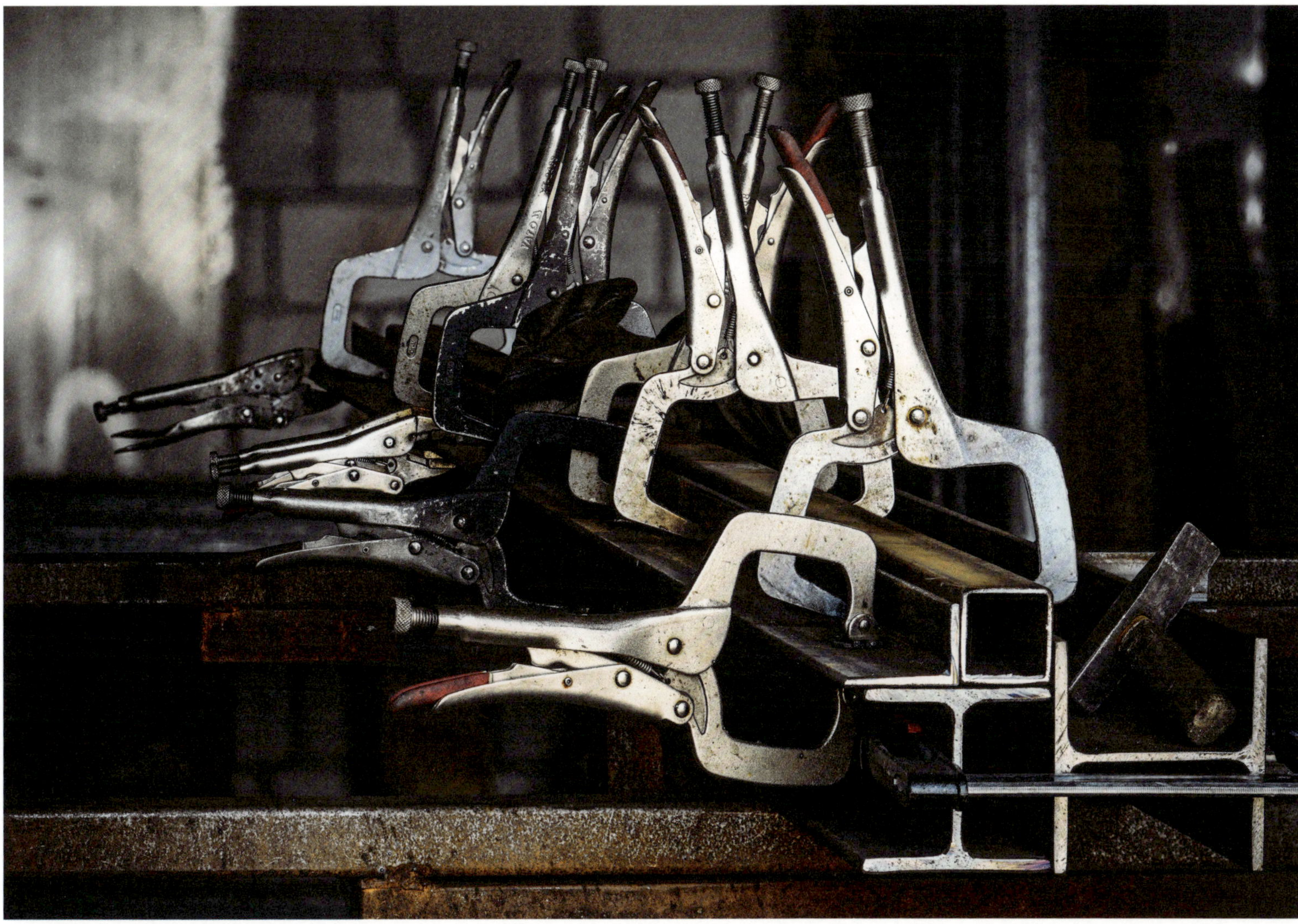

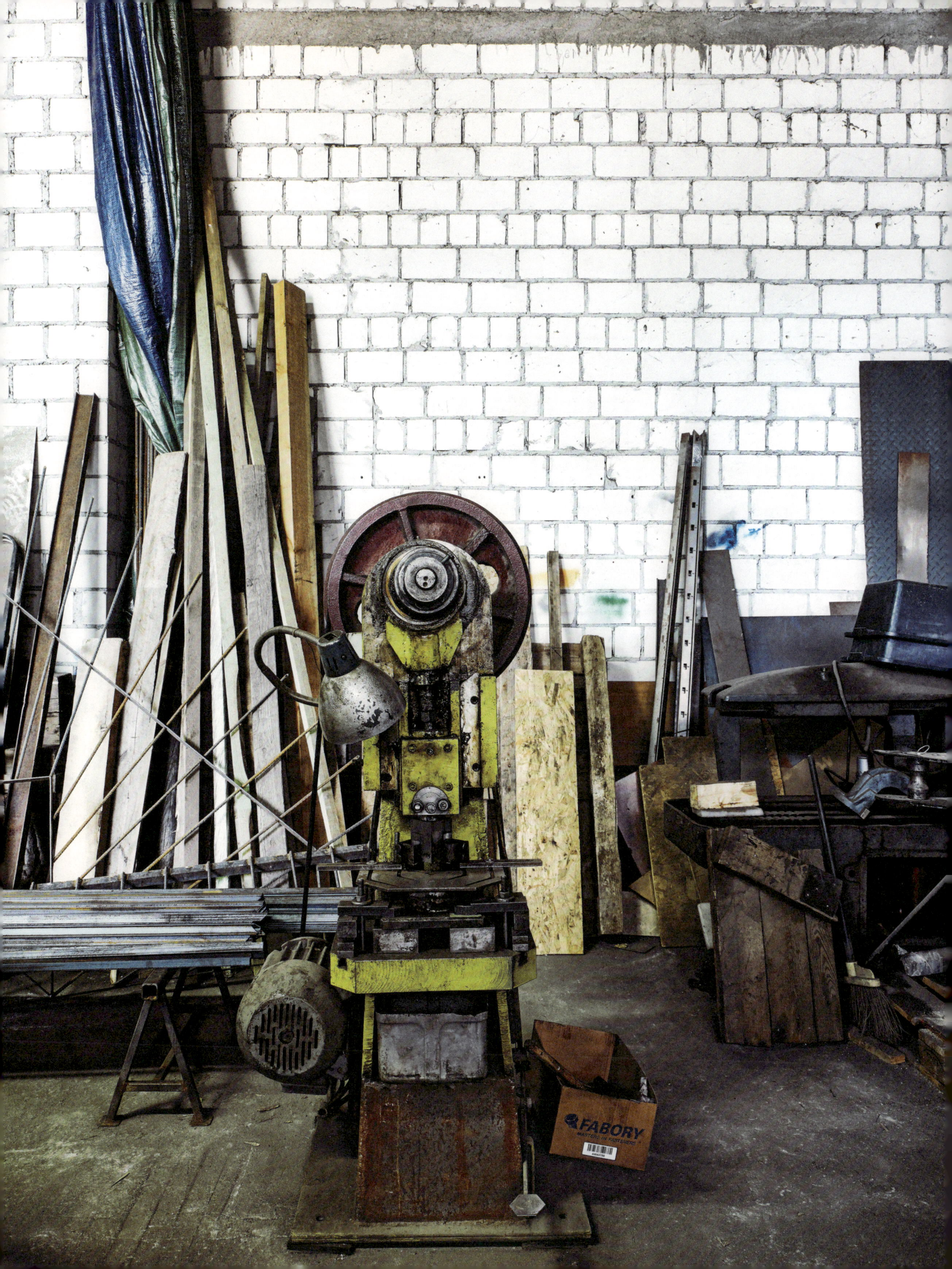
FABORY

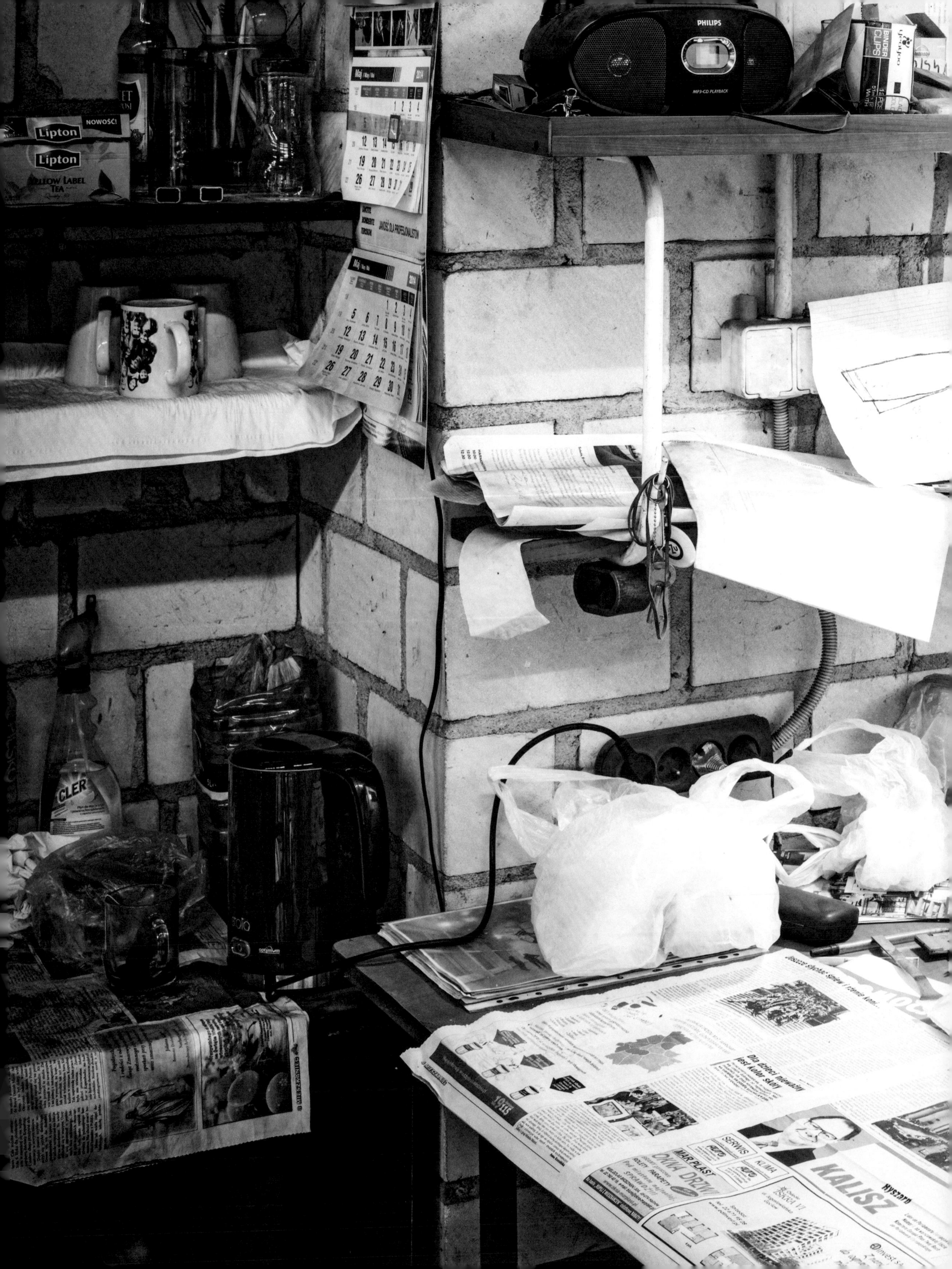

Lipton
NOWOŚĆ!
Lipton
PHILIPS
MP3-CD PLAYBACK
BINDER CLIPS
MAR PLAST
SERWIS
KLIMA
KALISZ

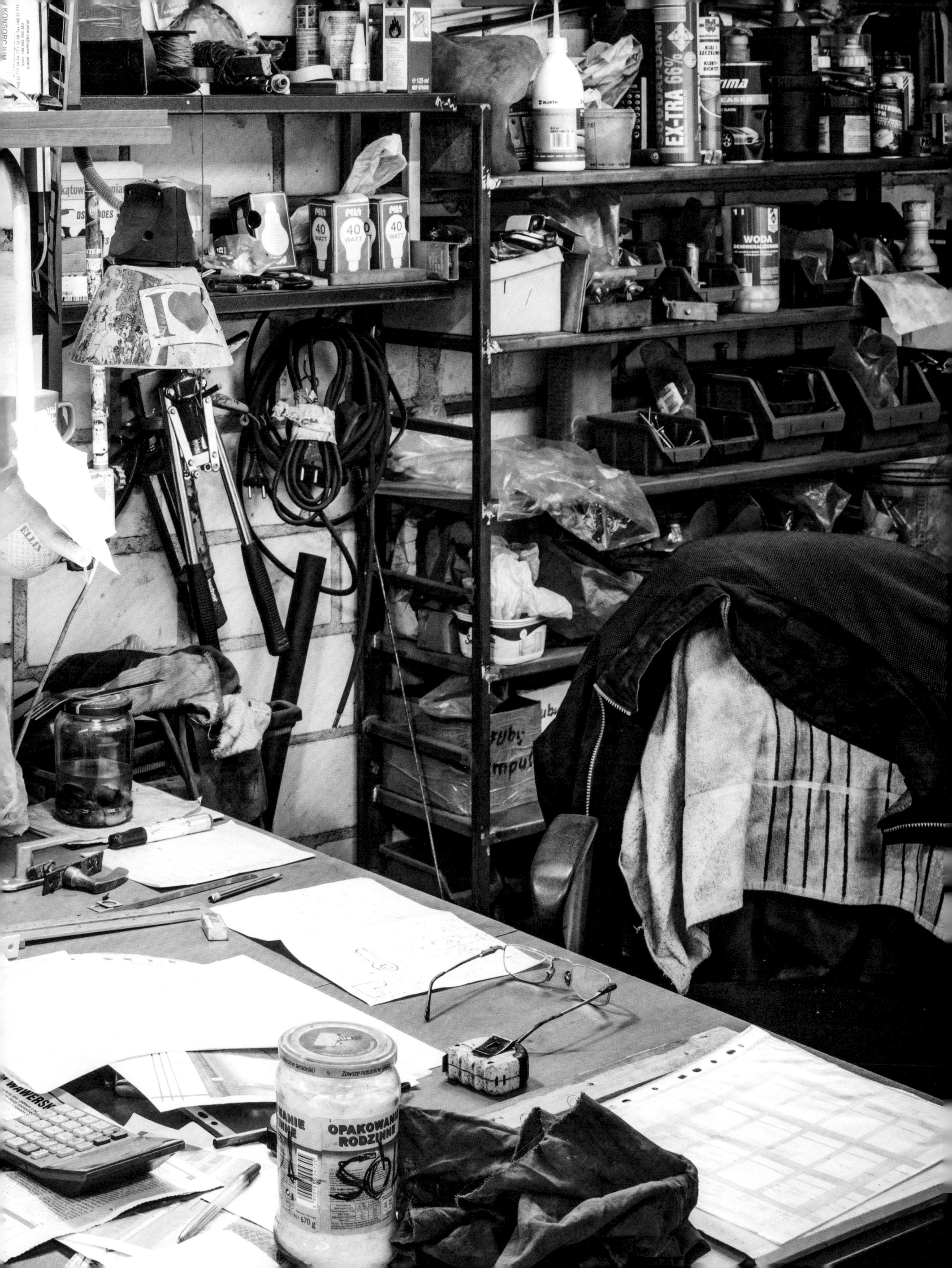
40 WATT
40 WATT
40 WATT
WODA
EX-TRA 66%
OPAKOWANIE RODZINNE
670 g

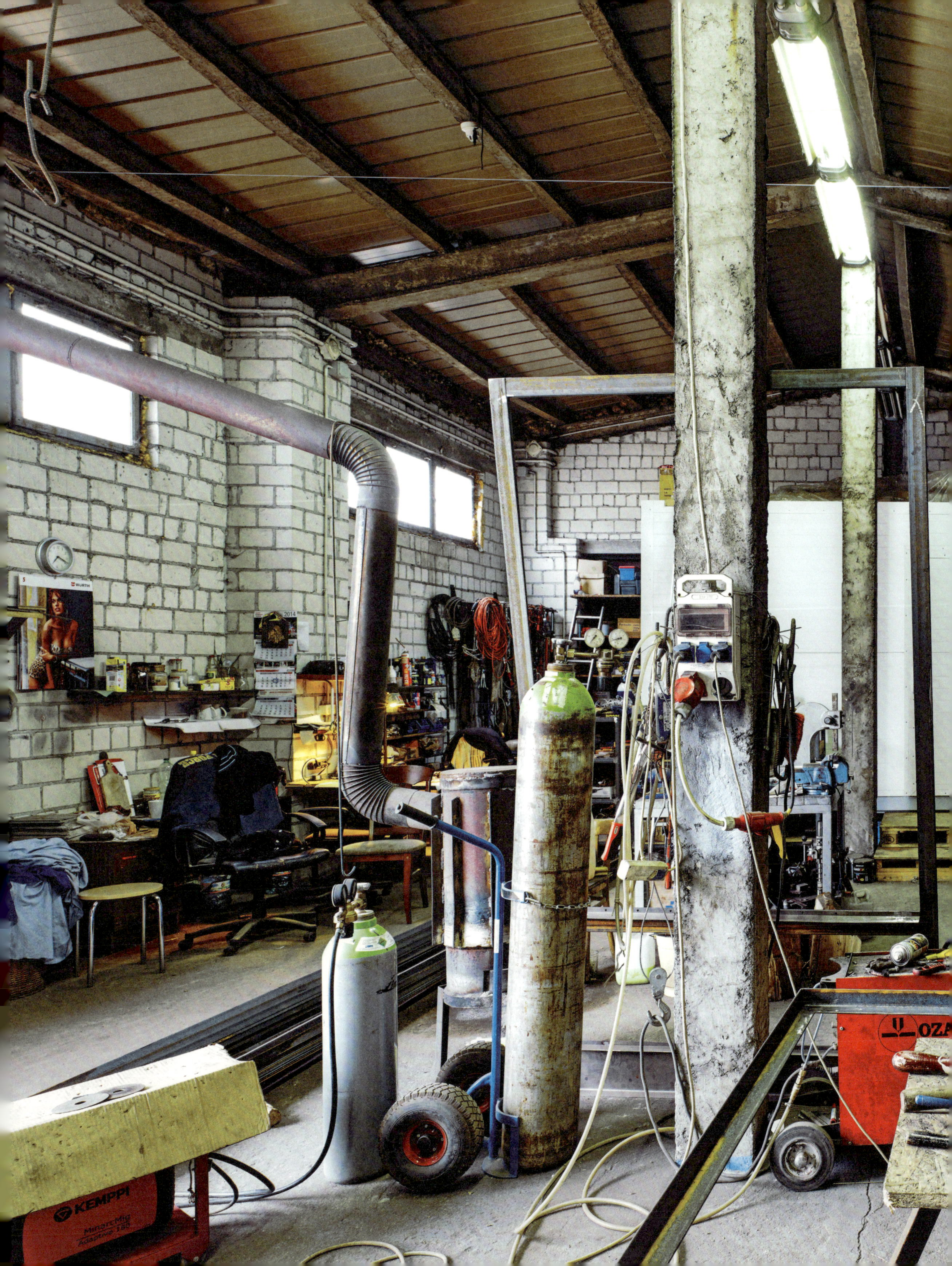
WÜRTH
2014
KEMPPI

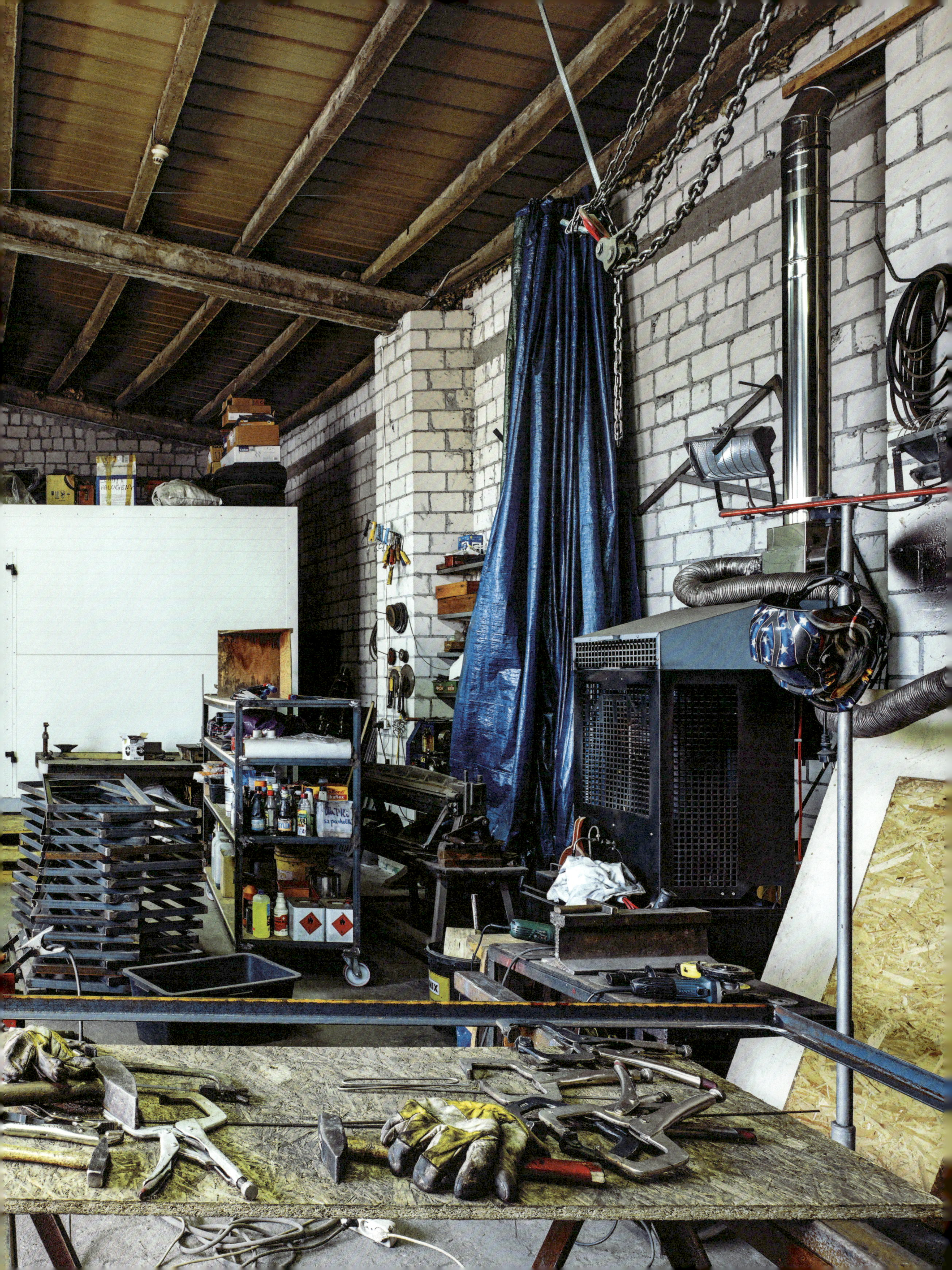

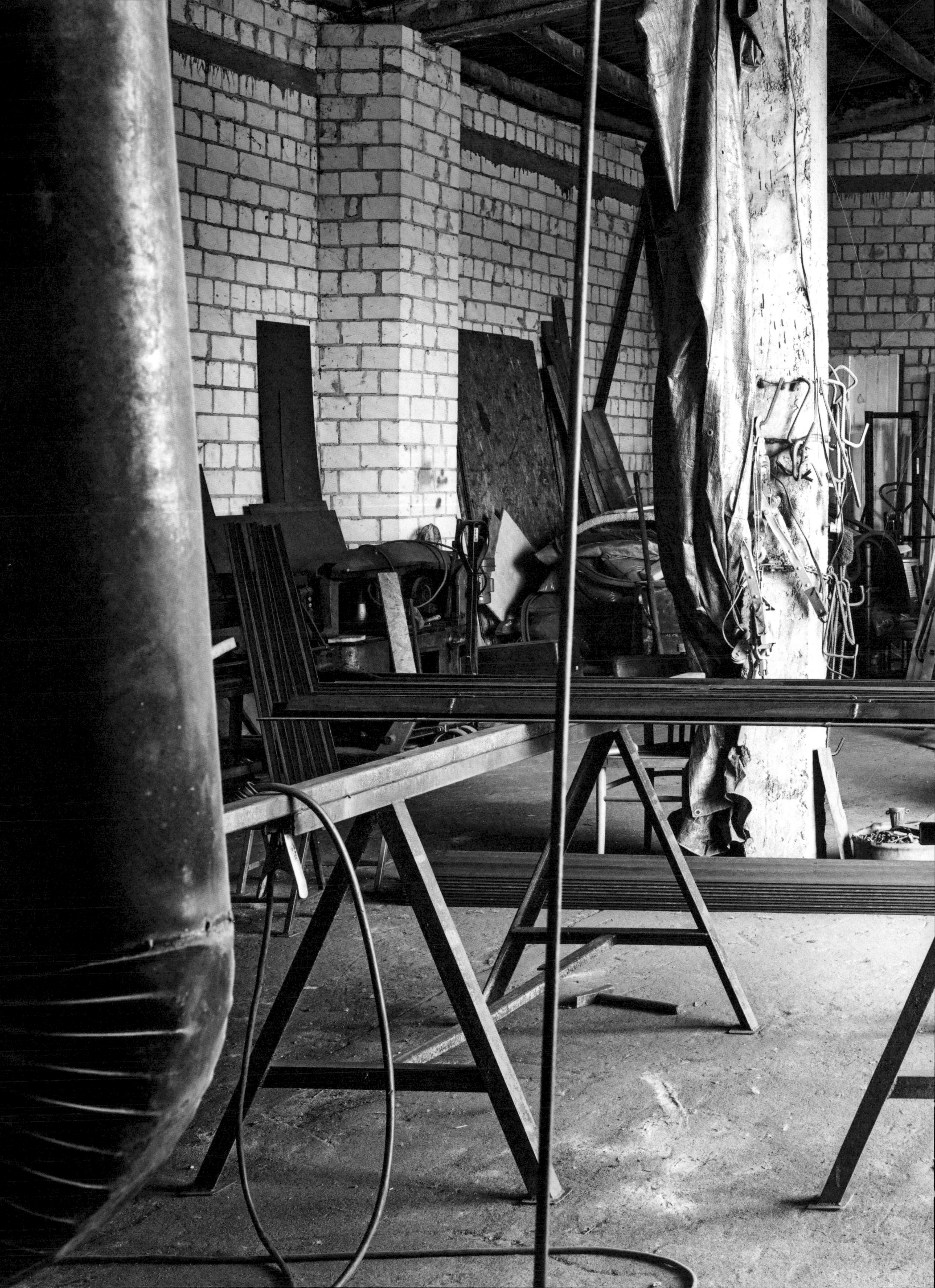

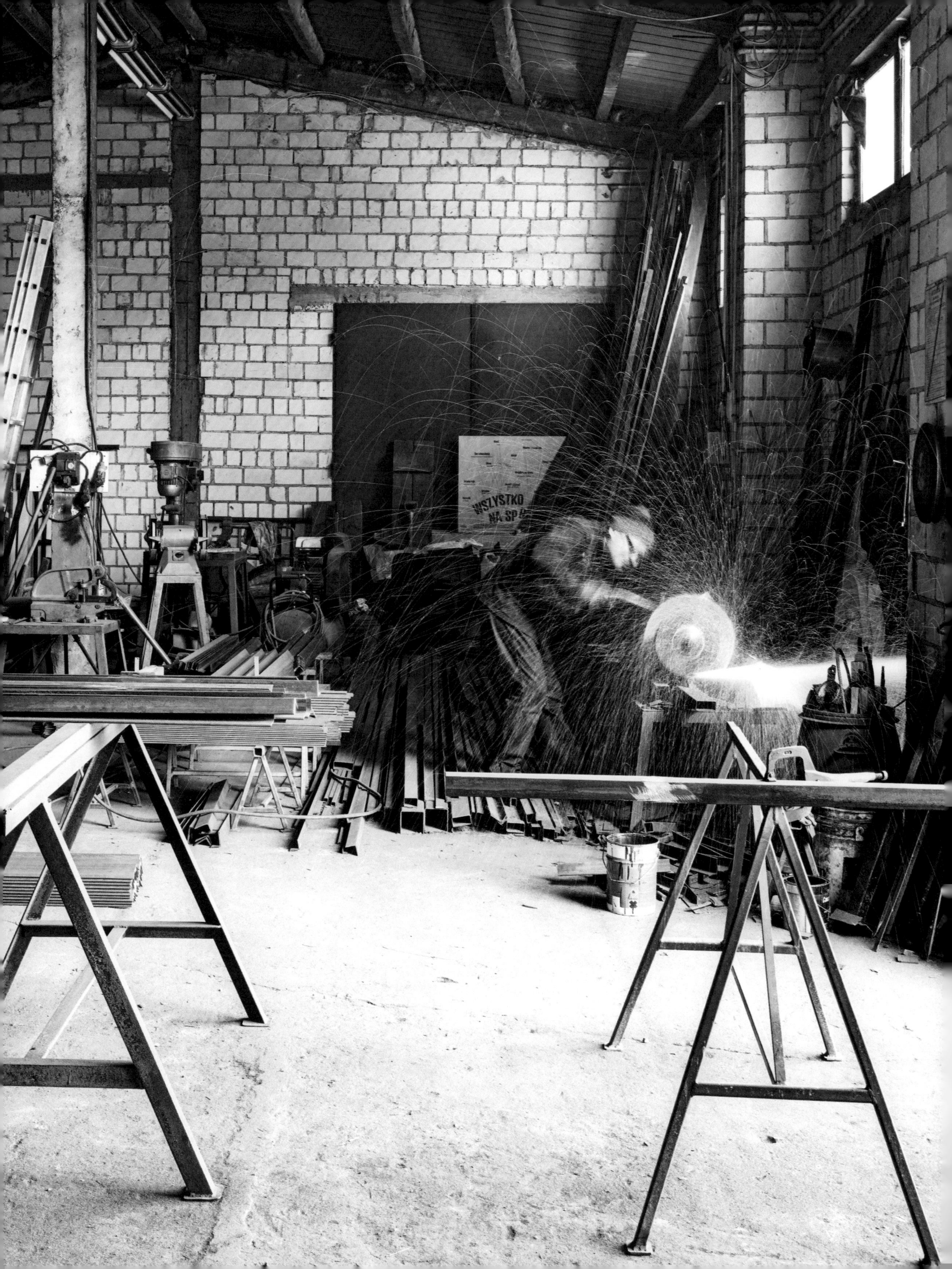
WSZYSTKO
NA SP

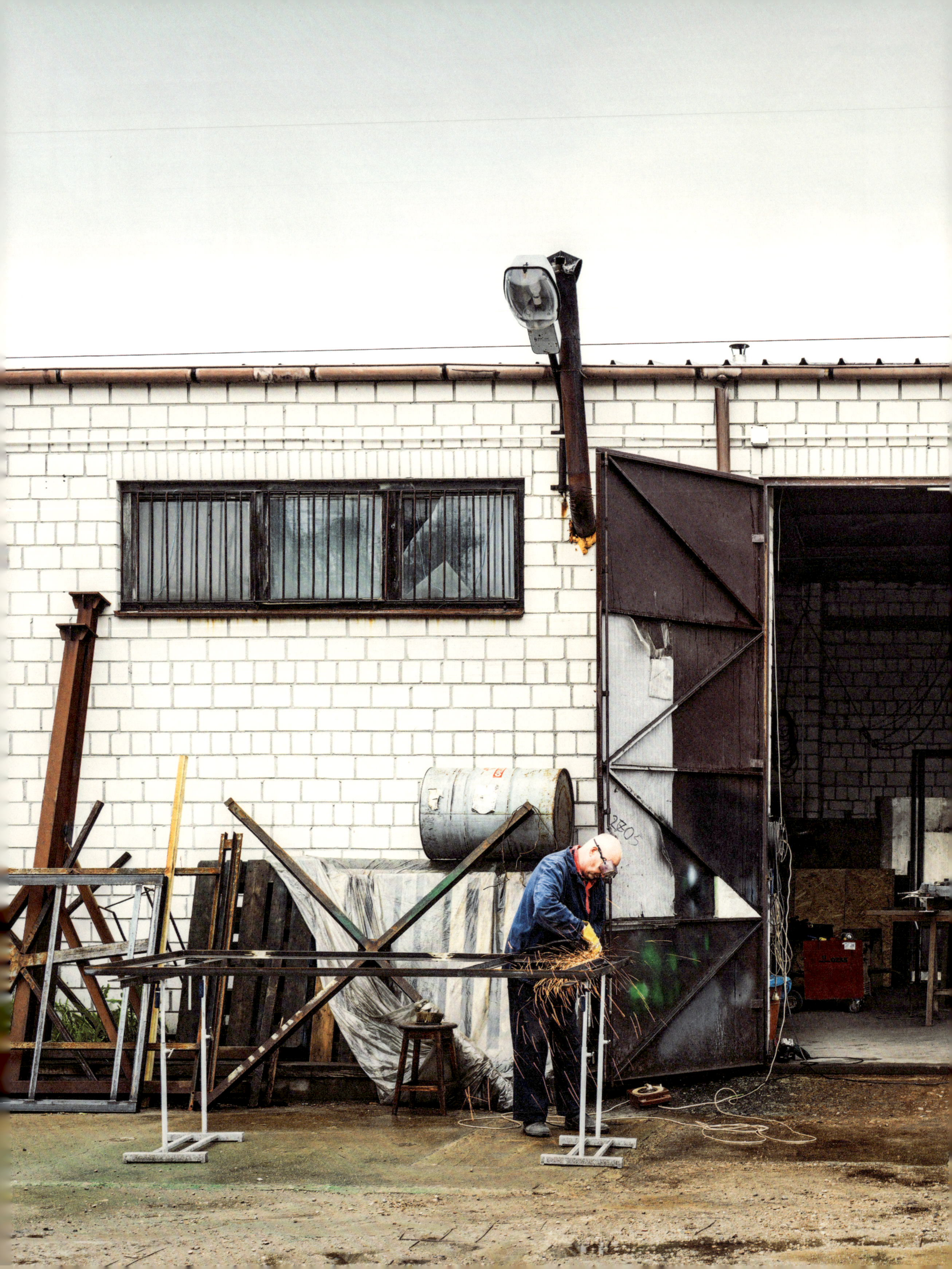

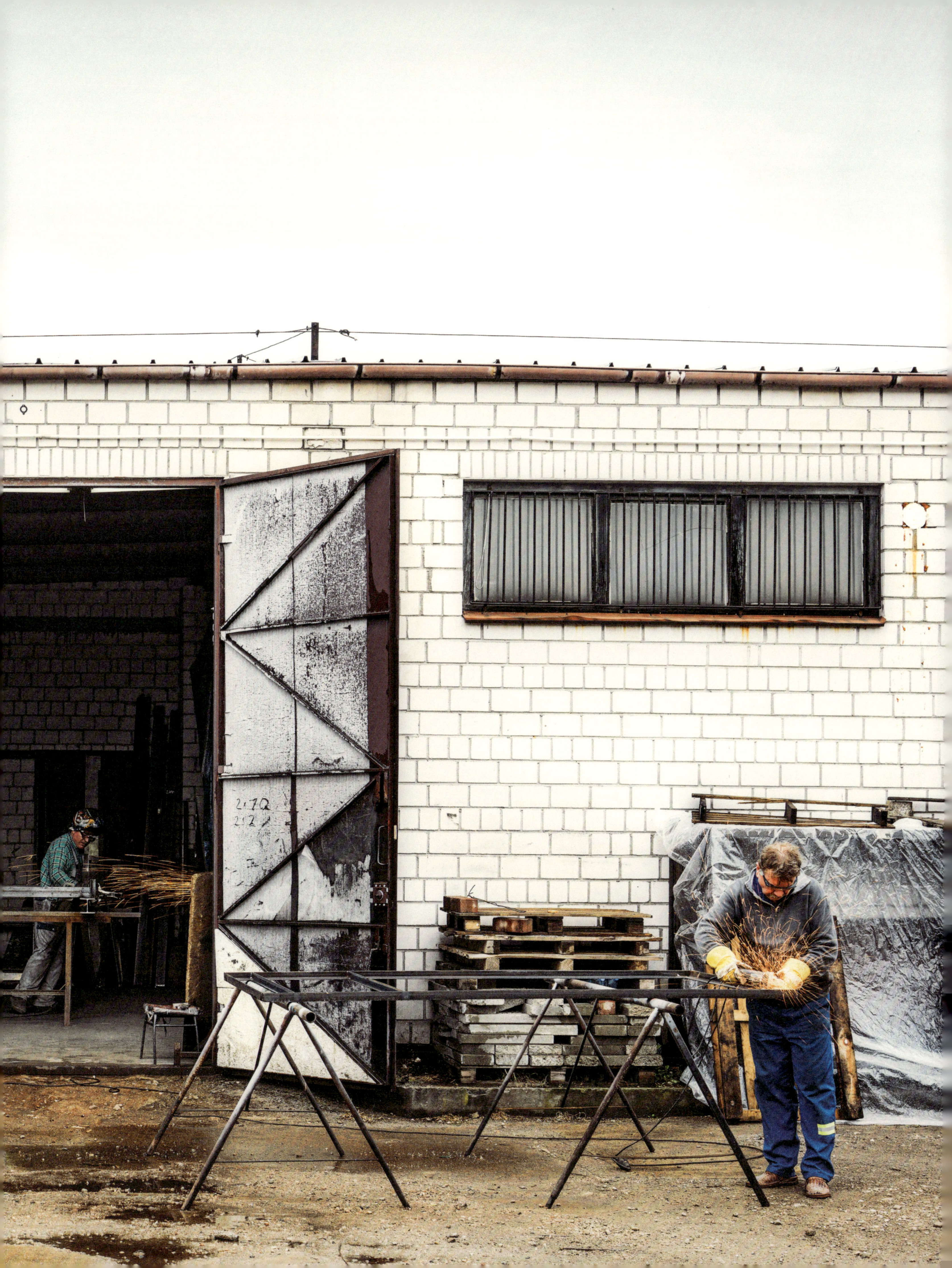

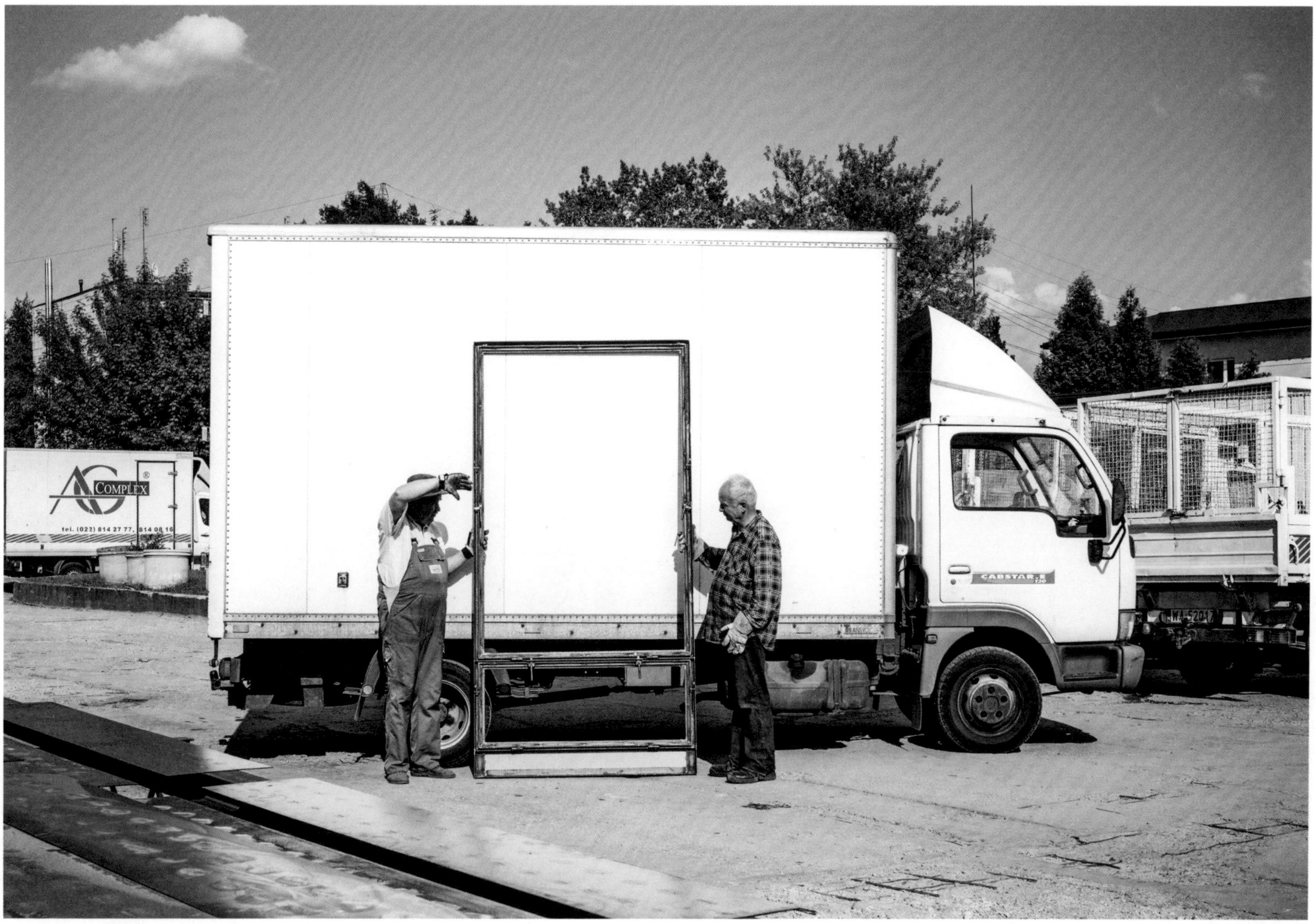
AG COMPLEX
tel. (022) 814 27 77, 814 08 16
CABSTAR

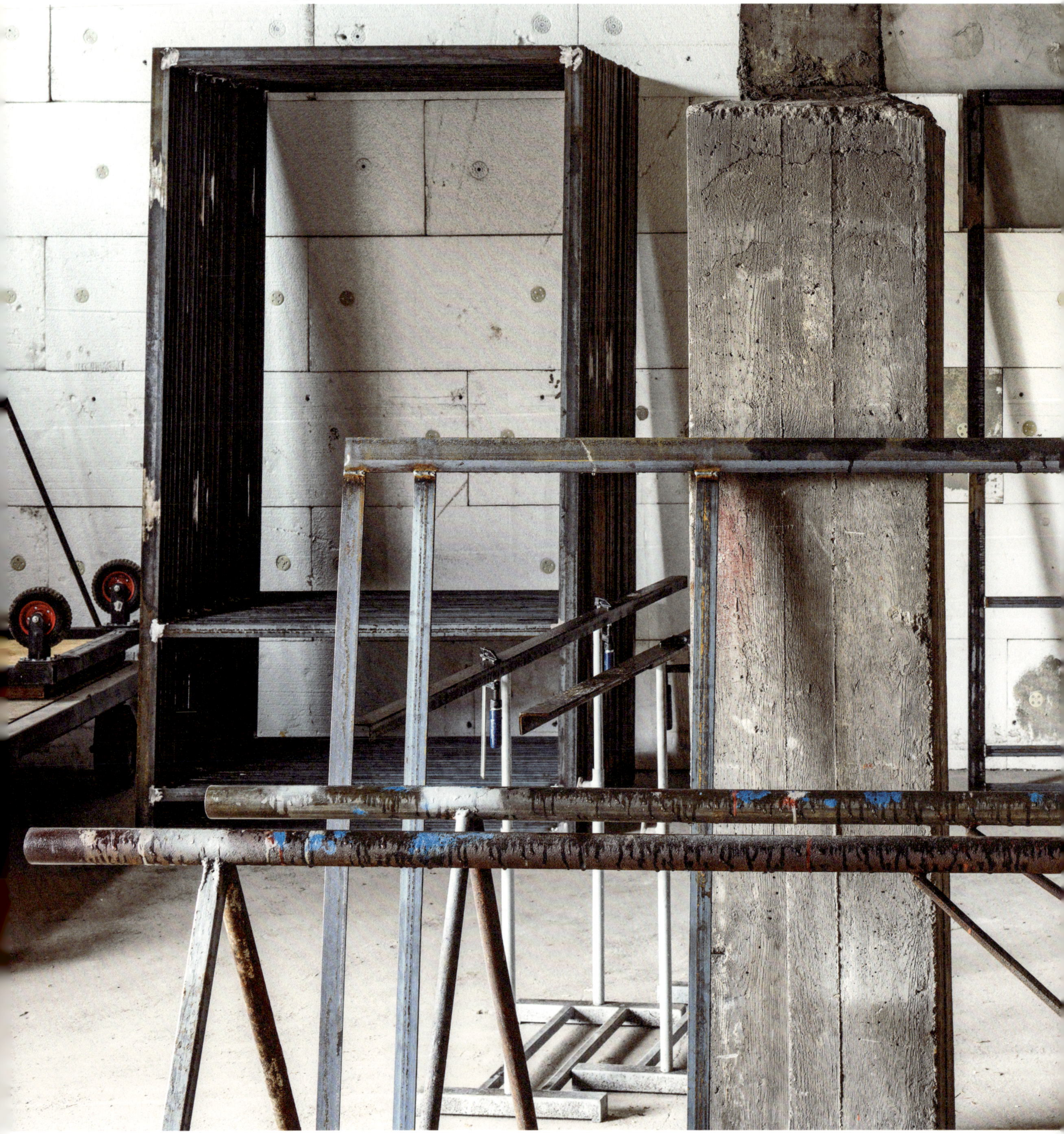

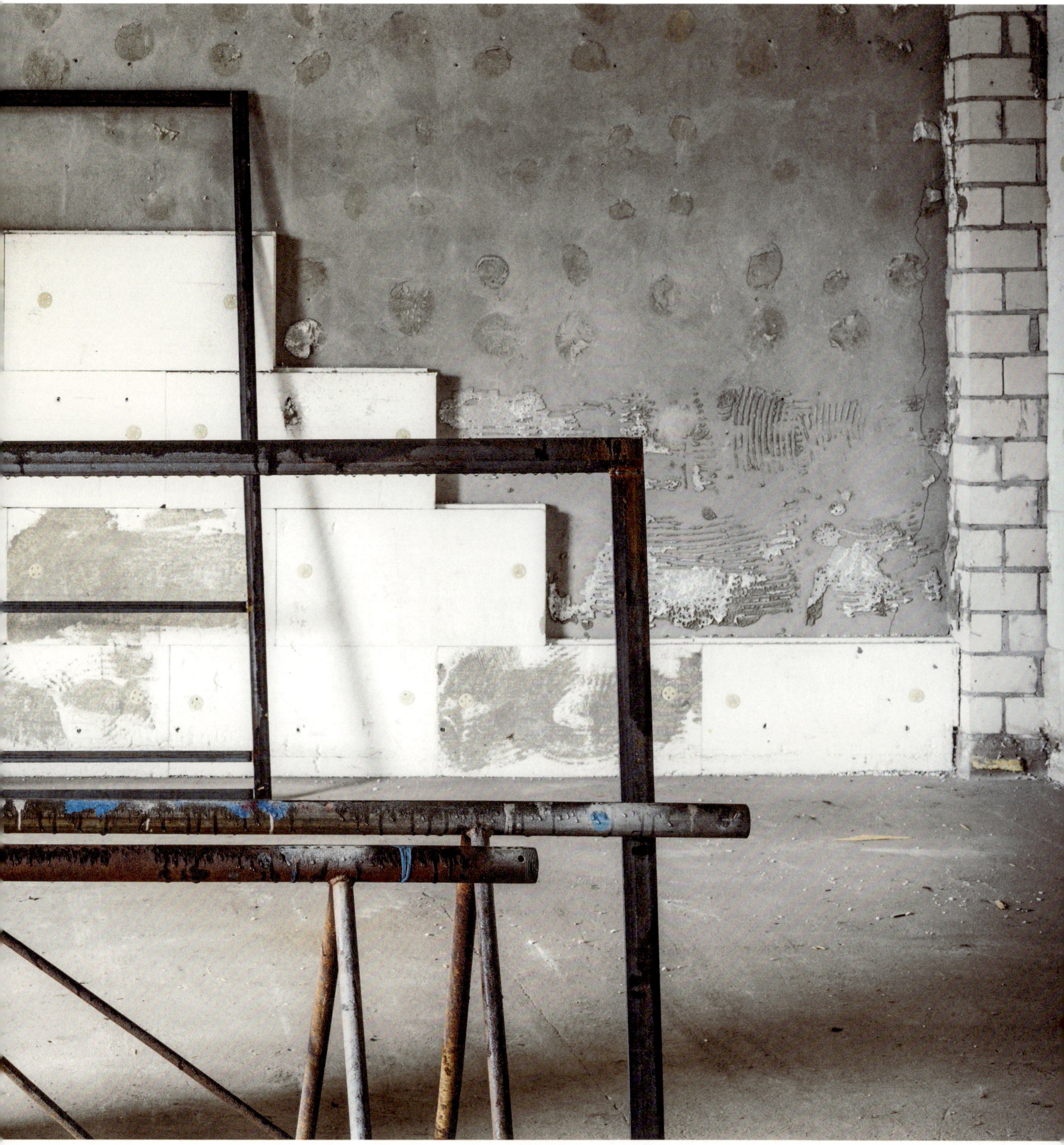

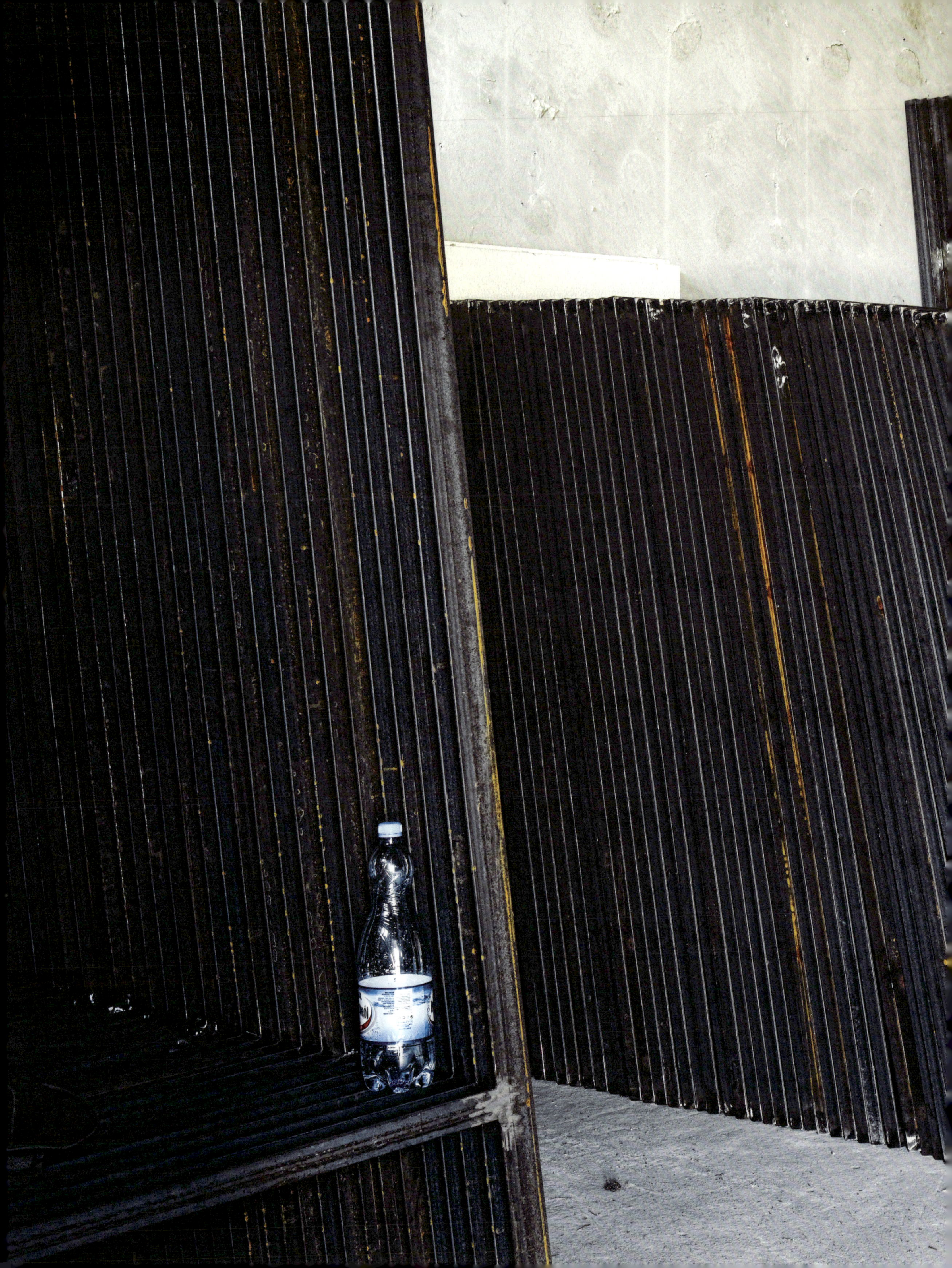

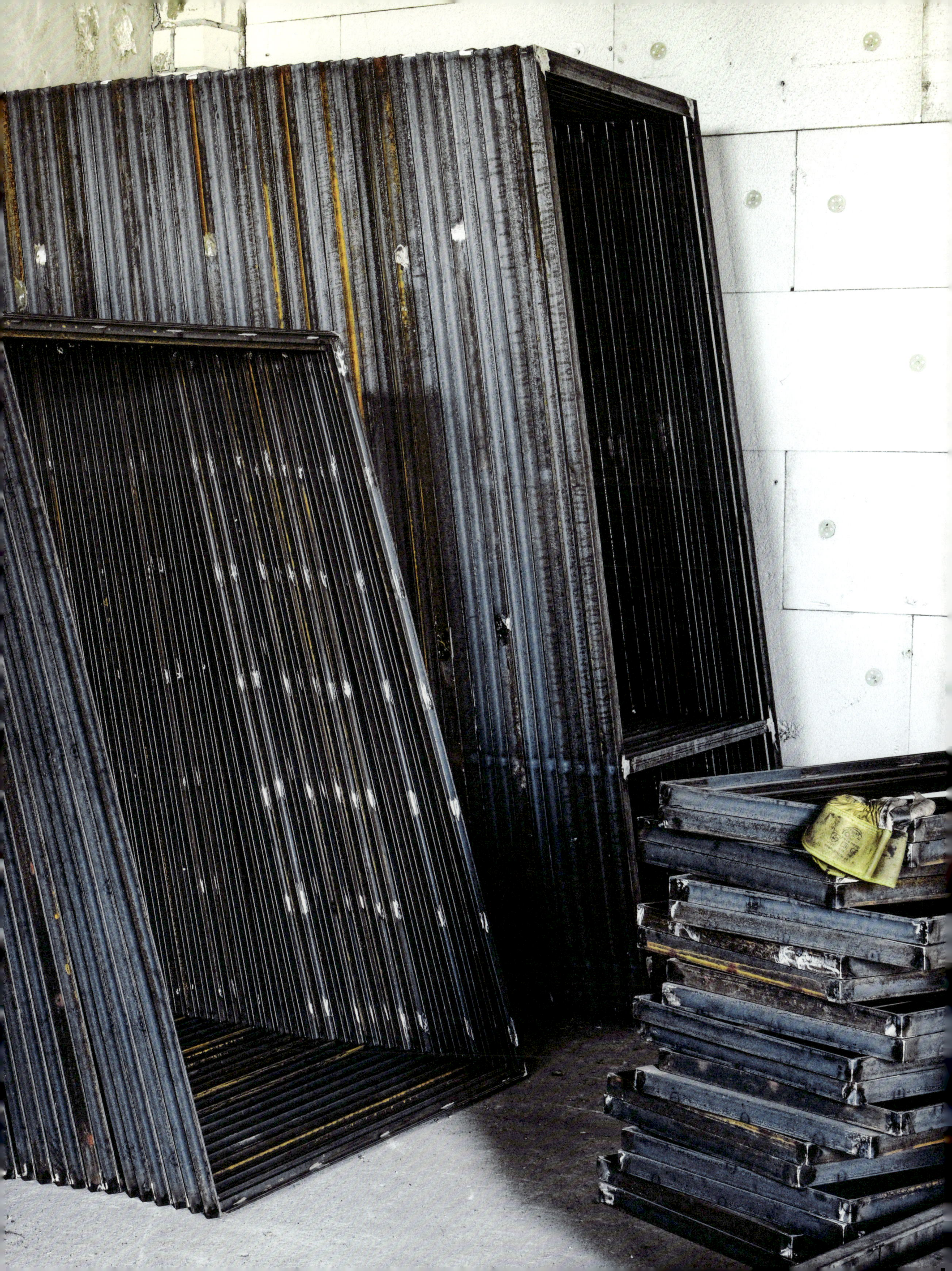

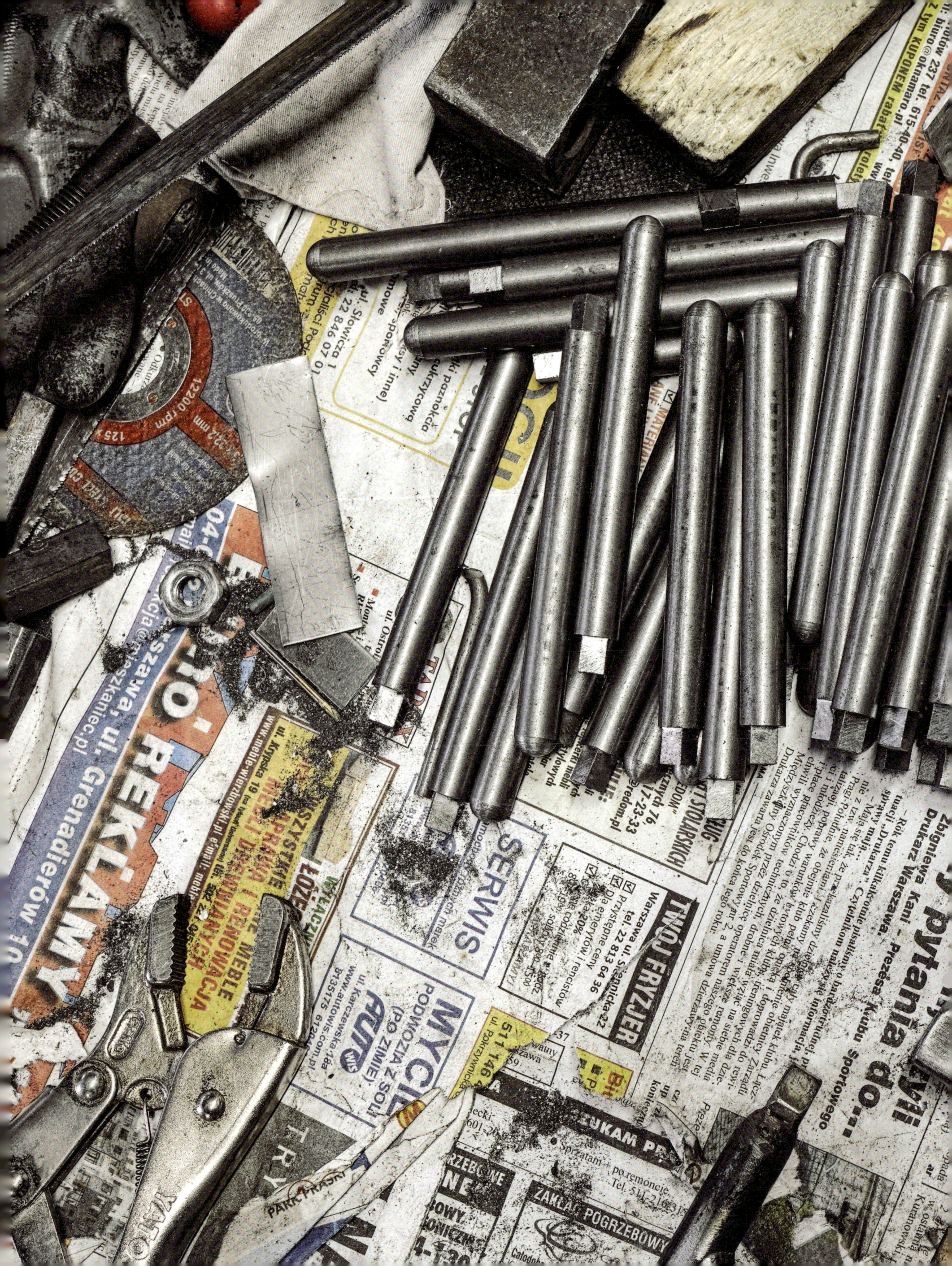
REKLAMY
SERWIS
TWÓJ FRYZJER
MYCIE
pytania do...
YATO

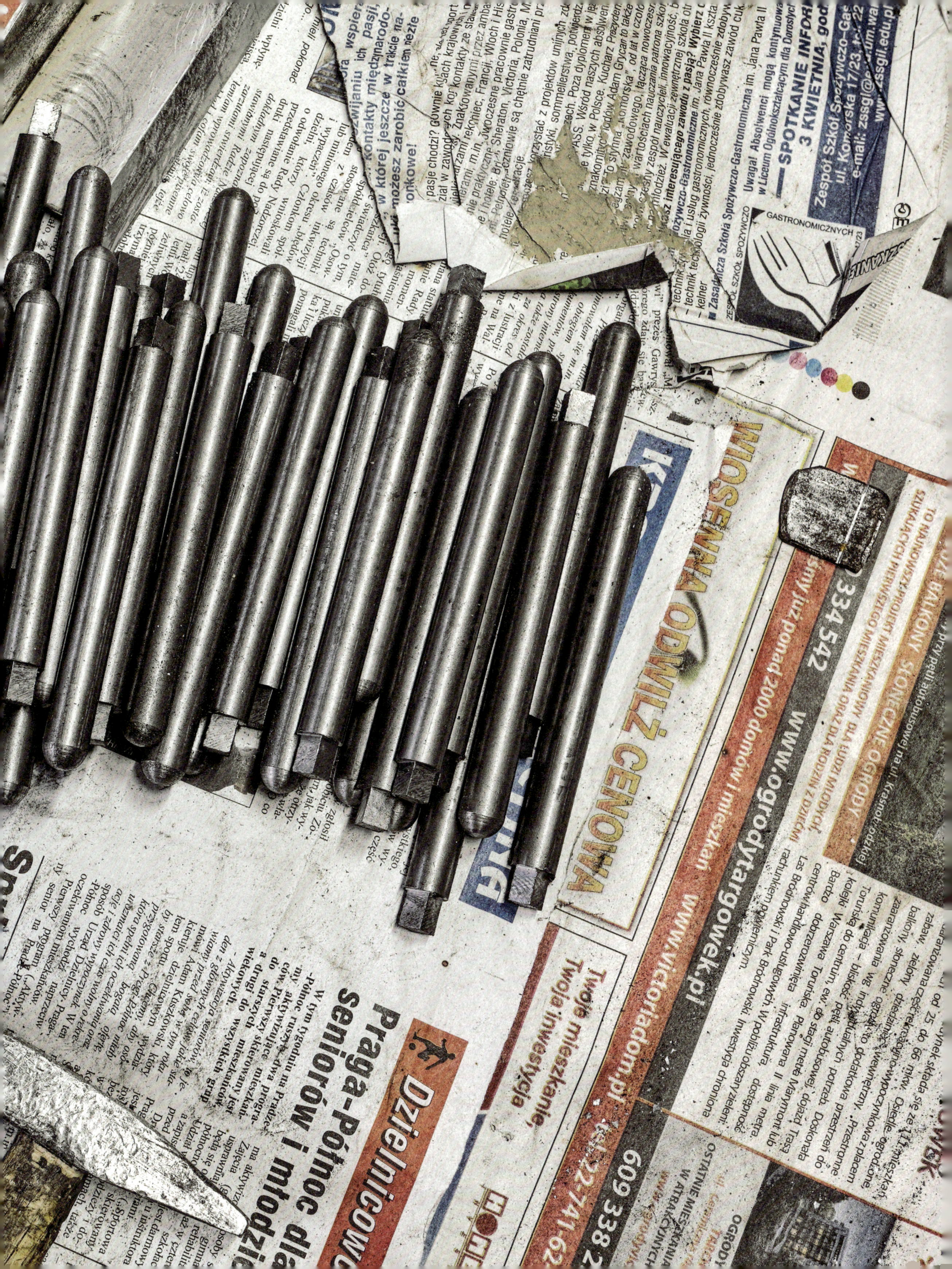
WIOSENNA ODWILŻ CENOWA
www.ogrodytargowek.pl
www.victoriadom.pl
Twoje mieszkanie, Twoja inwestycja
SPOTKANIE INFORMACYJNE
3 KWIETNIA
334 542

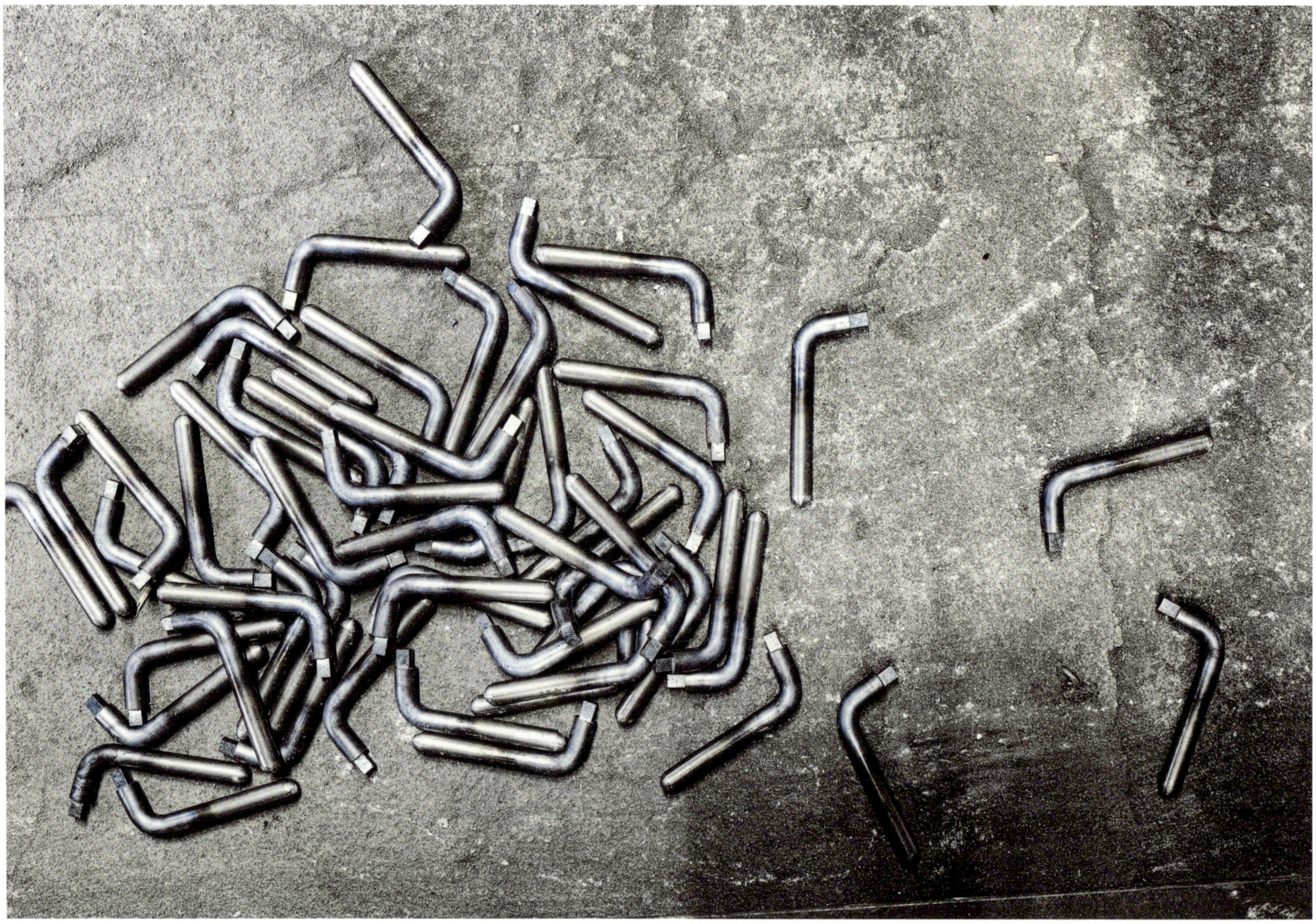

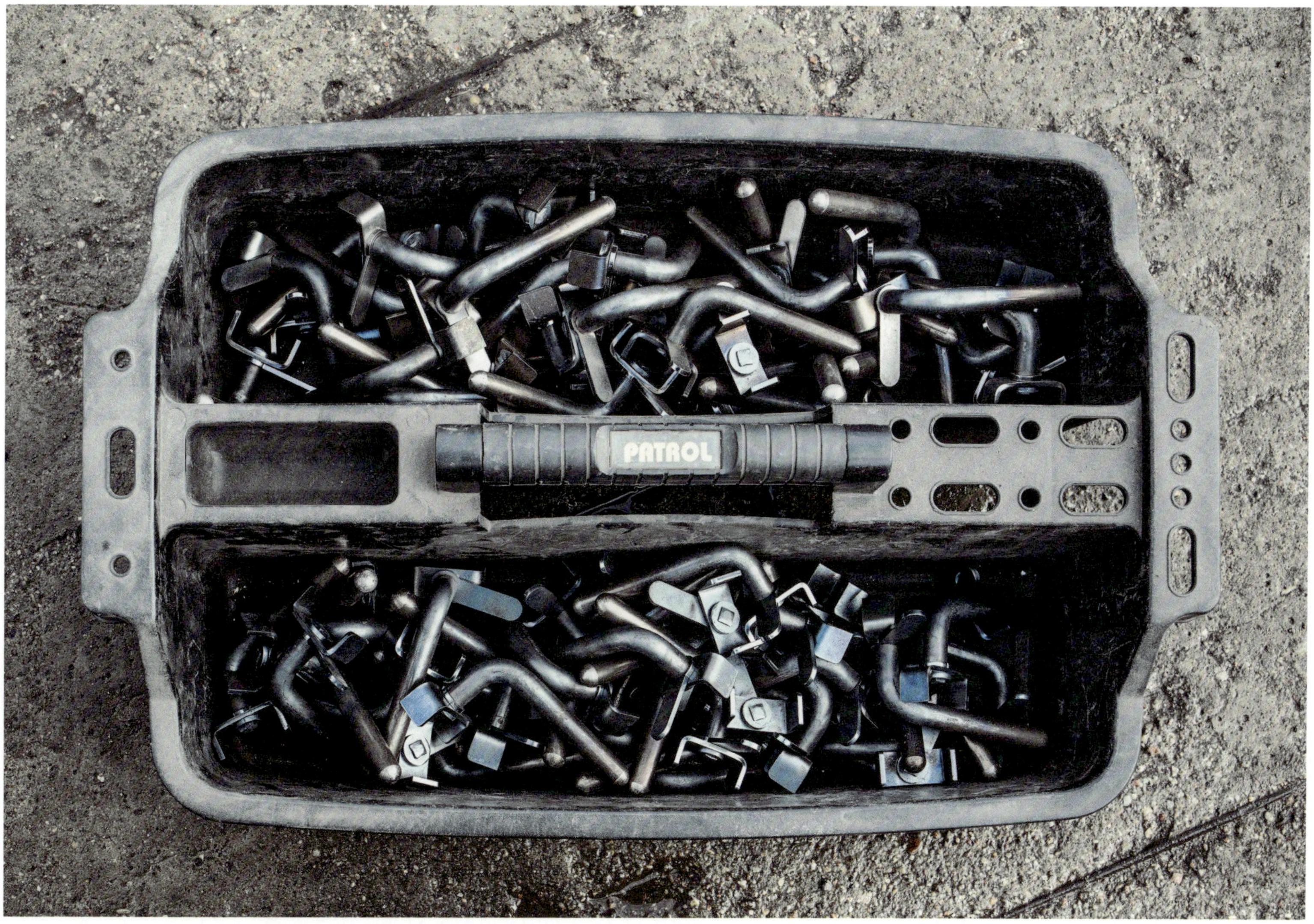
PATROL

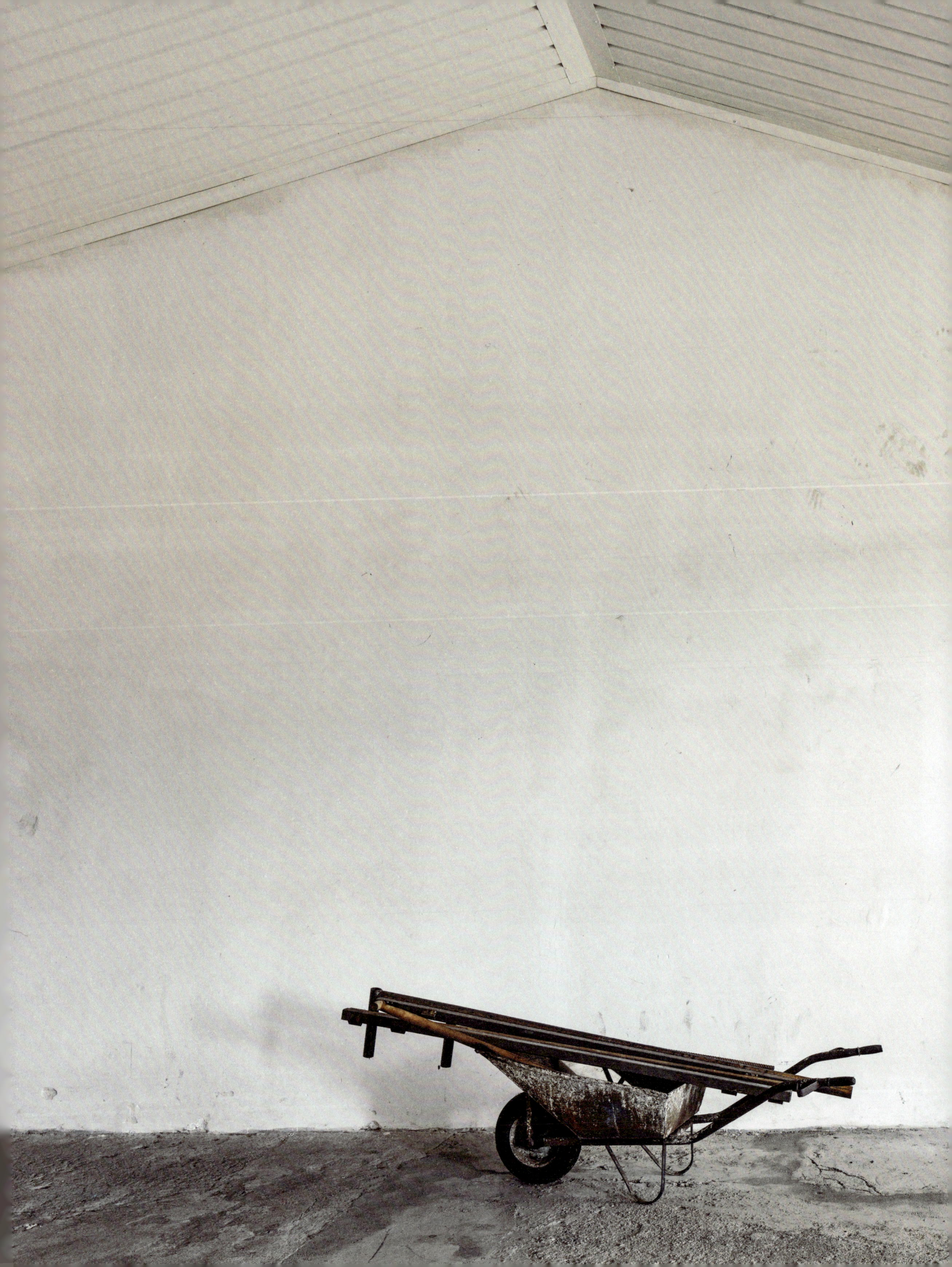

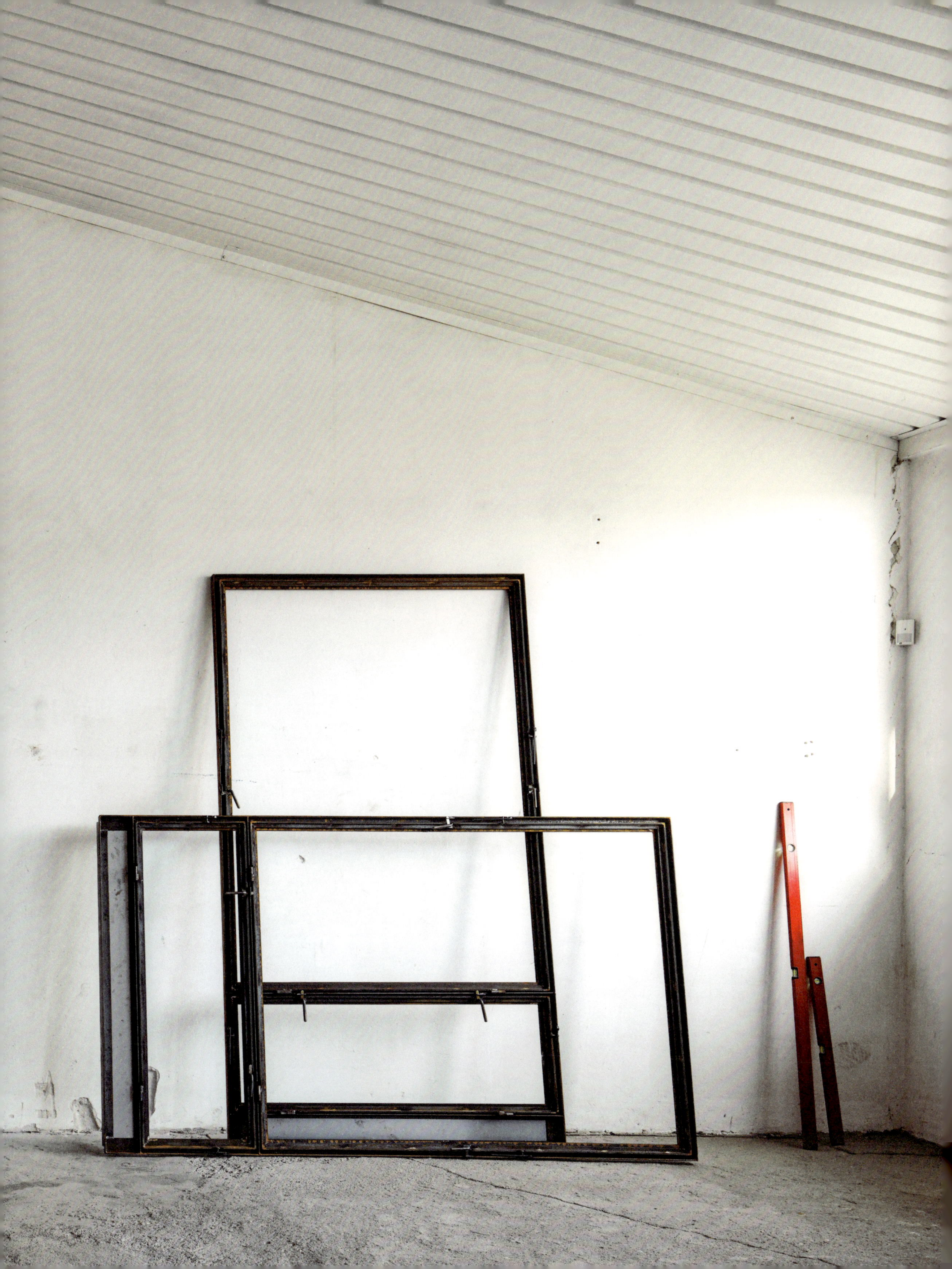

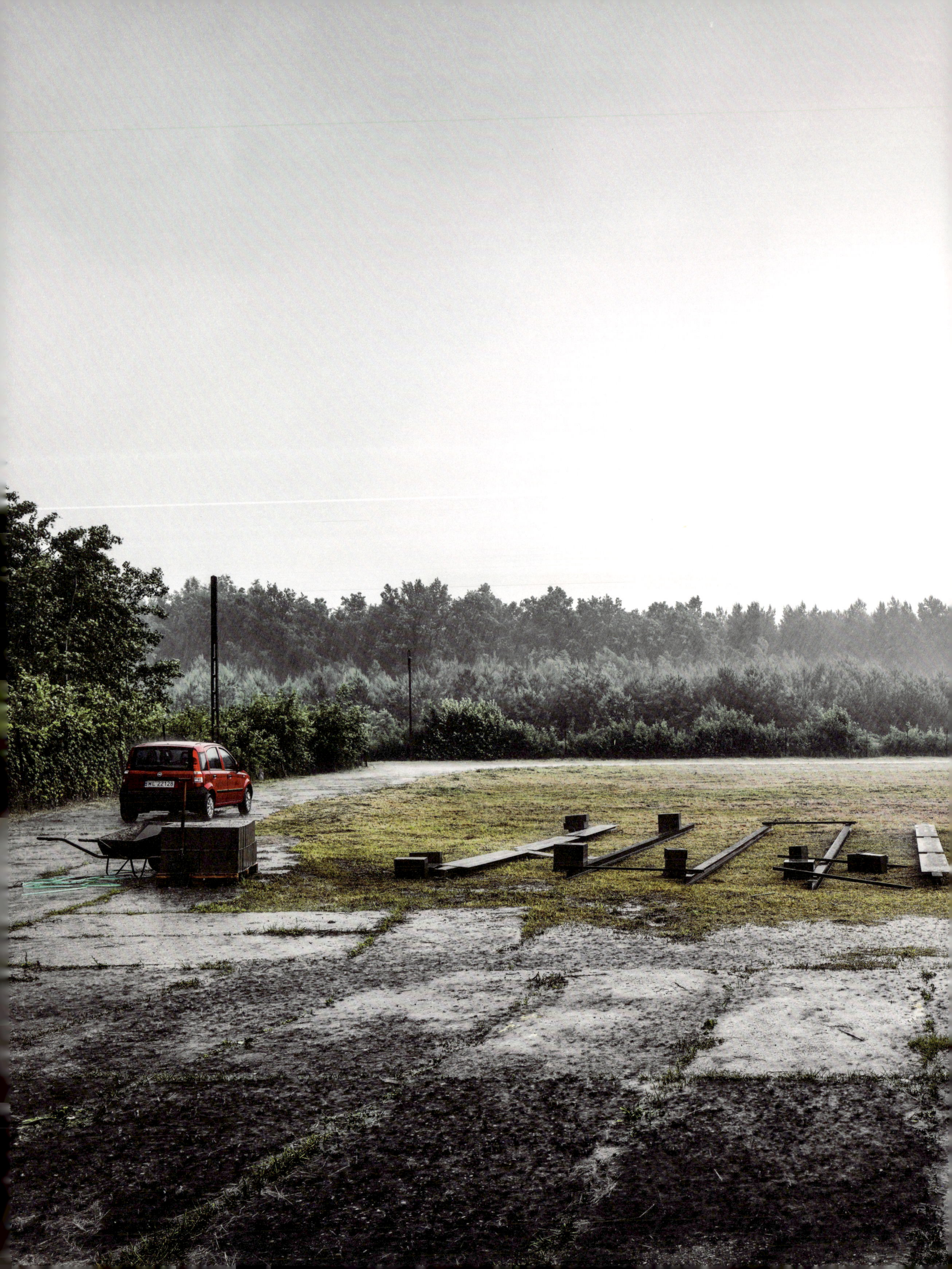

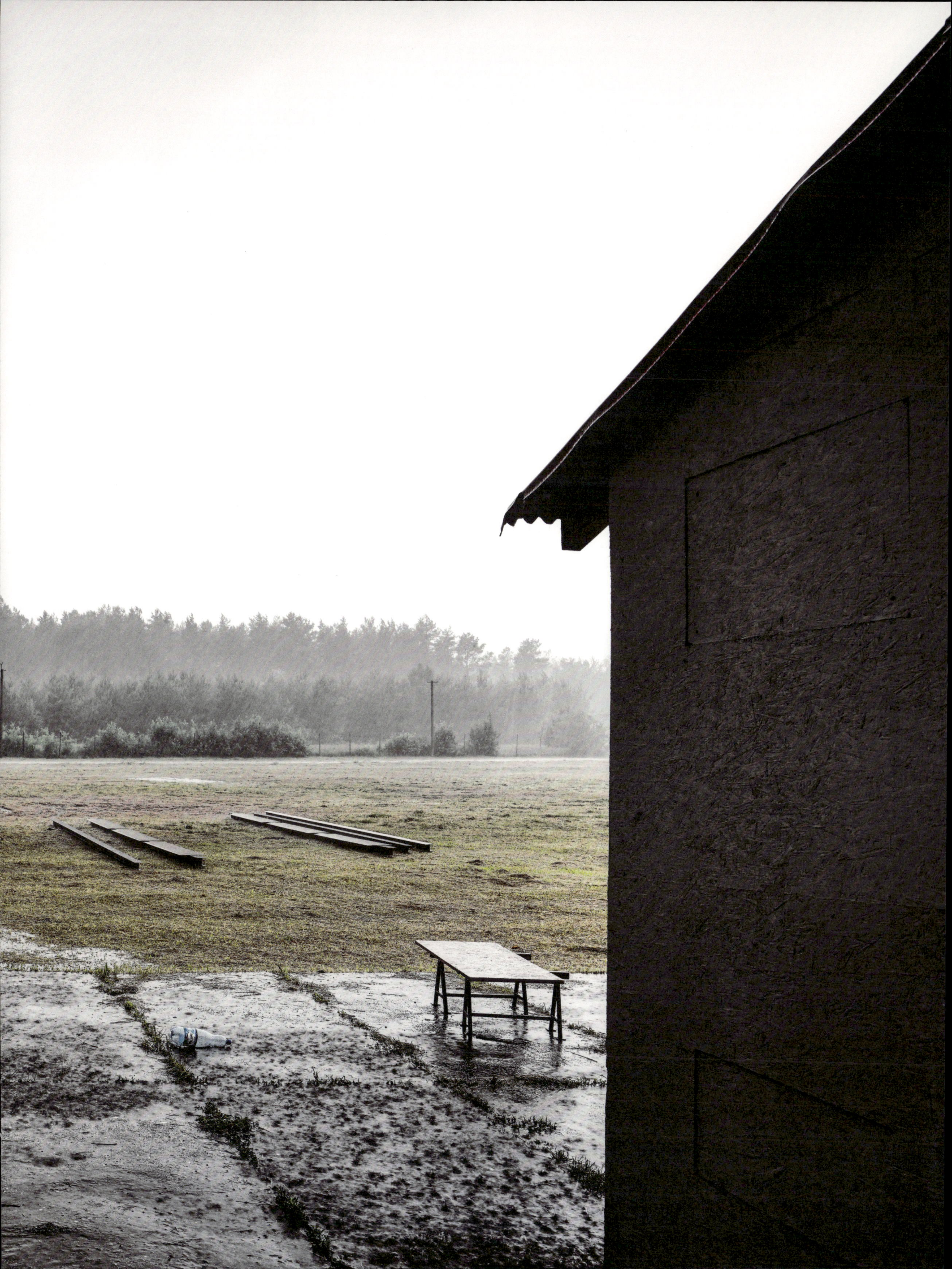

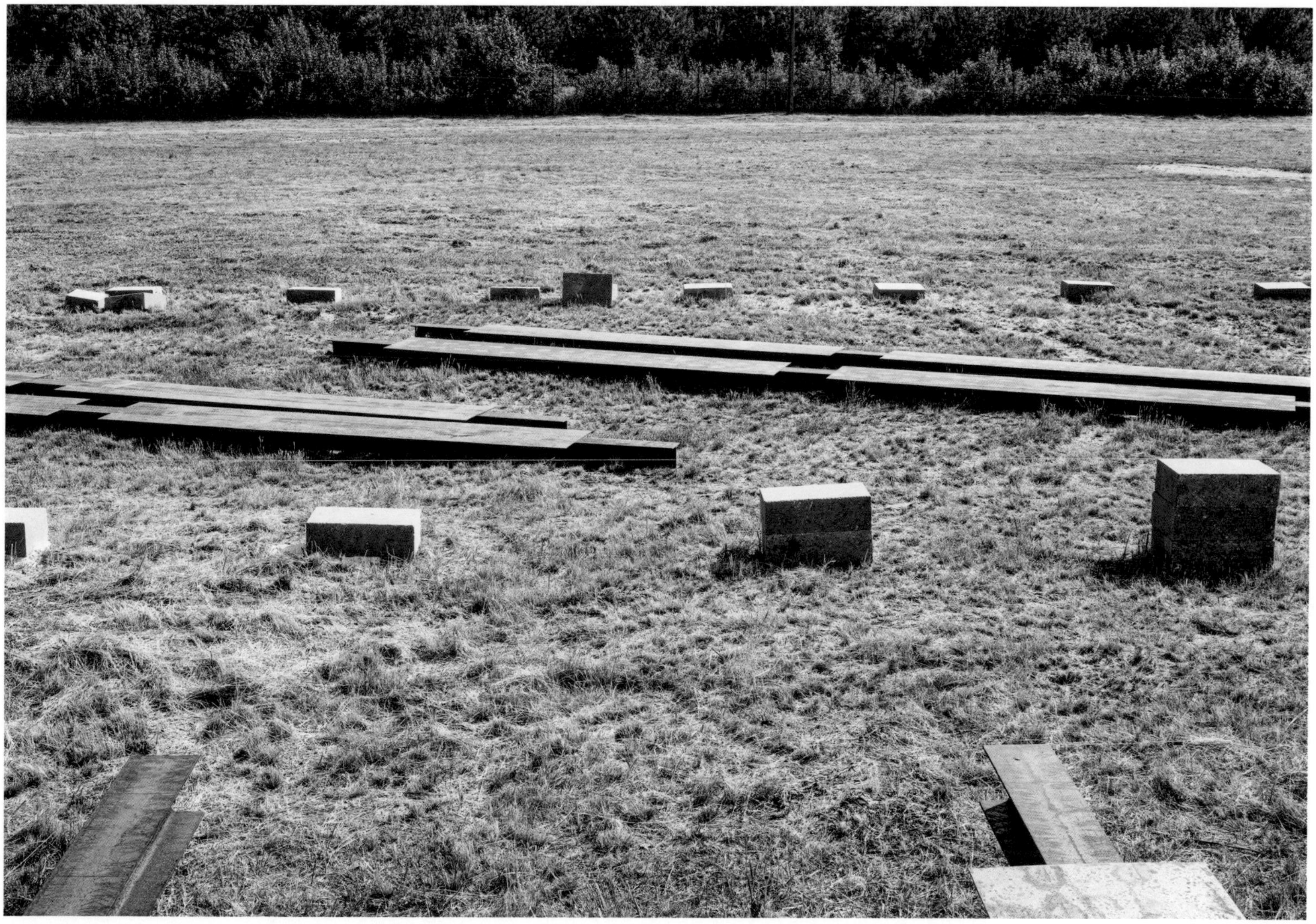

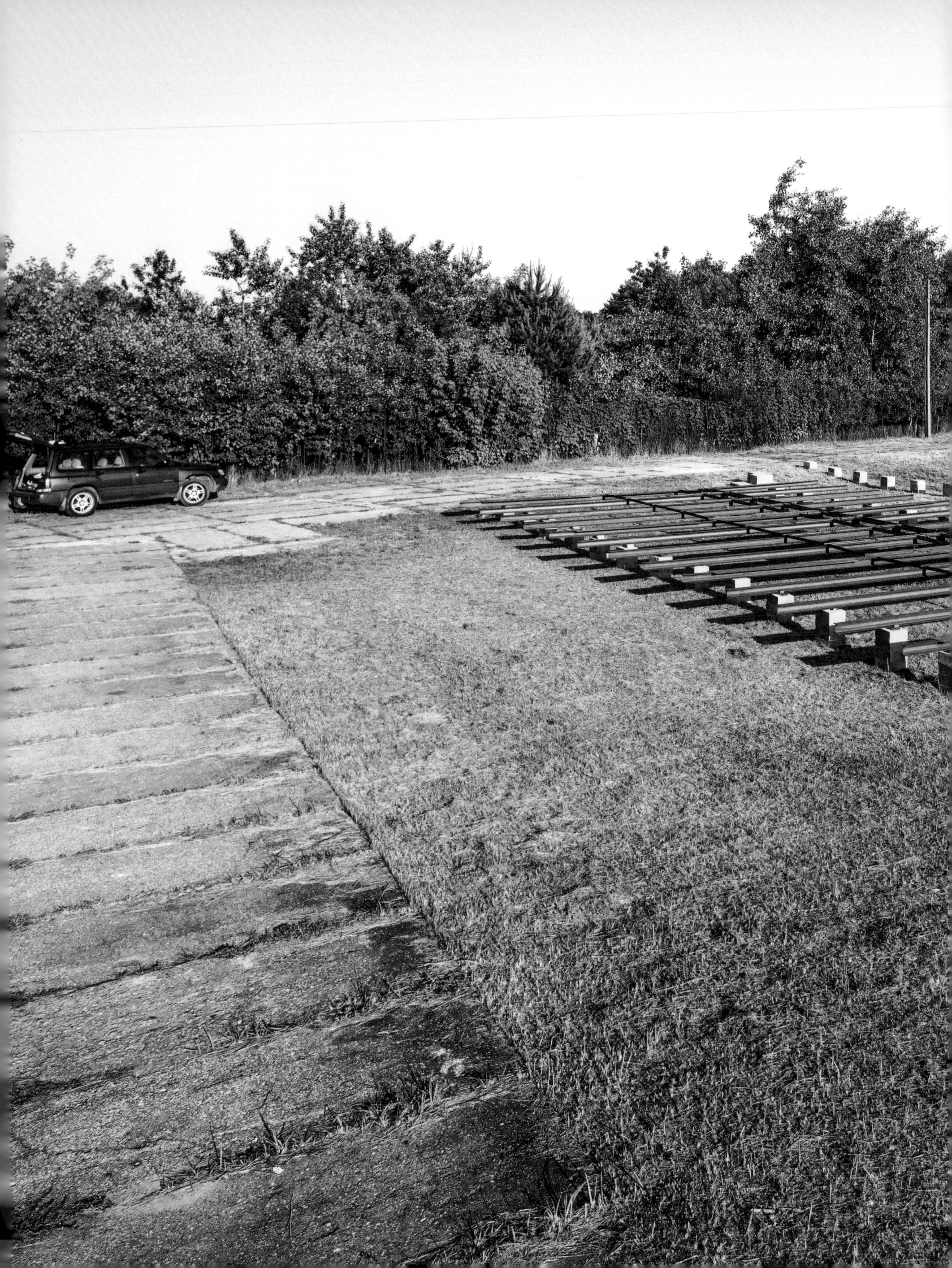

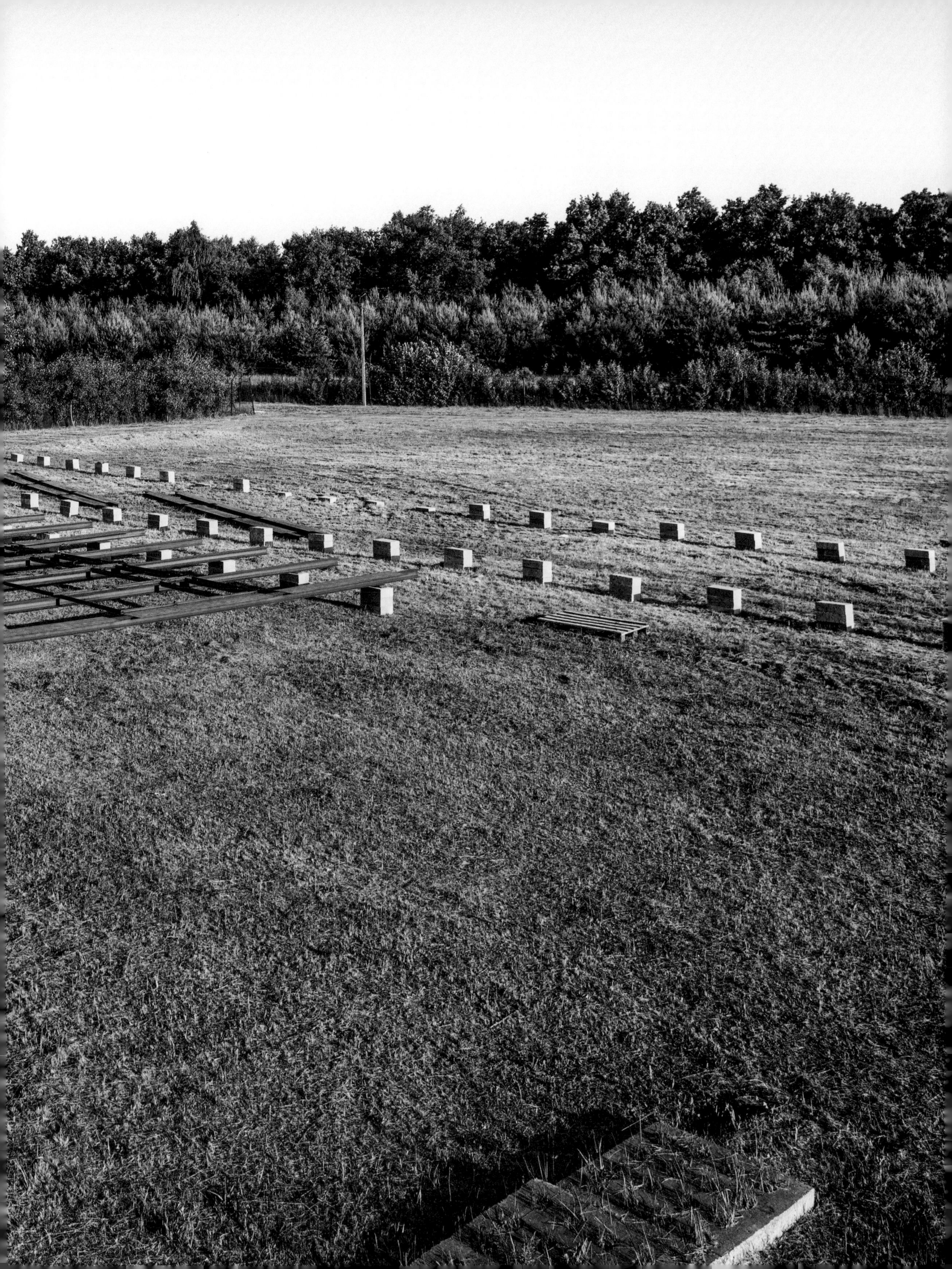

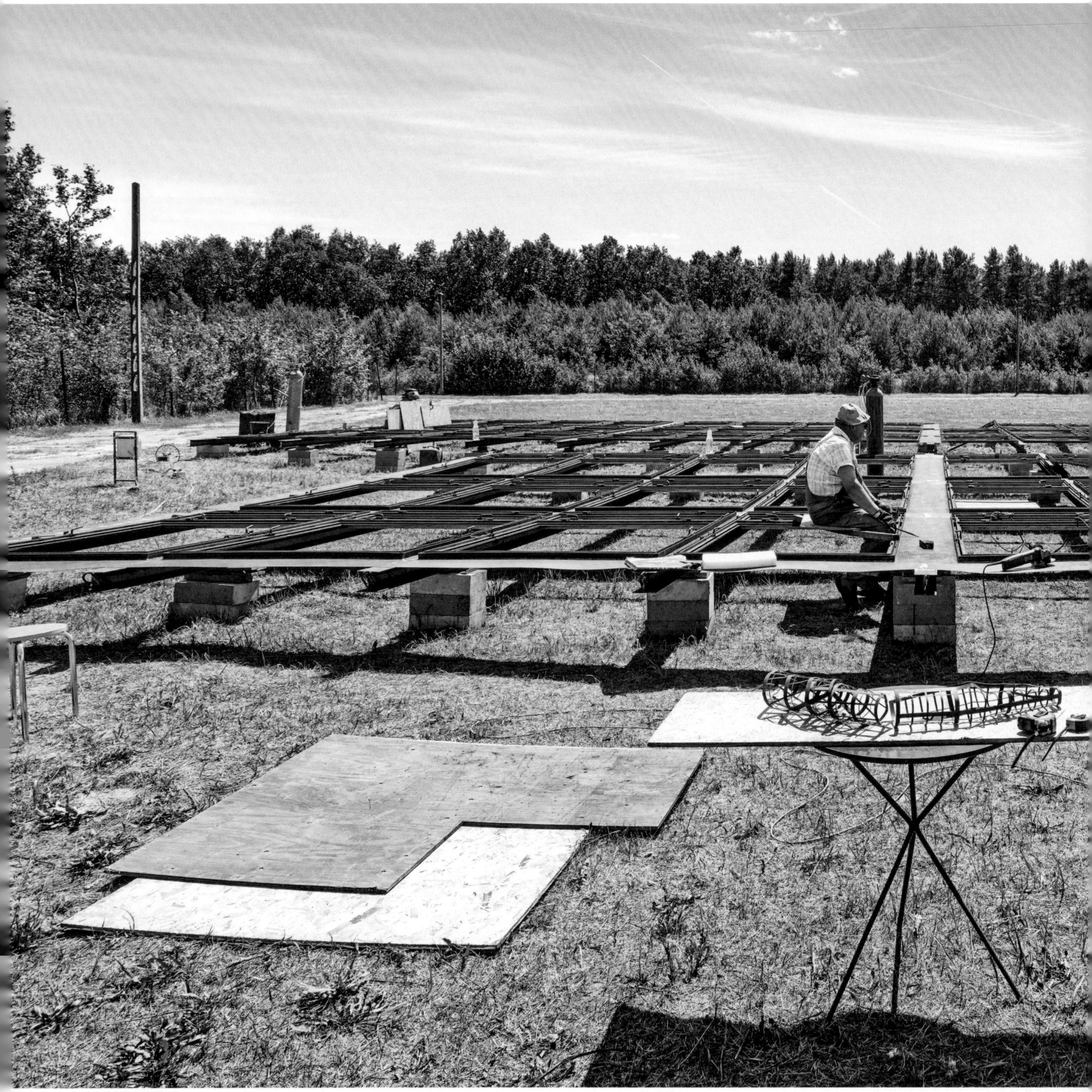

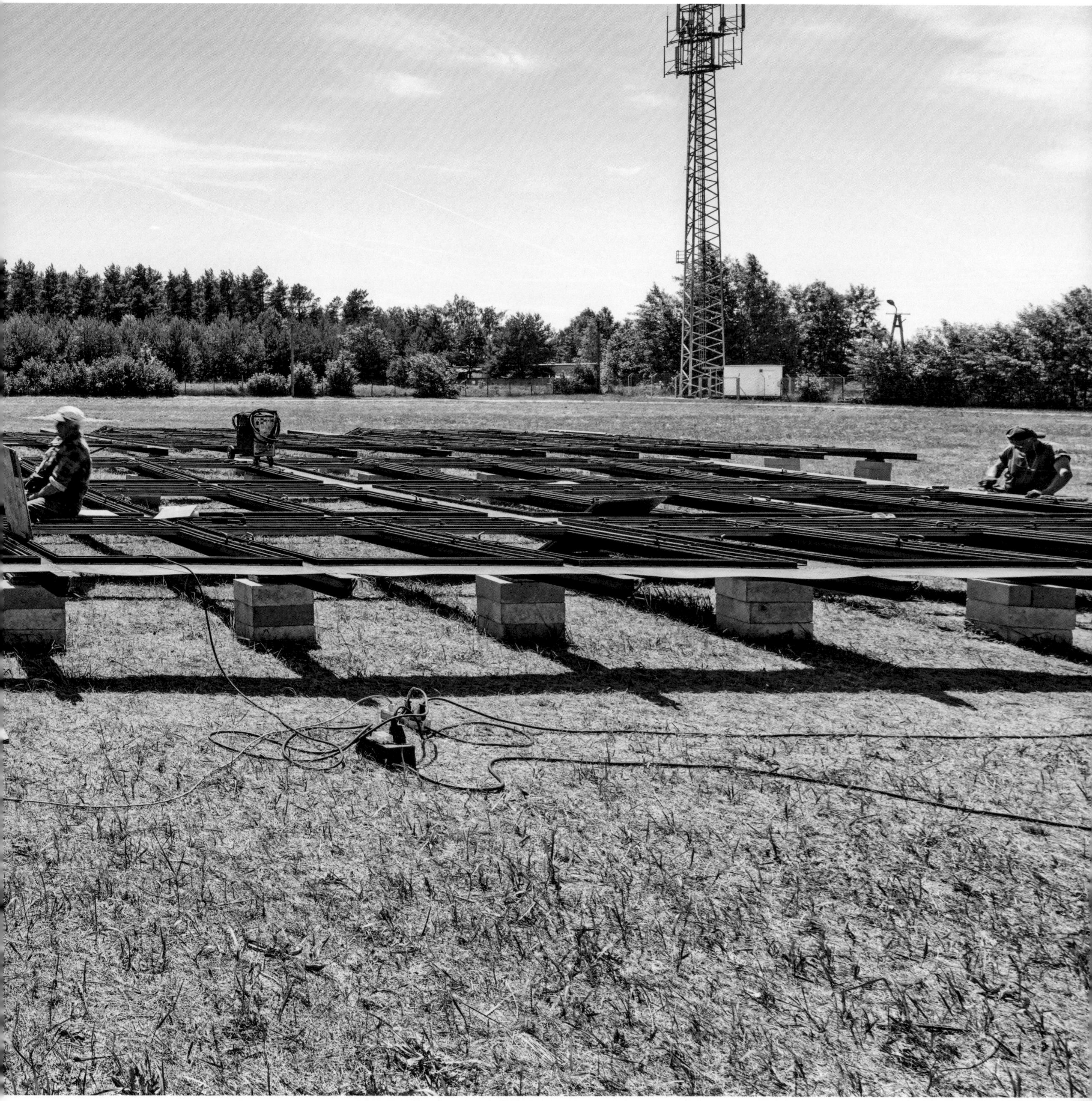

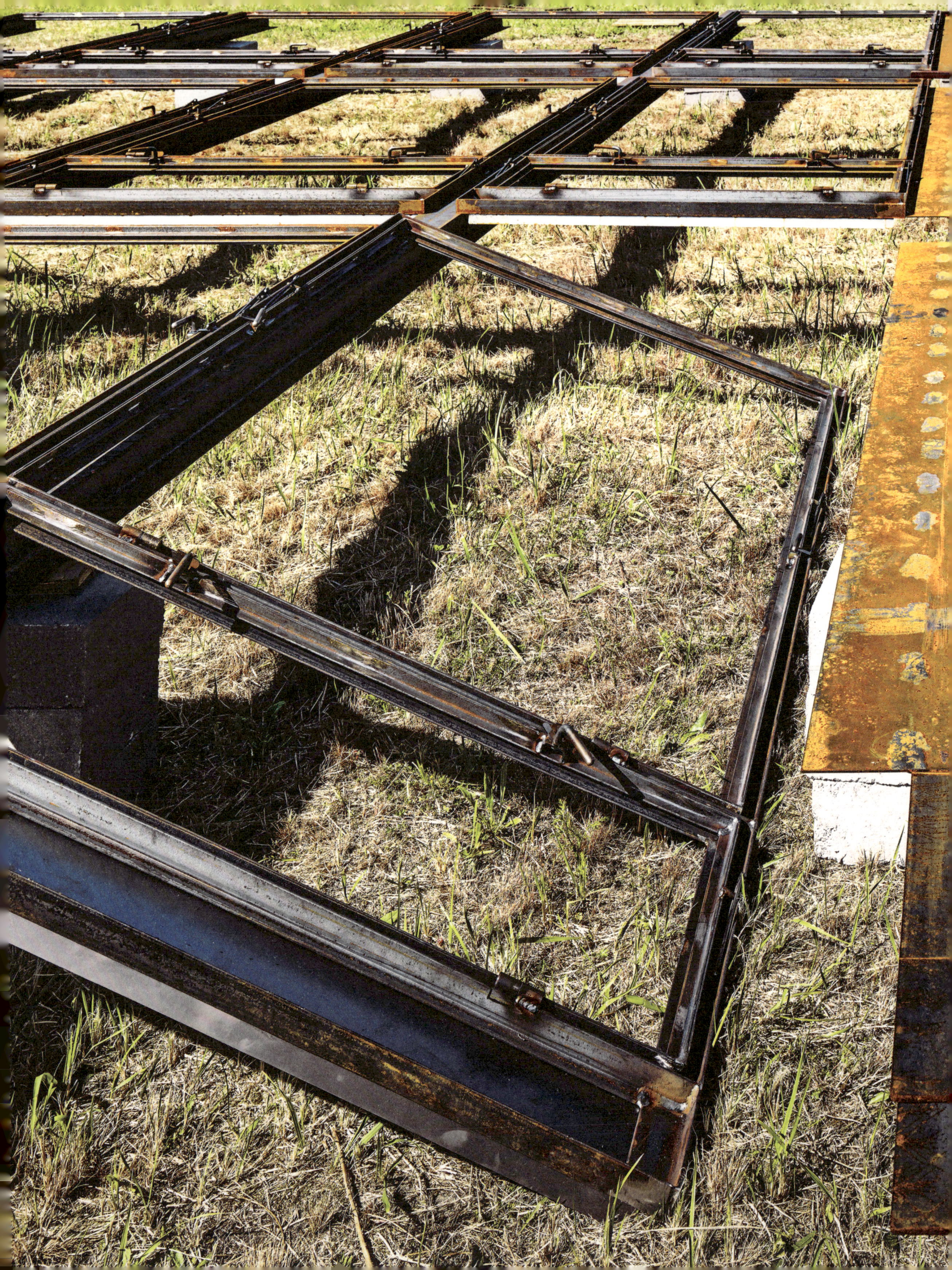

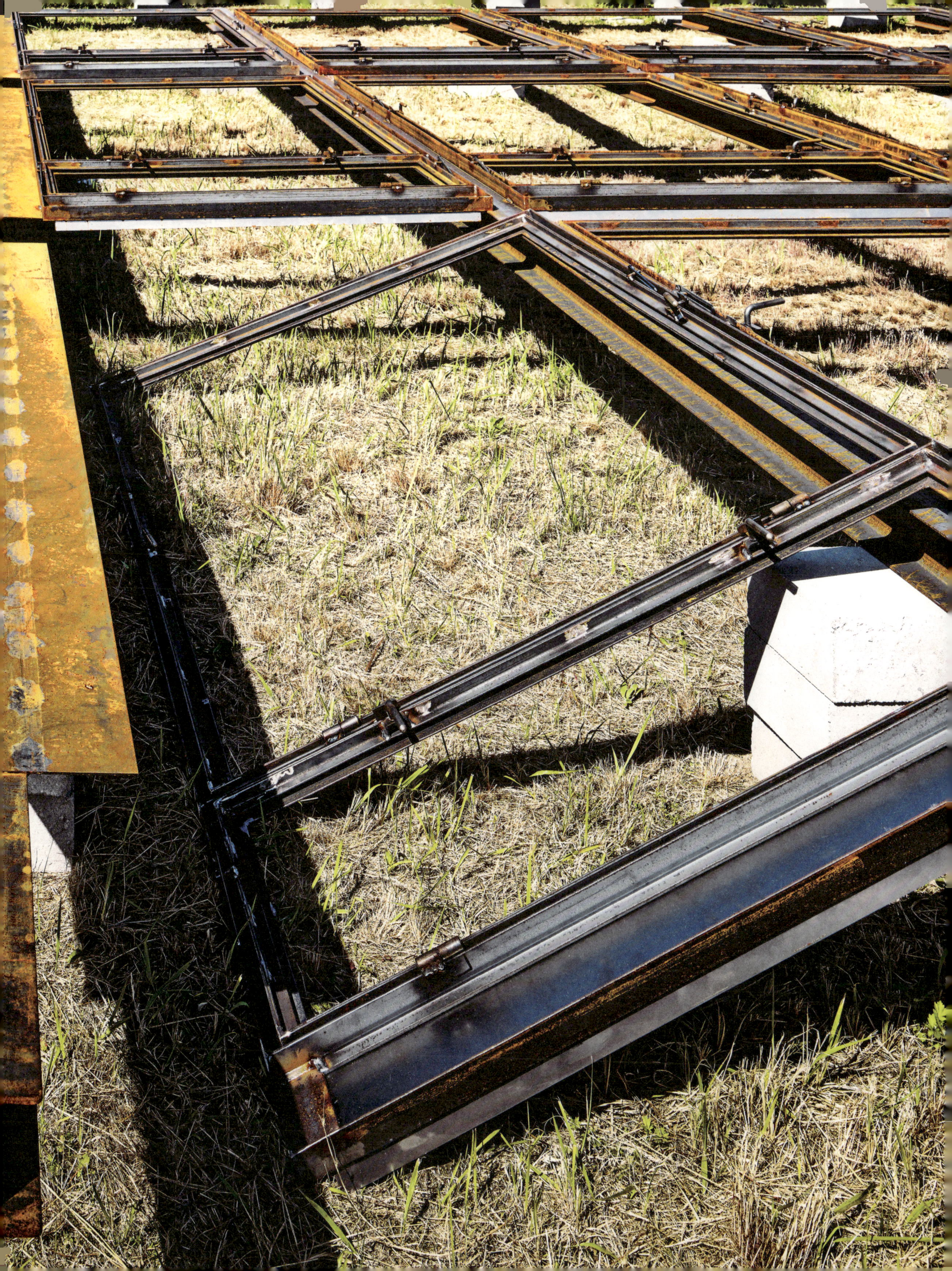

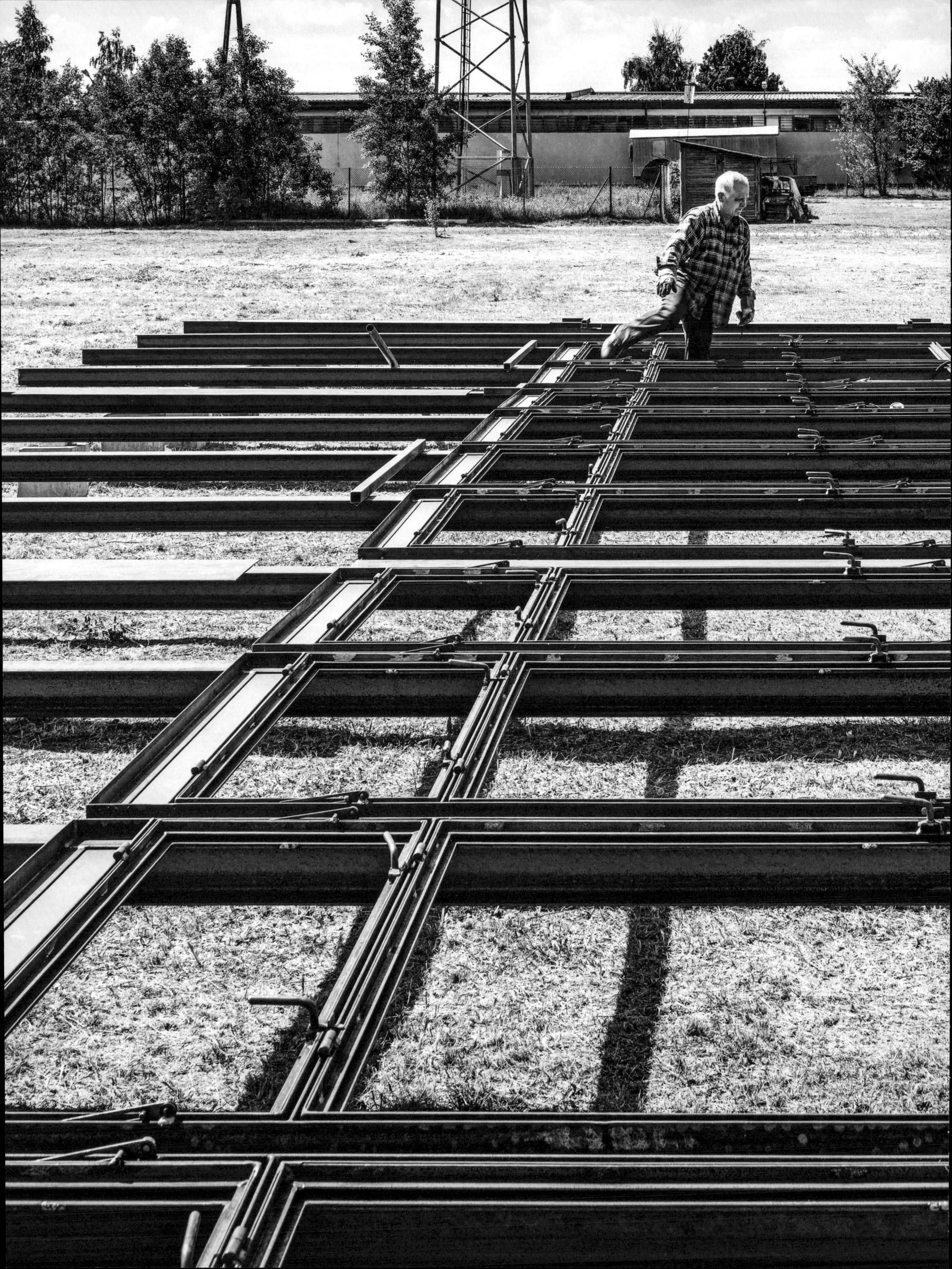

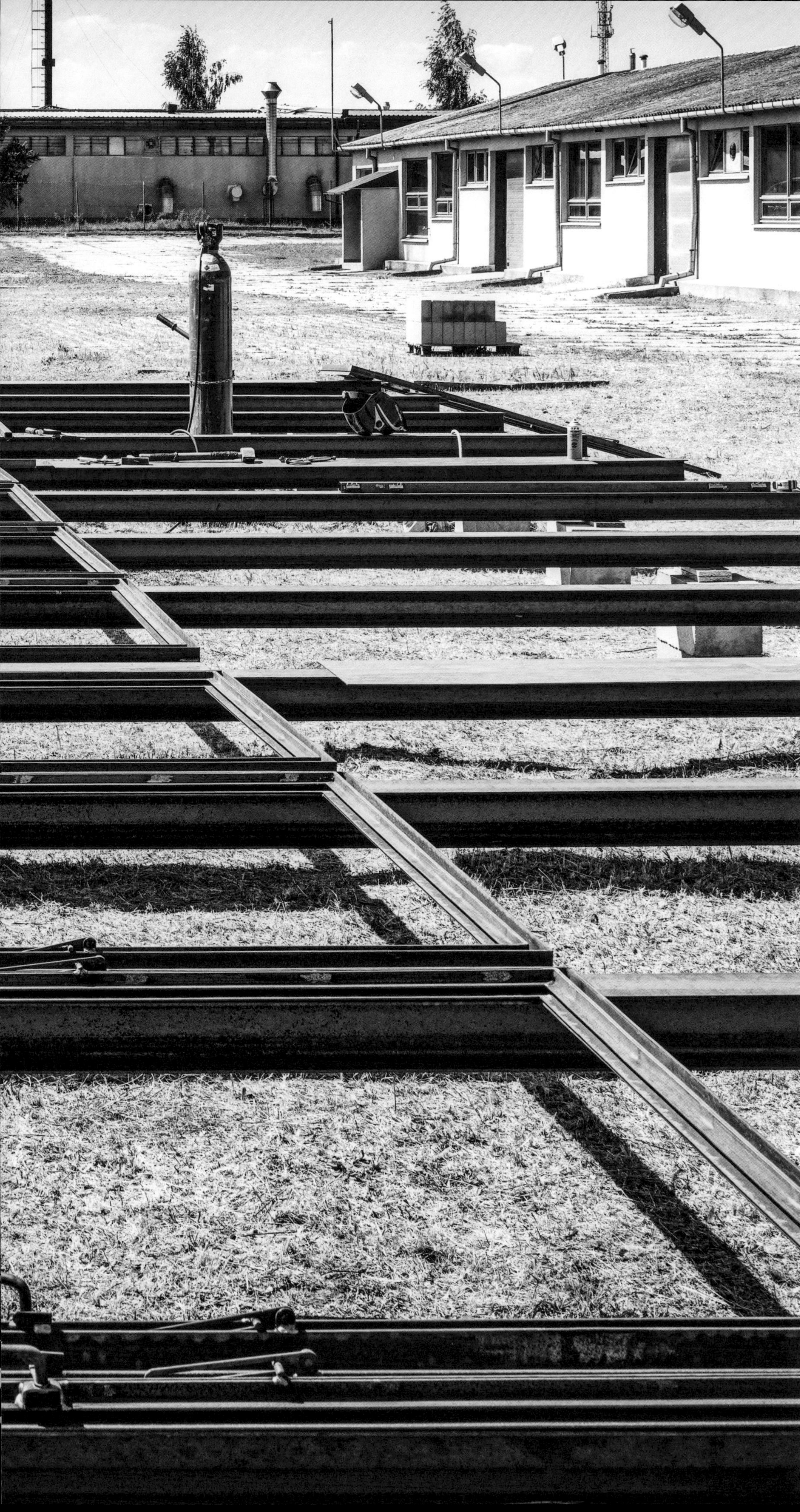

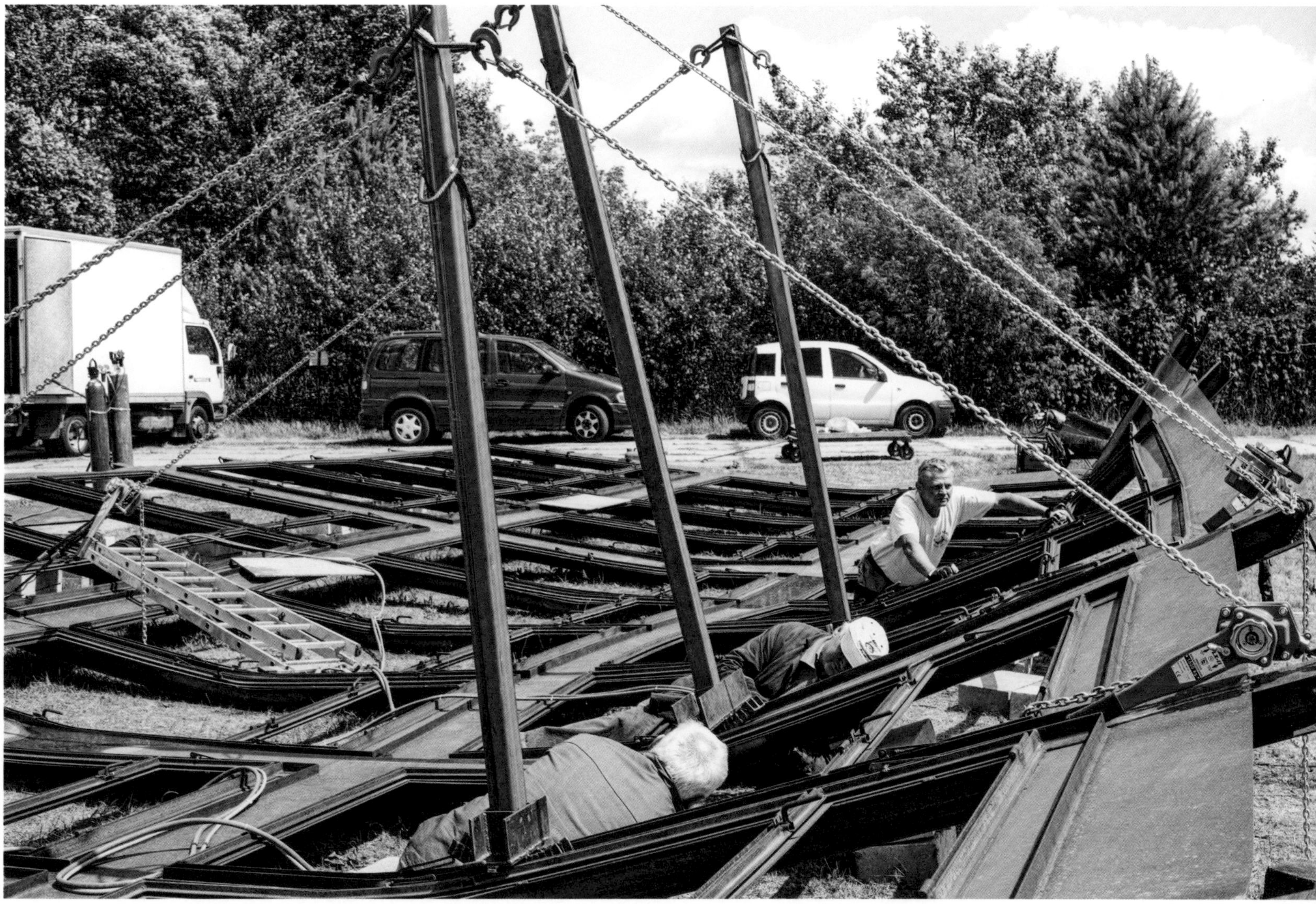

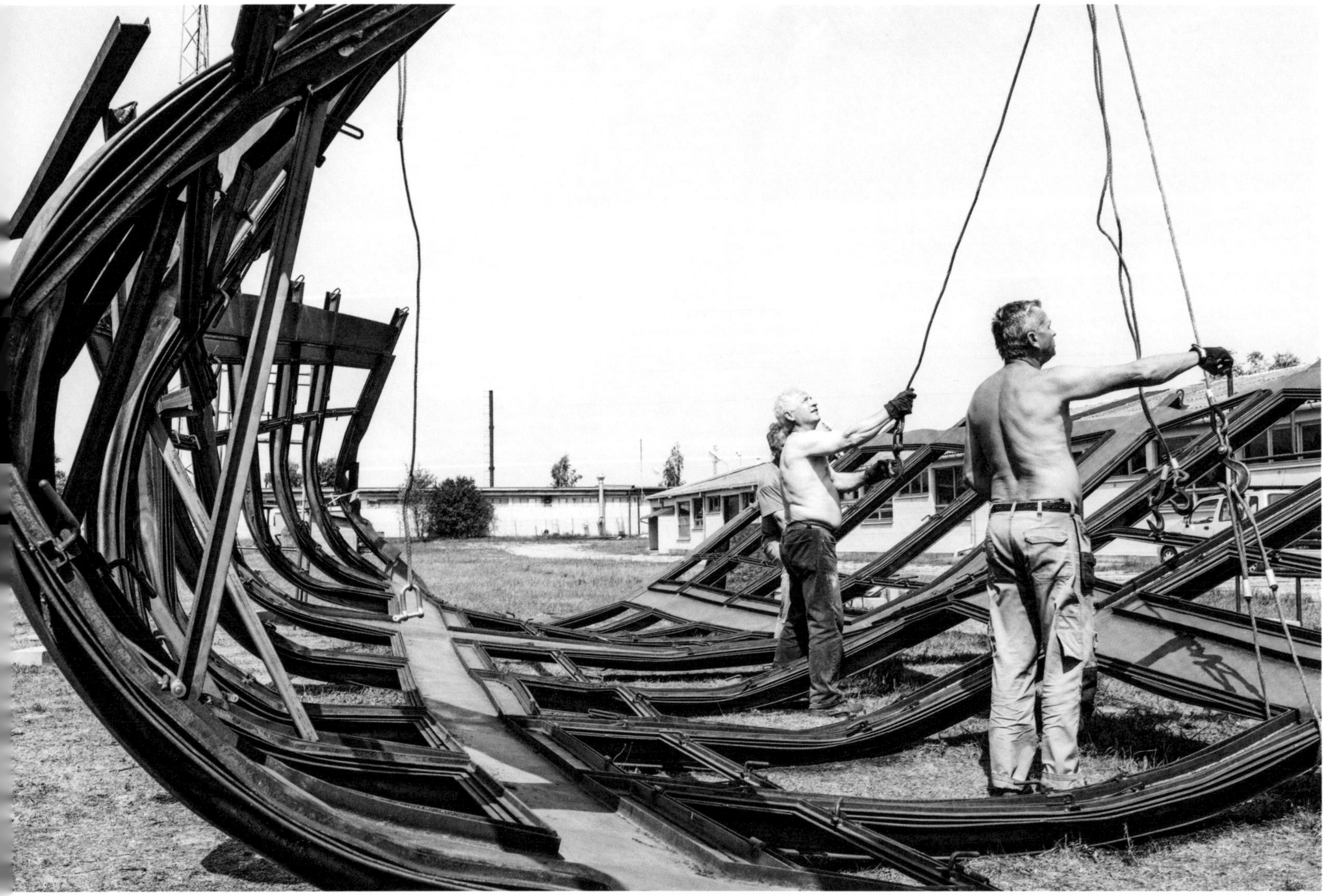

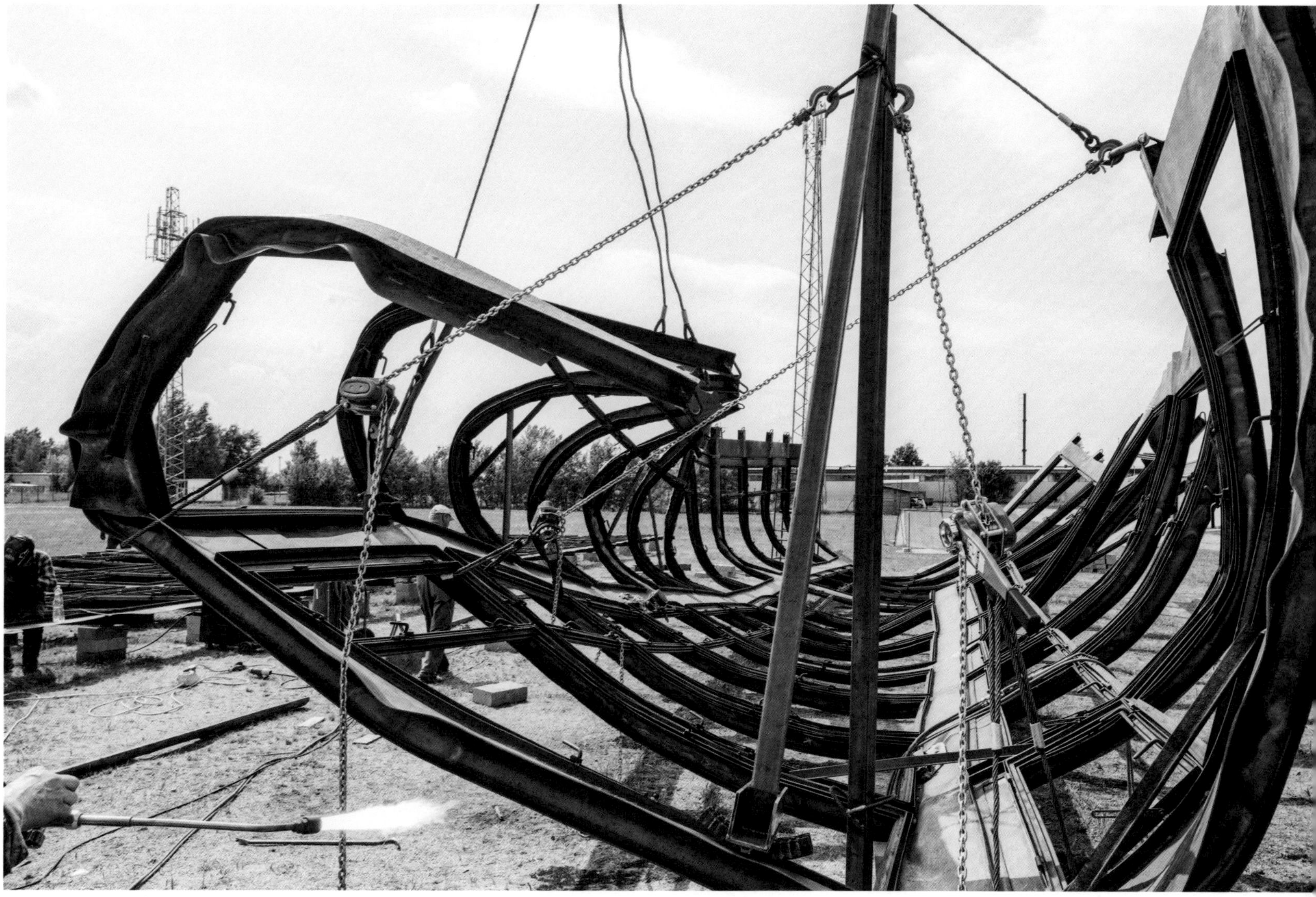

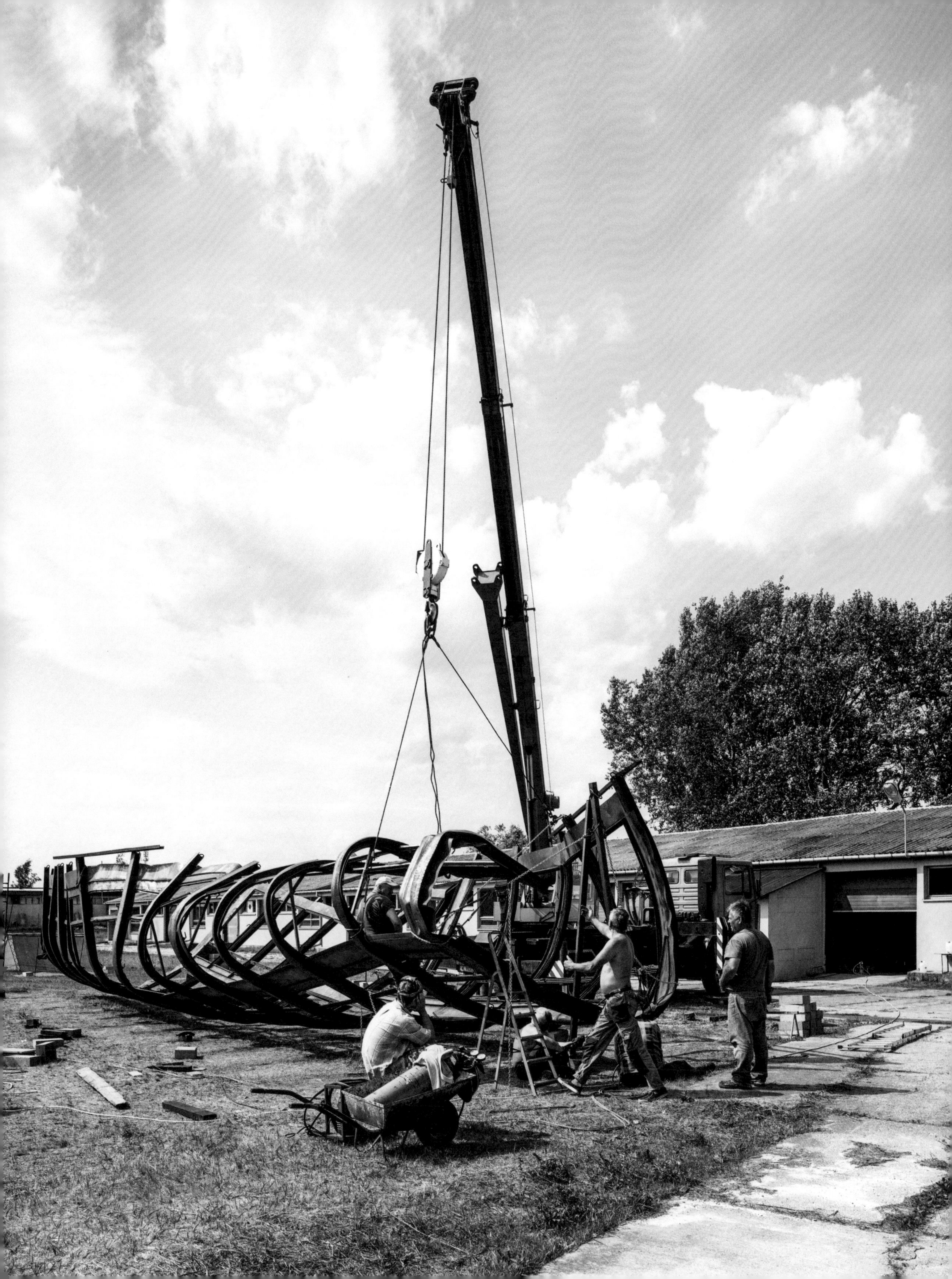

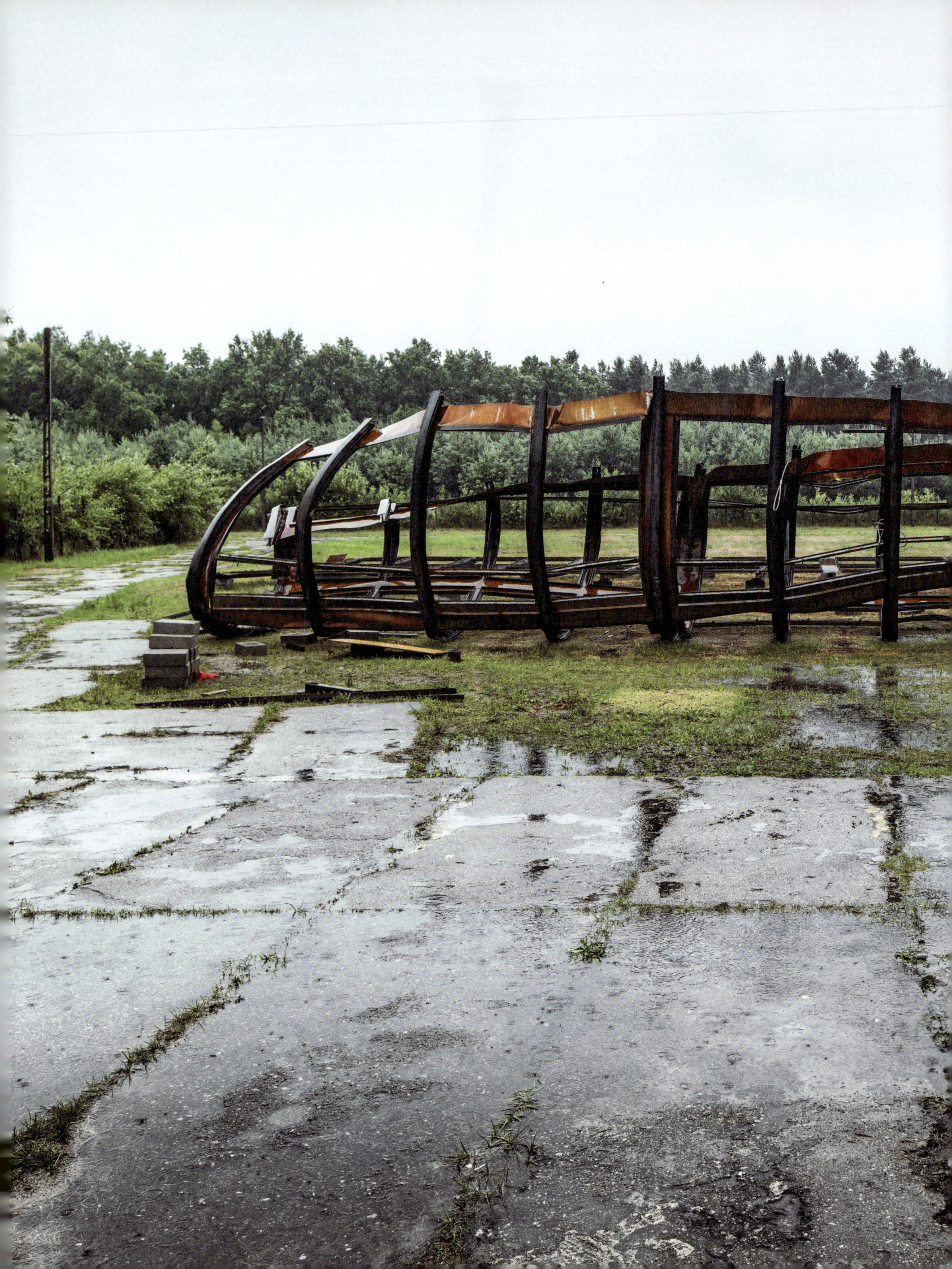

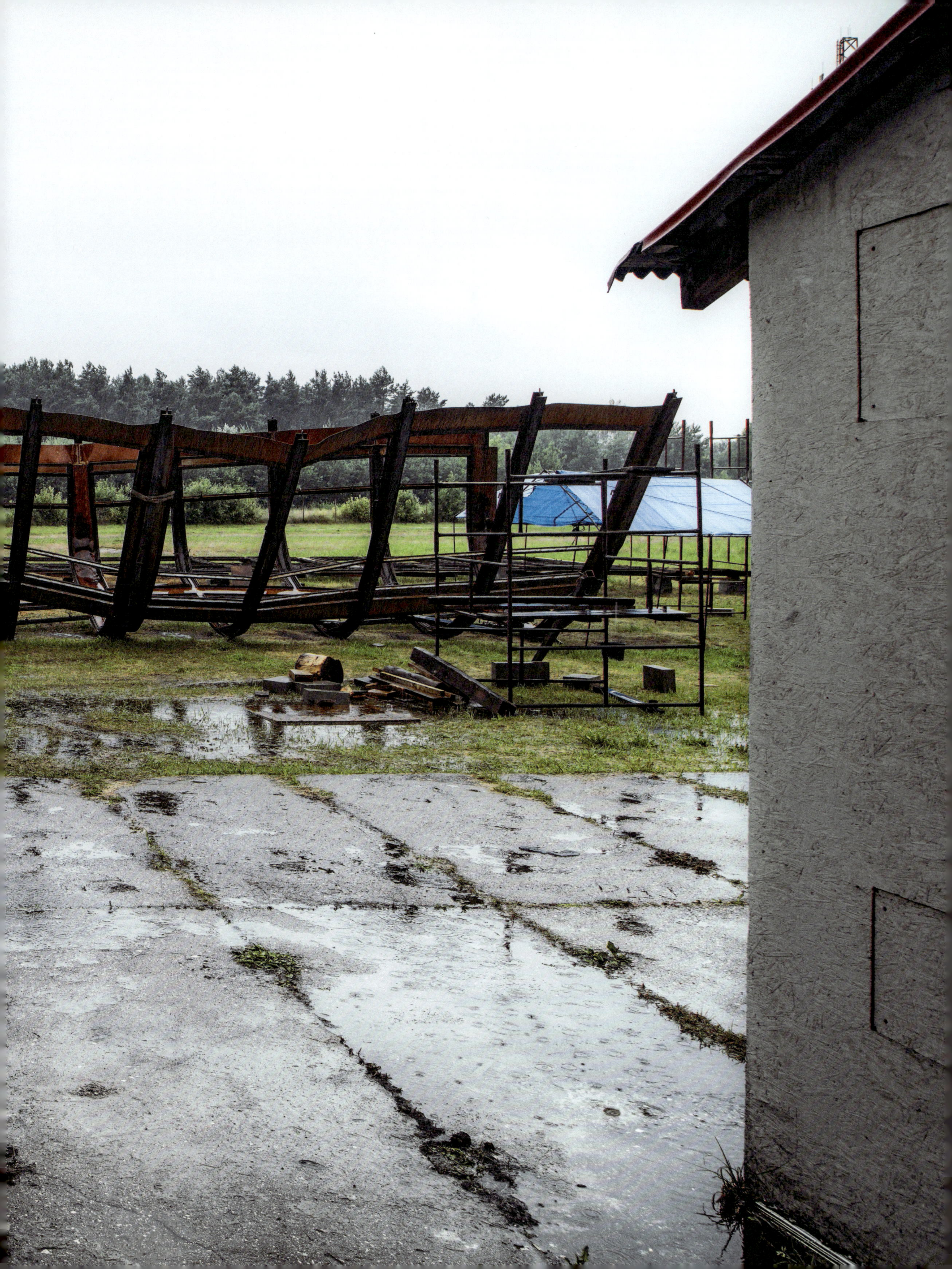

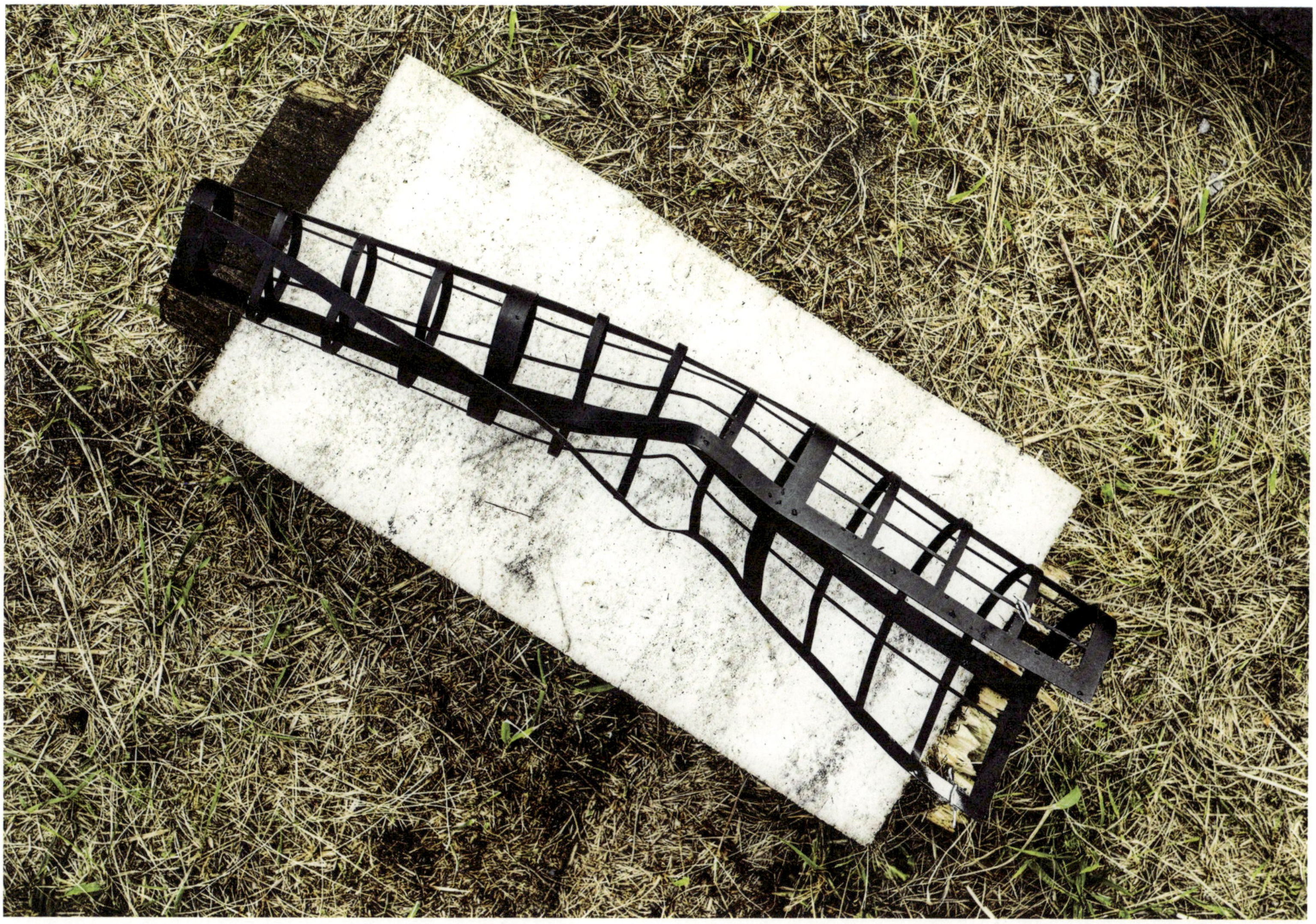

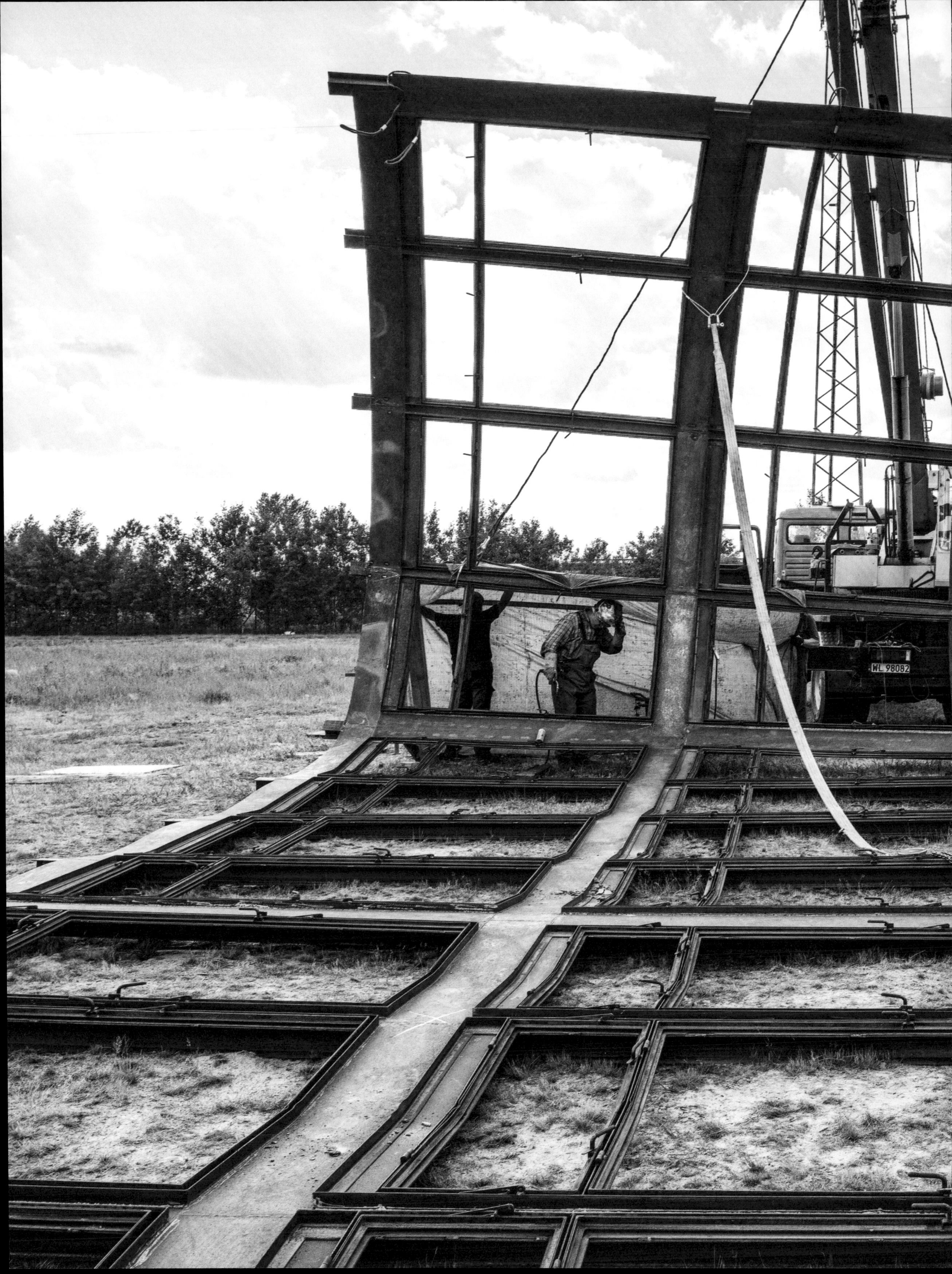
WL 98082

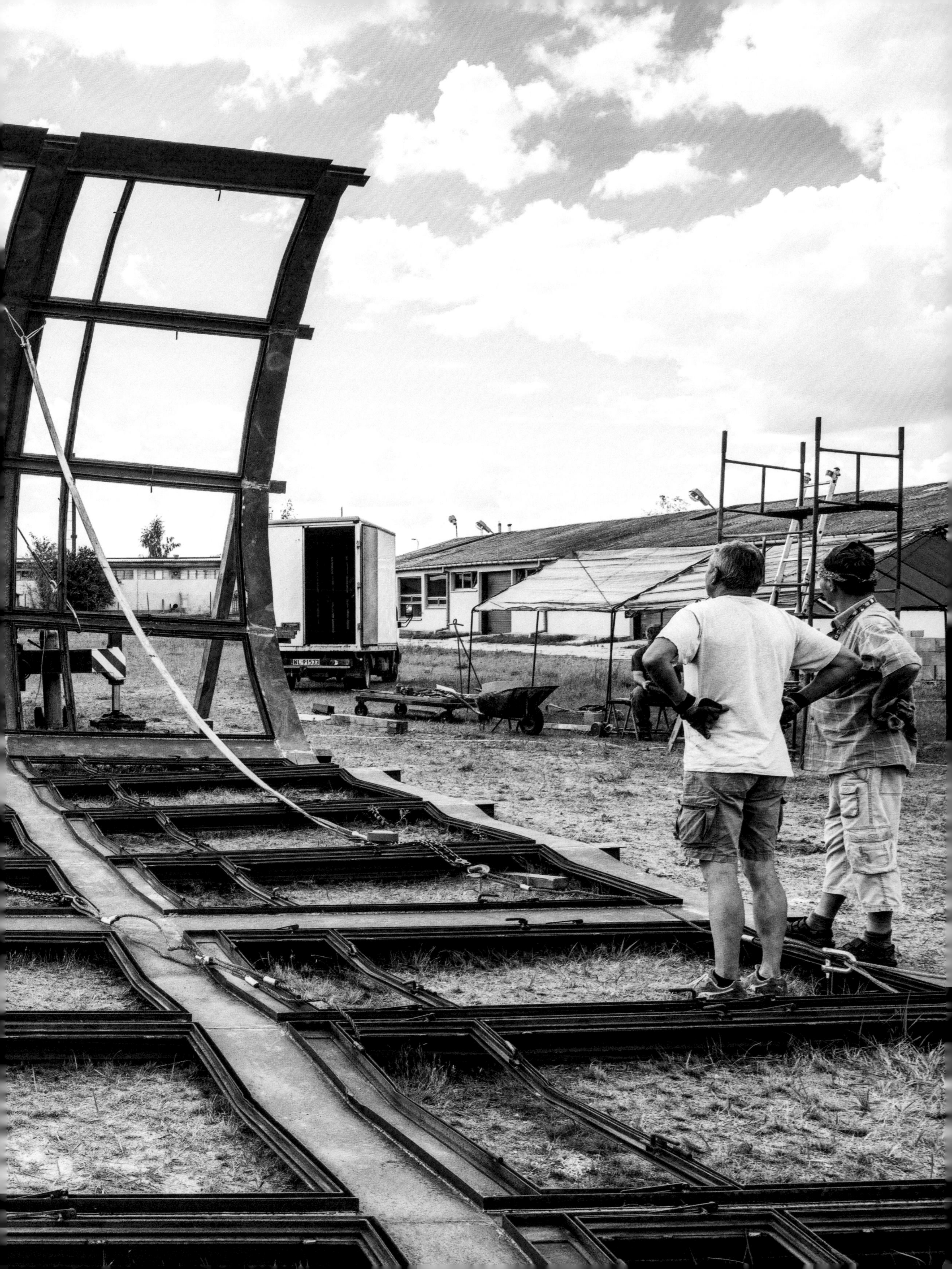
WL 91533

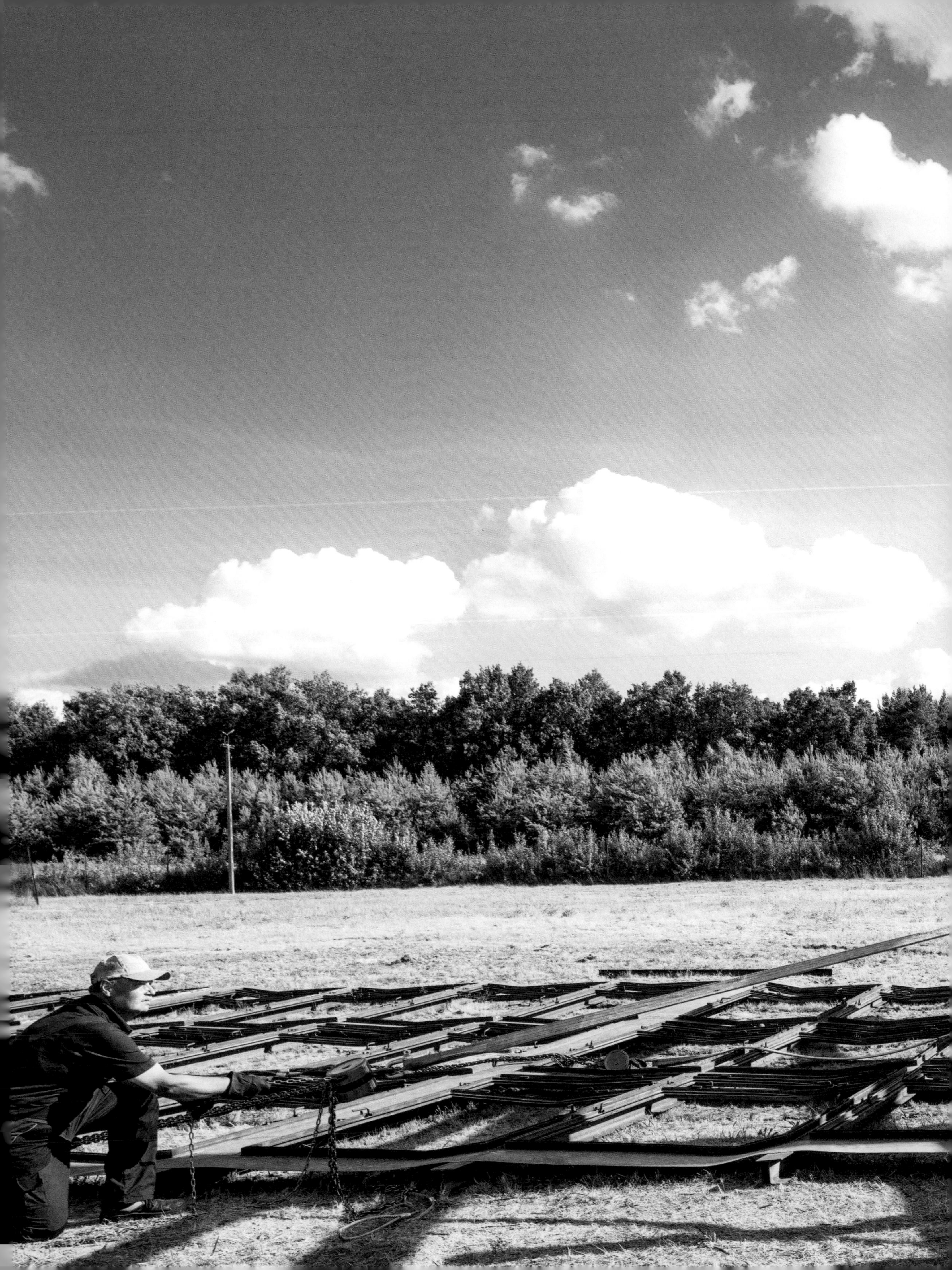

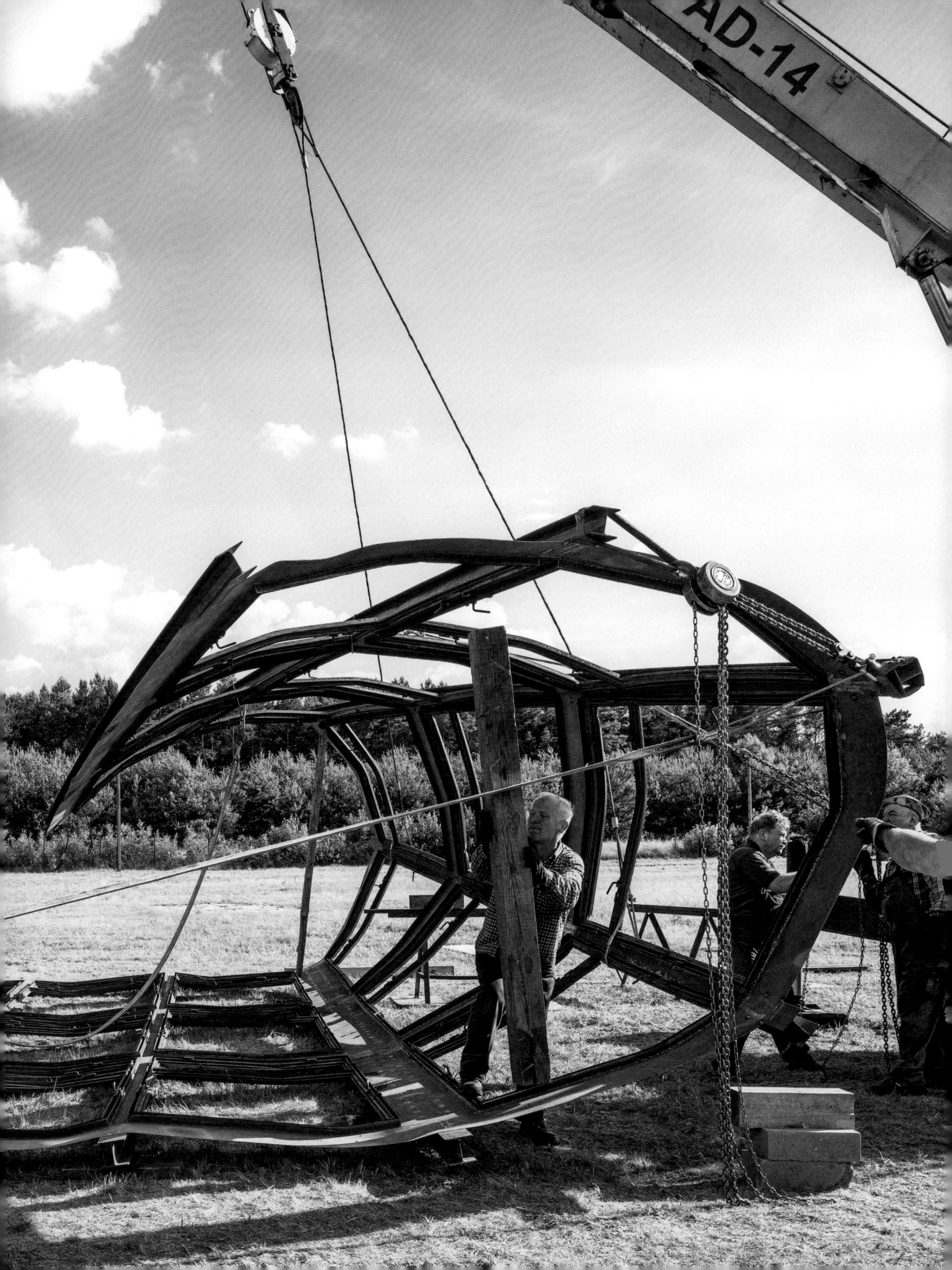
AD-14

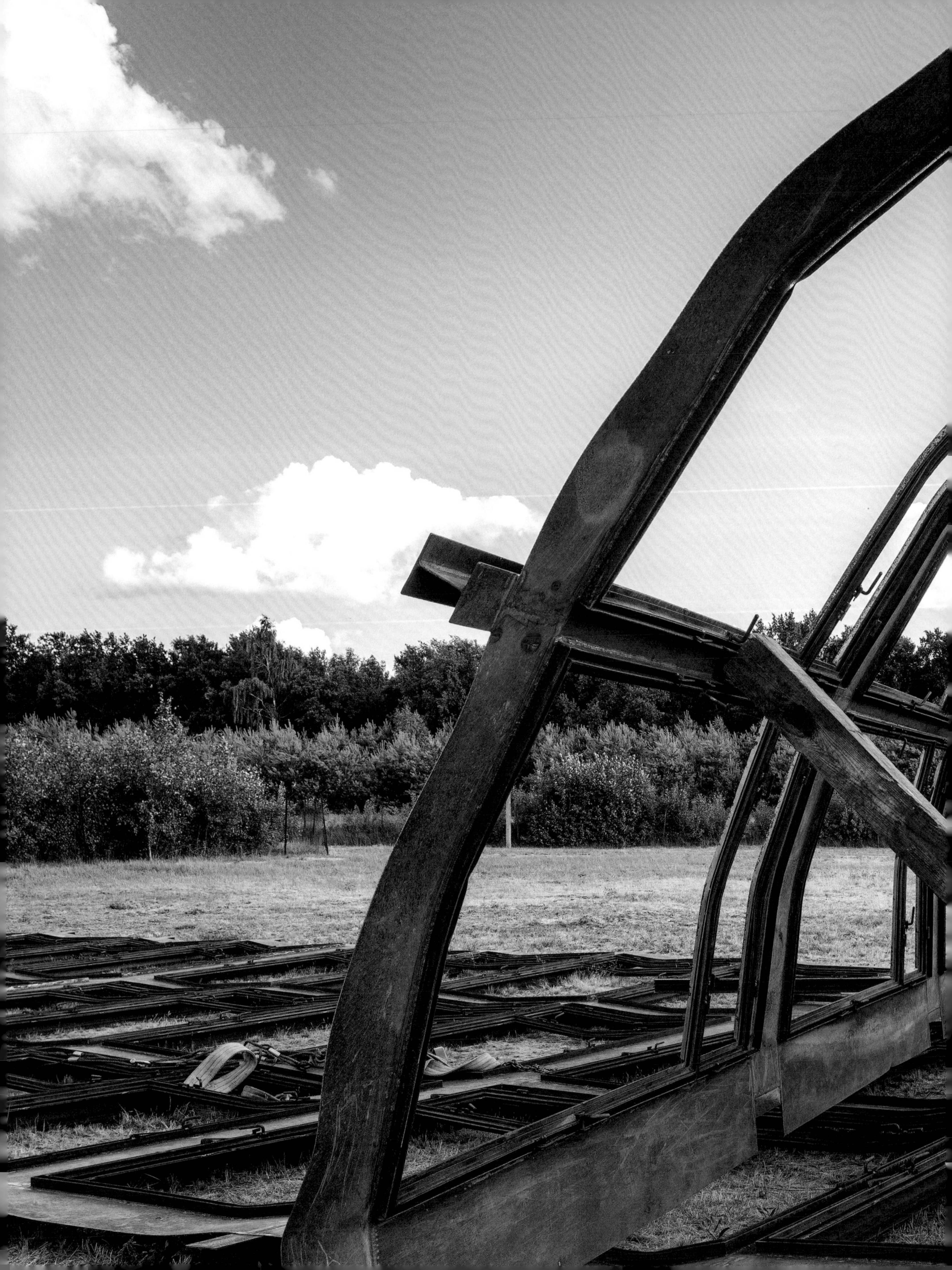

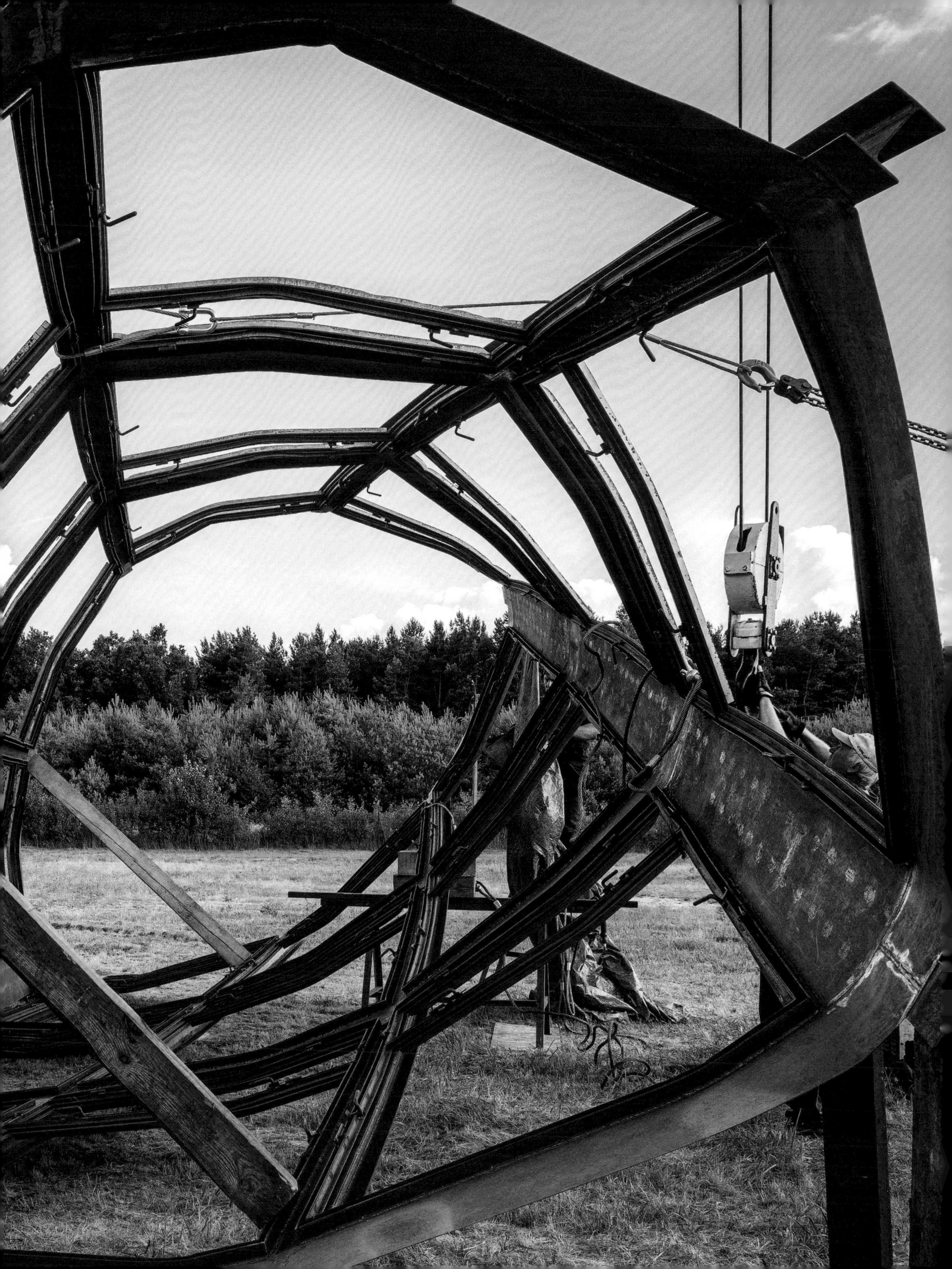

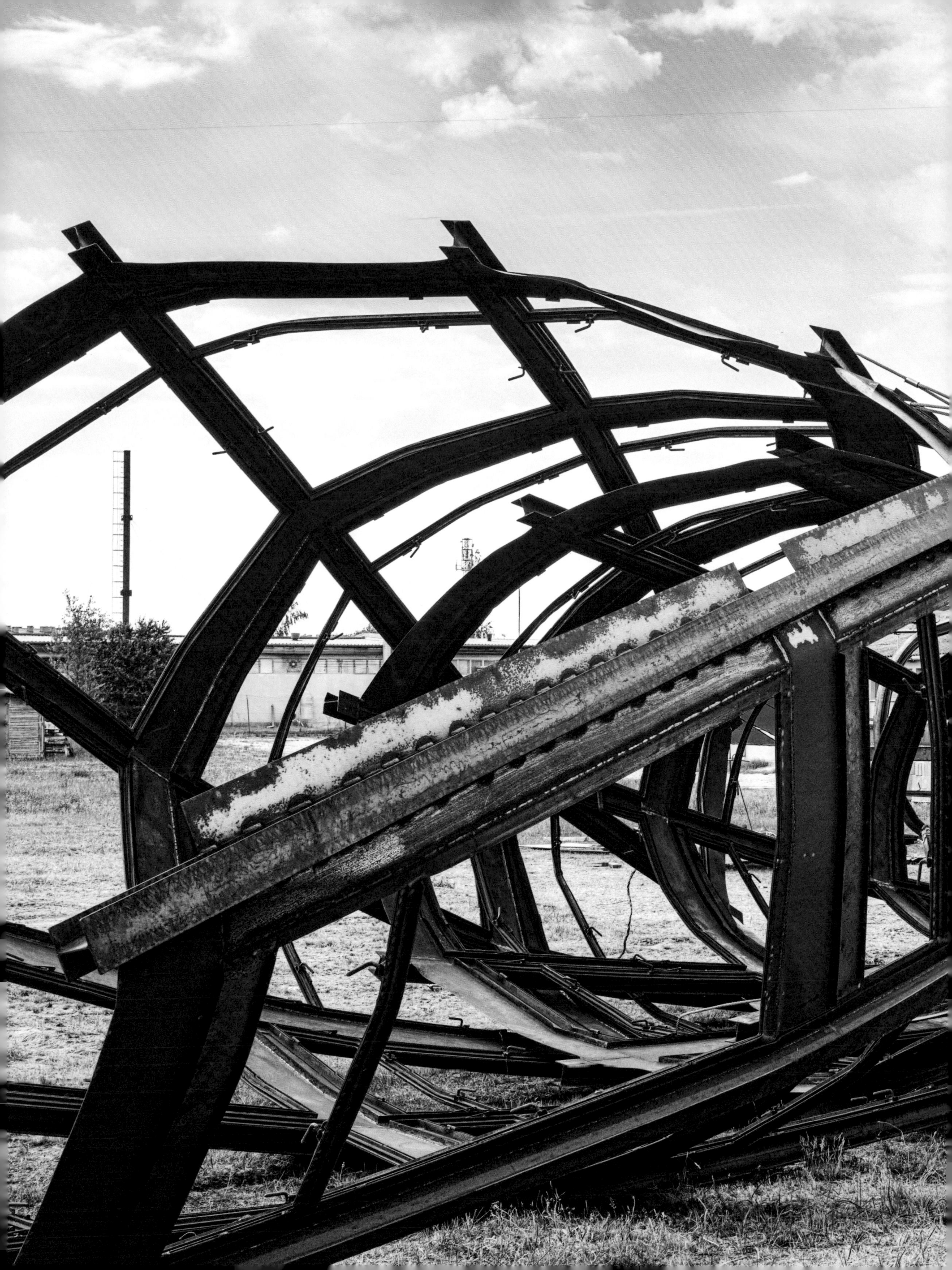

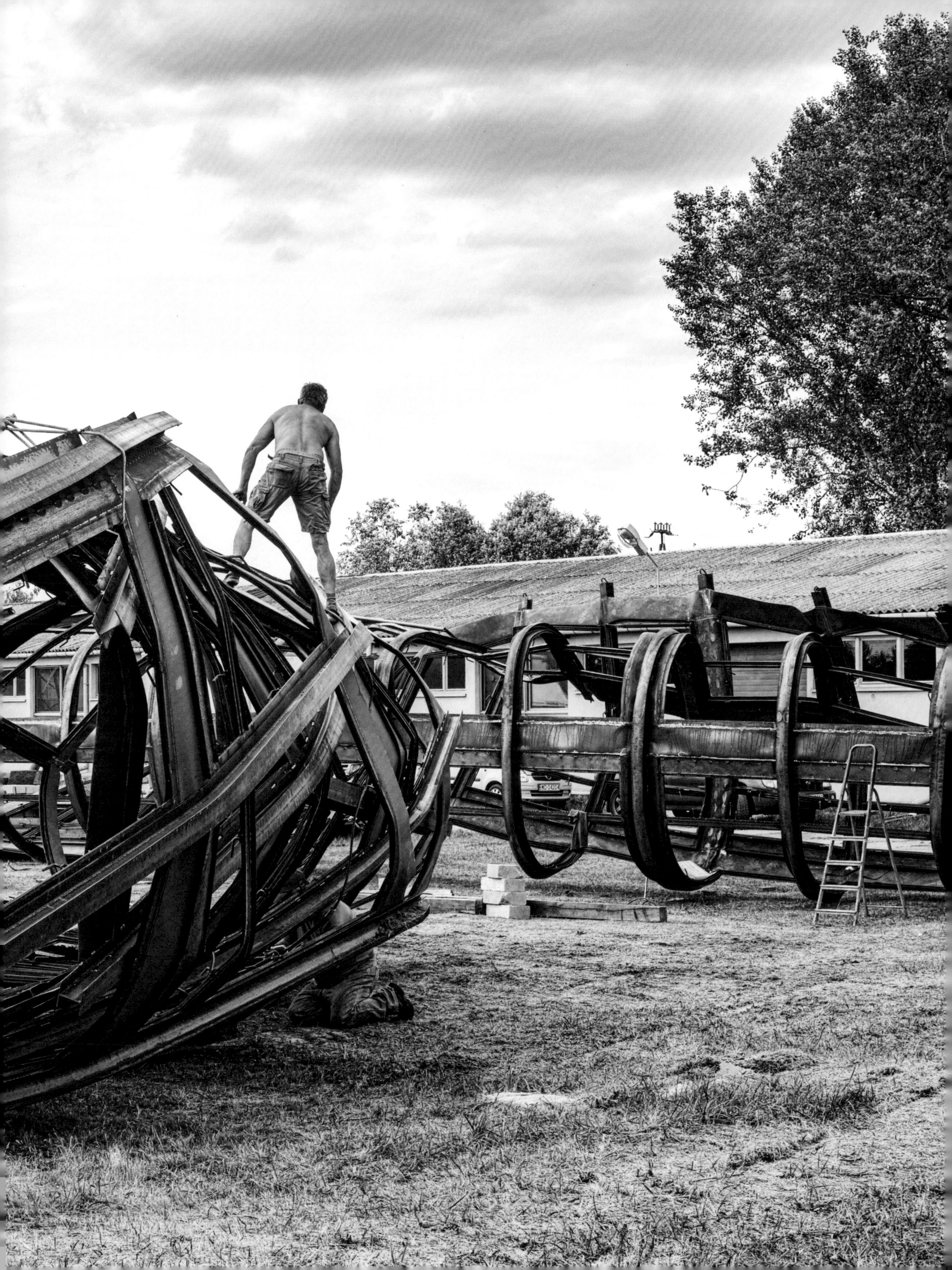

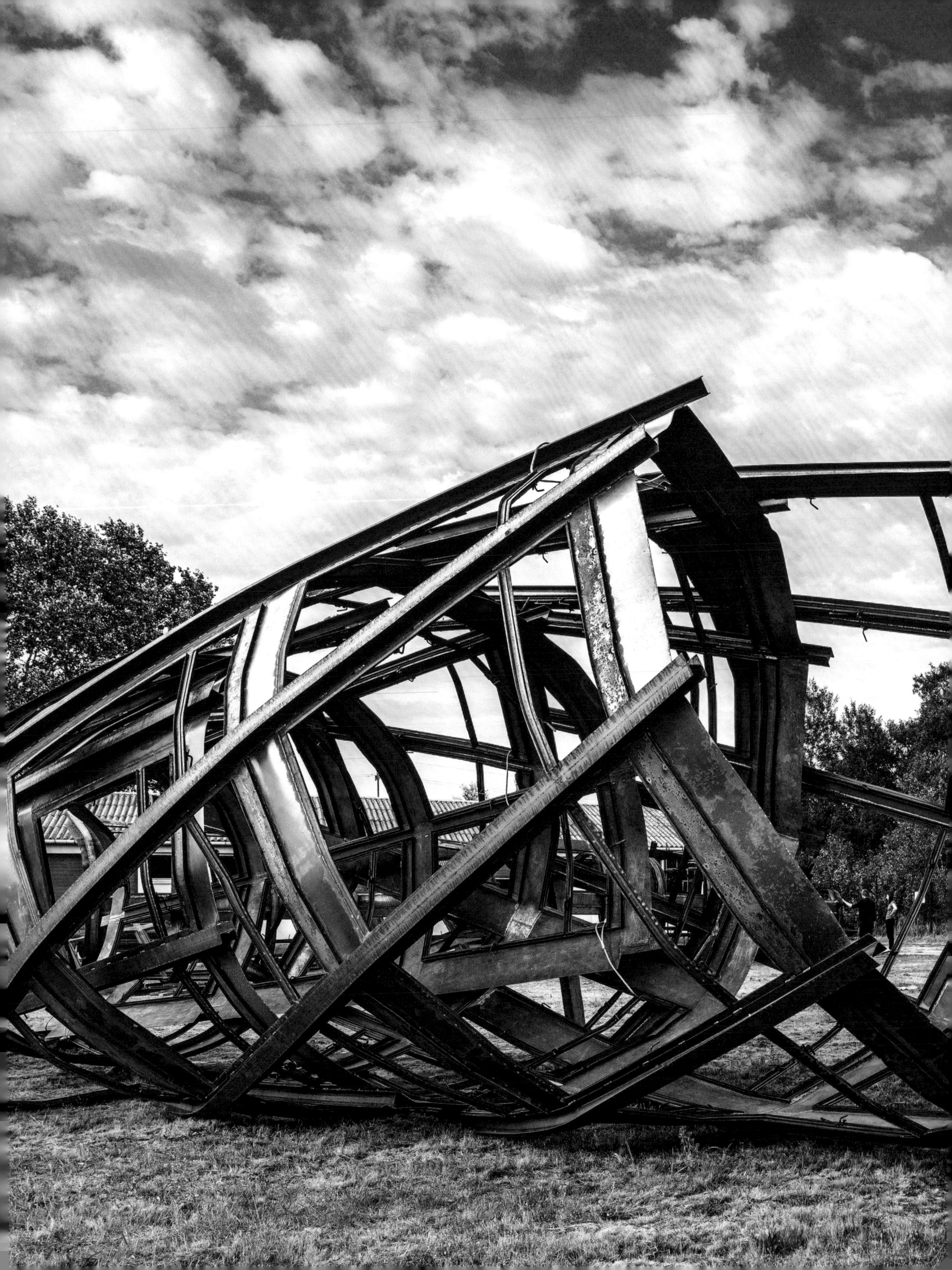

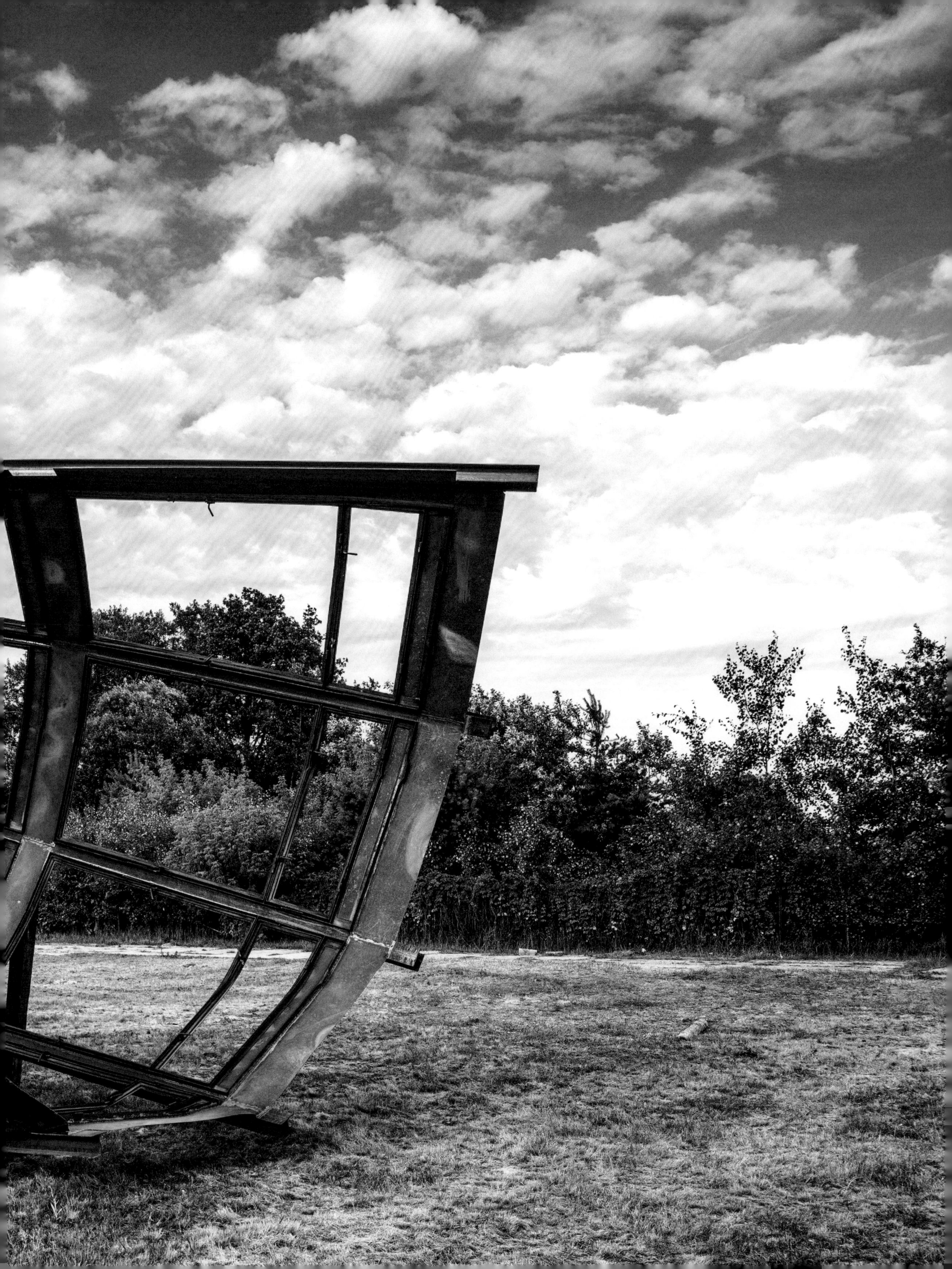

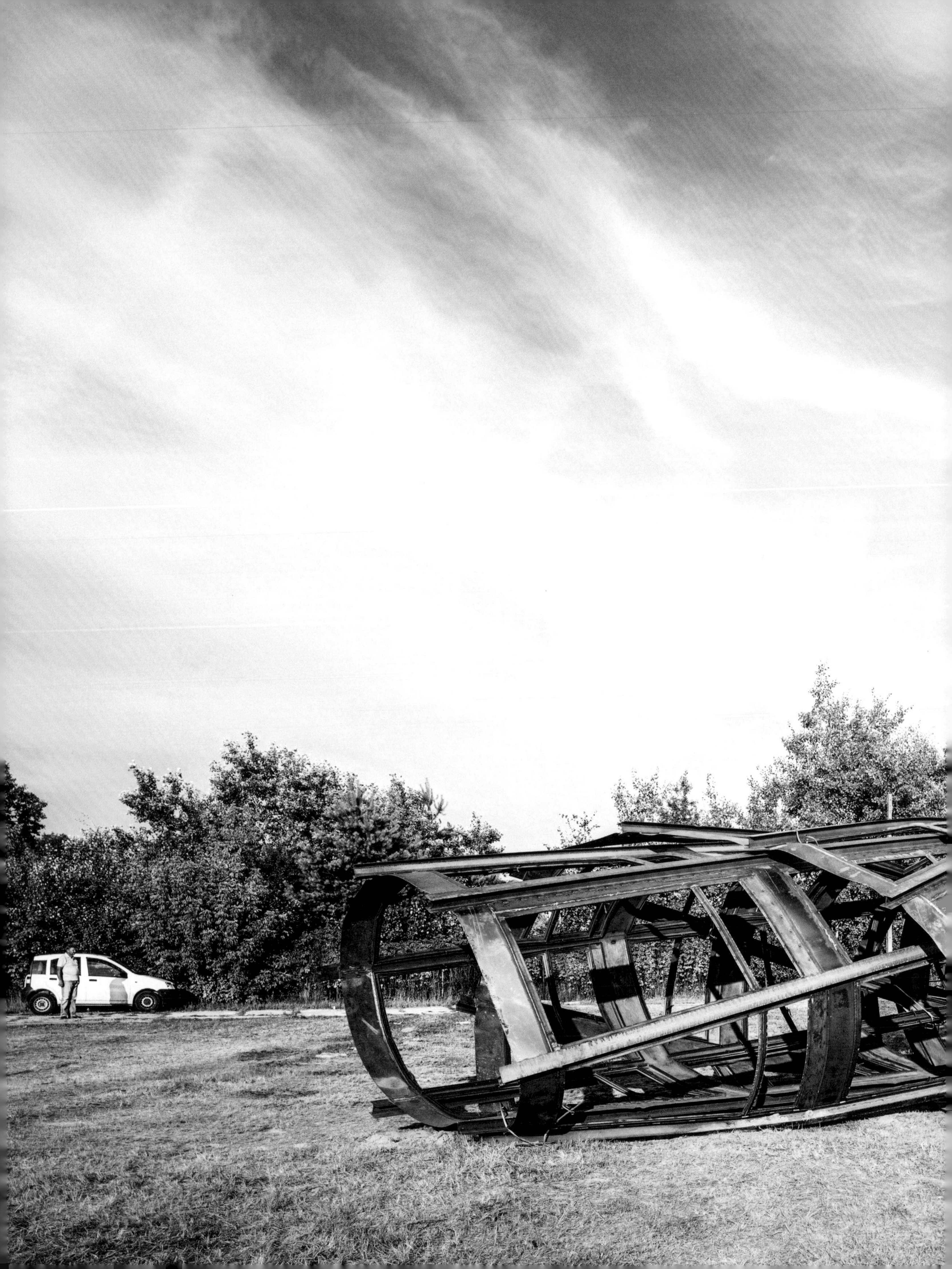

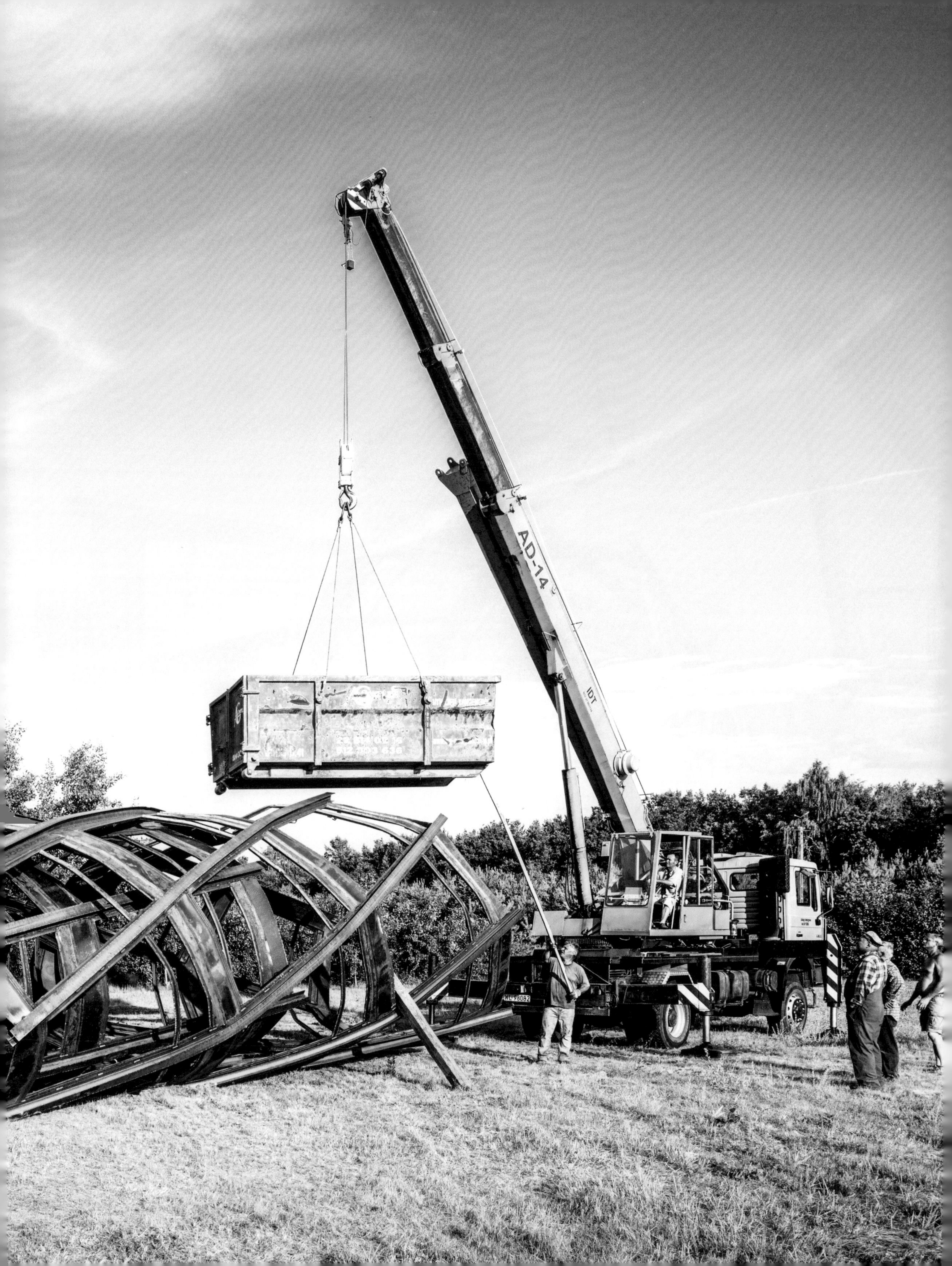
AD-14
IDT

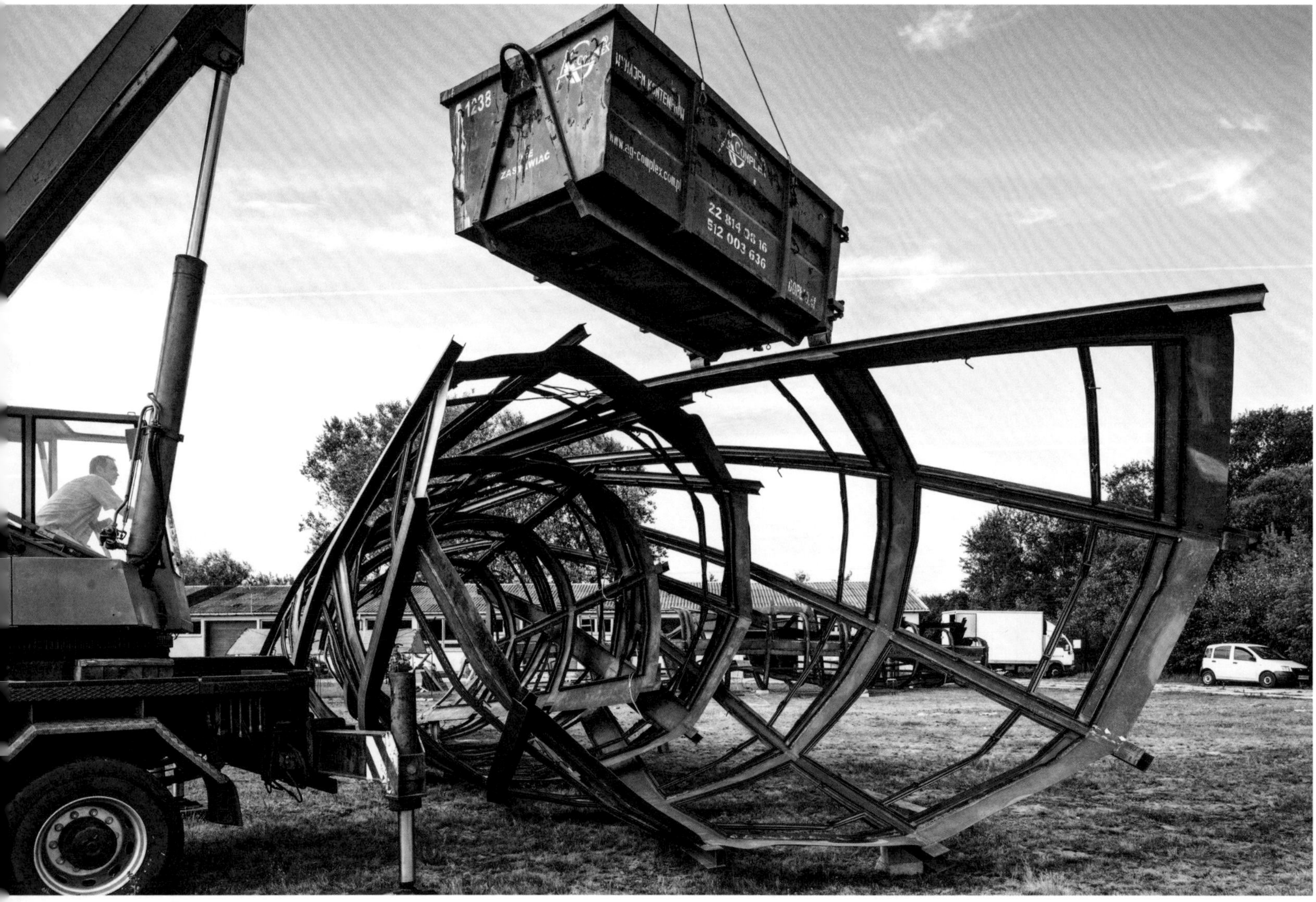
1238
www.ag-complex.com.pl
22 814 38 16
512 003 636

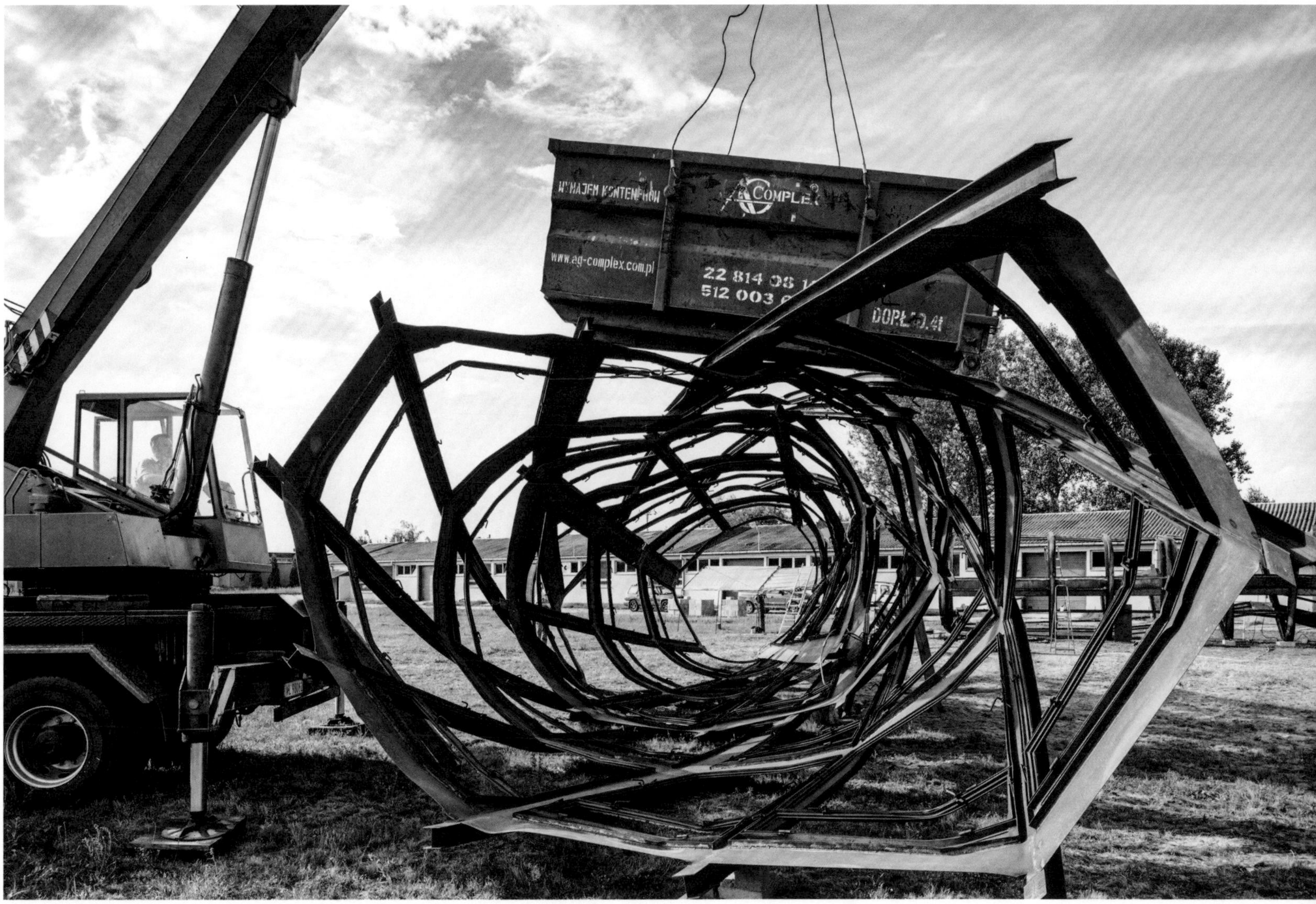
www.ag-complex.com.pl

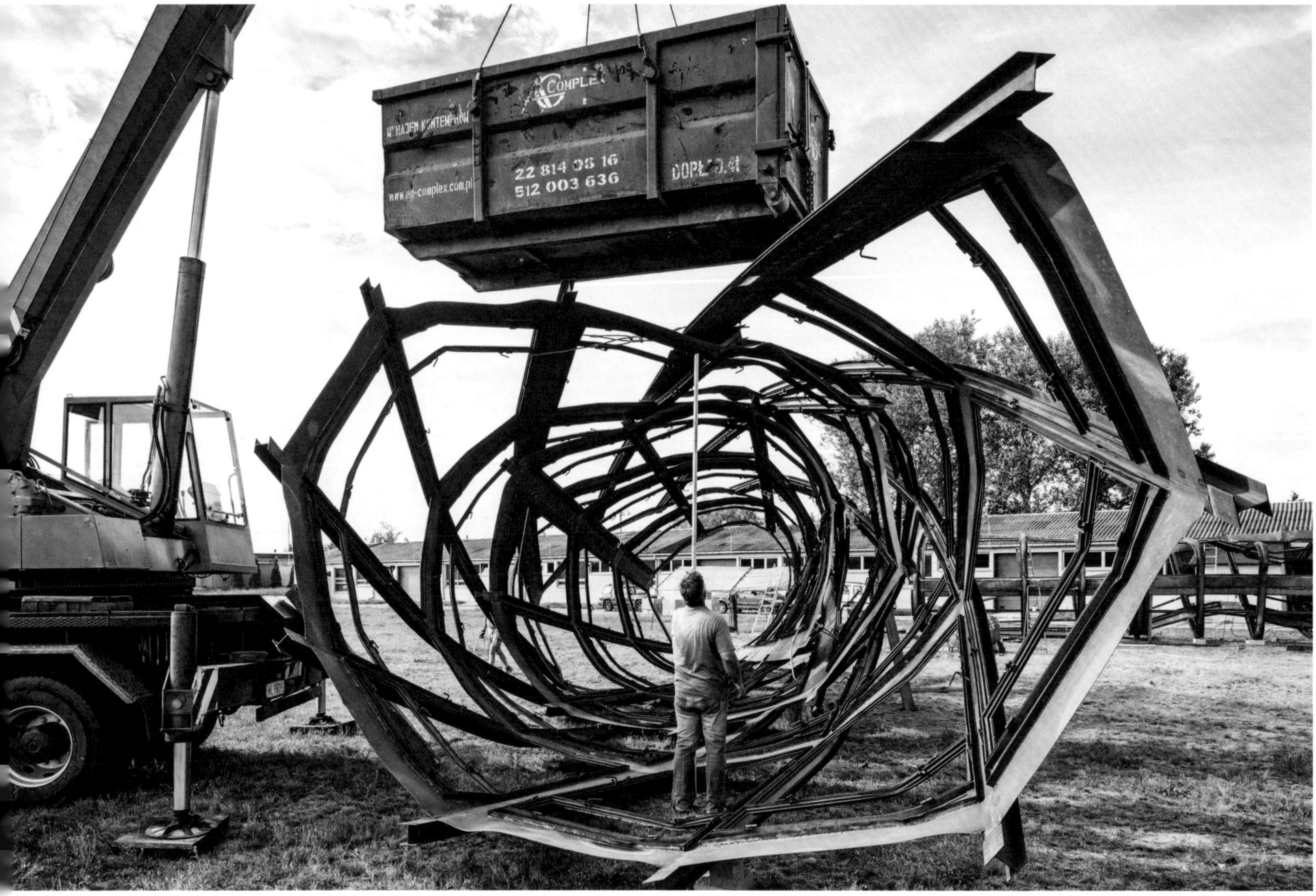
COMPLEX
512 003 636

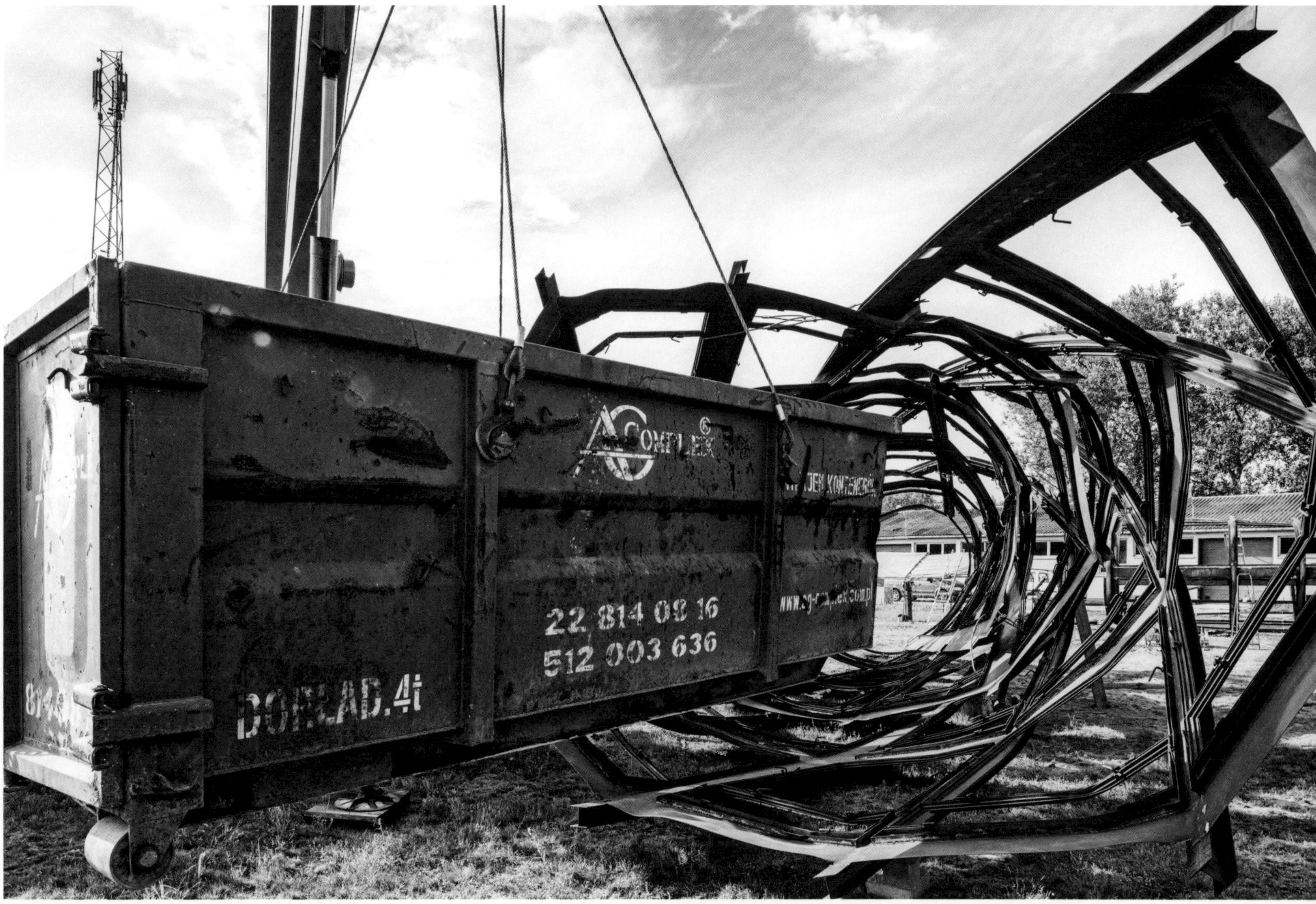
COMPLEX
22 814 08 16
512 003 636

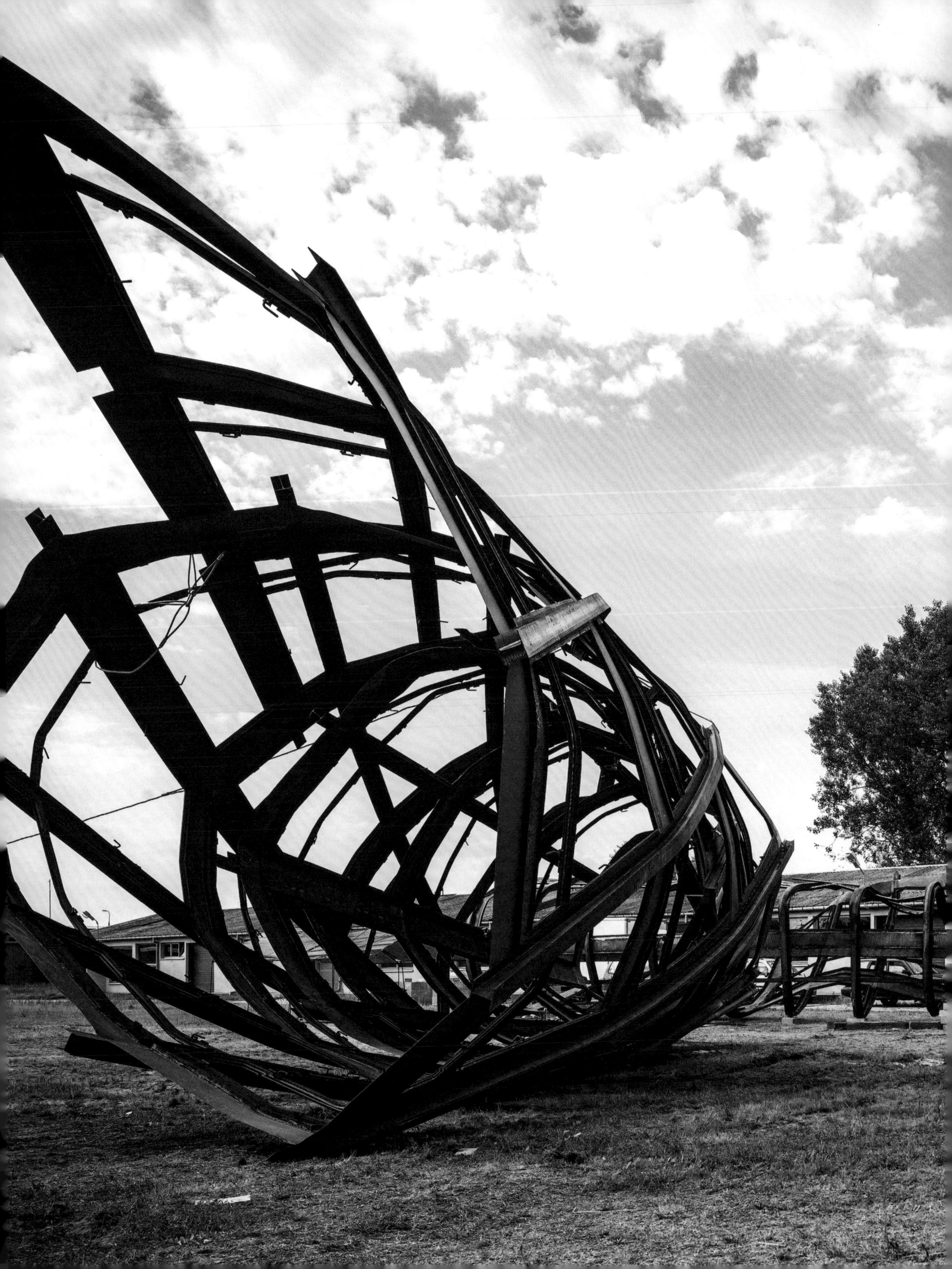

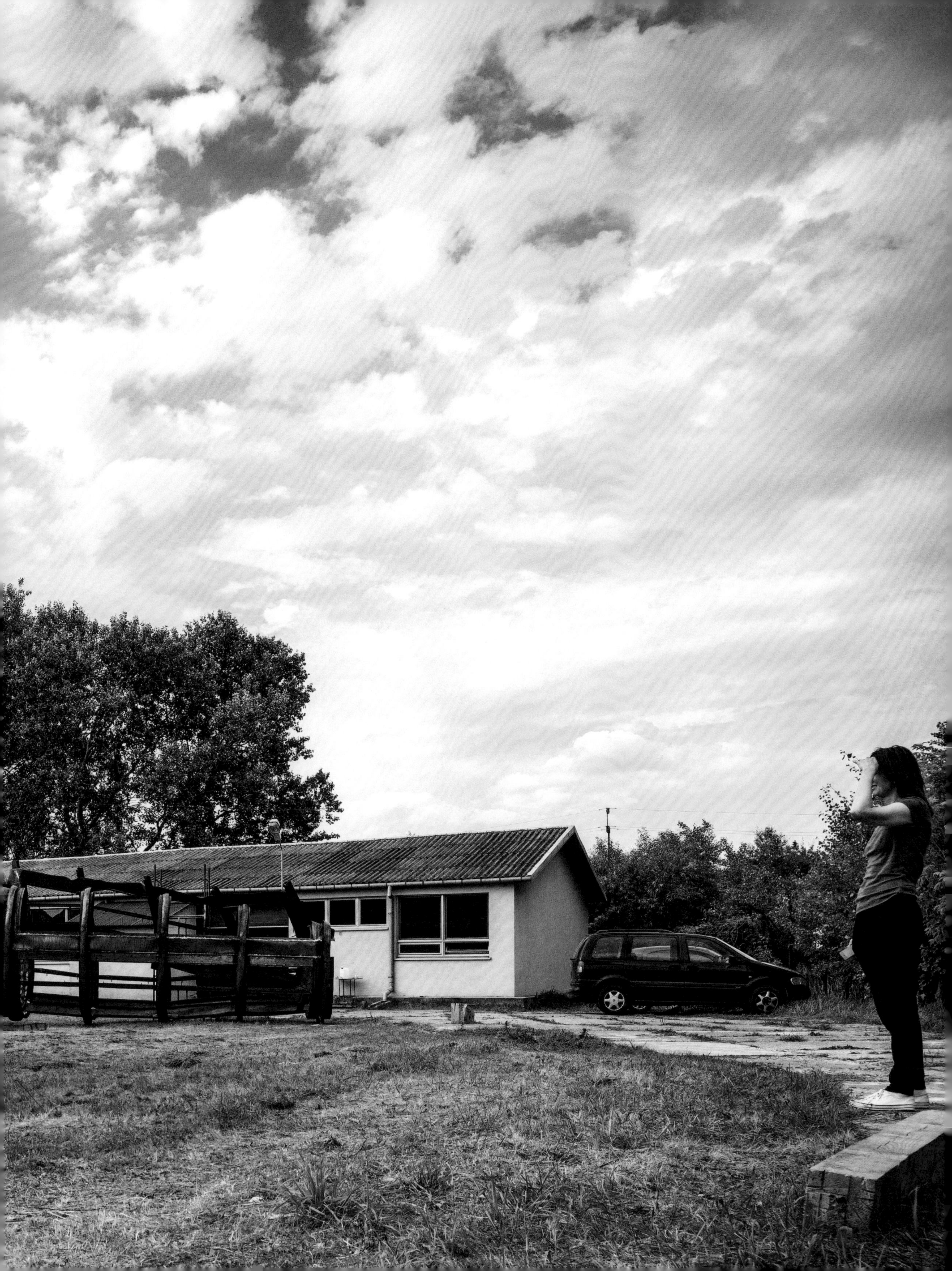

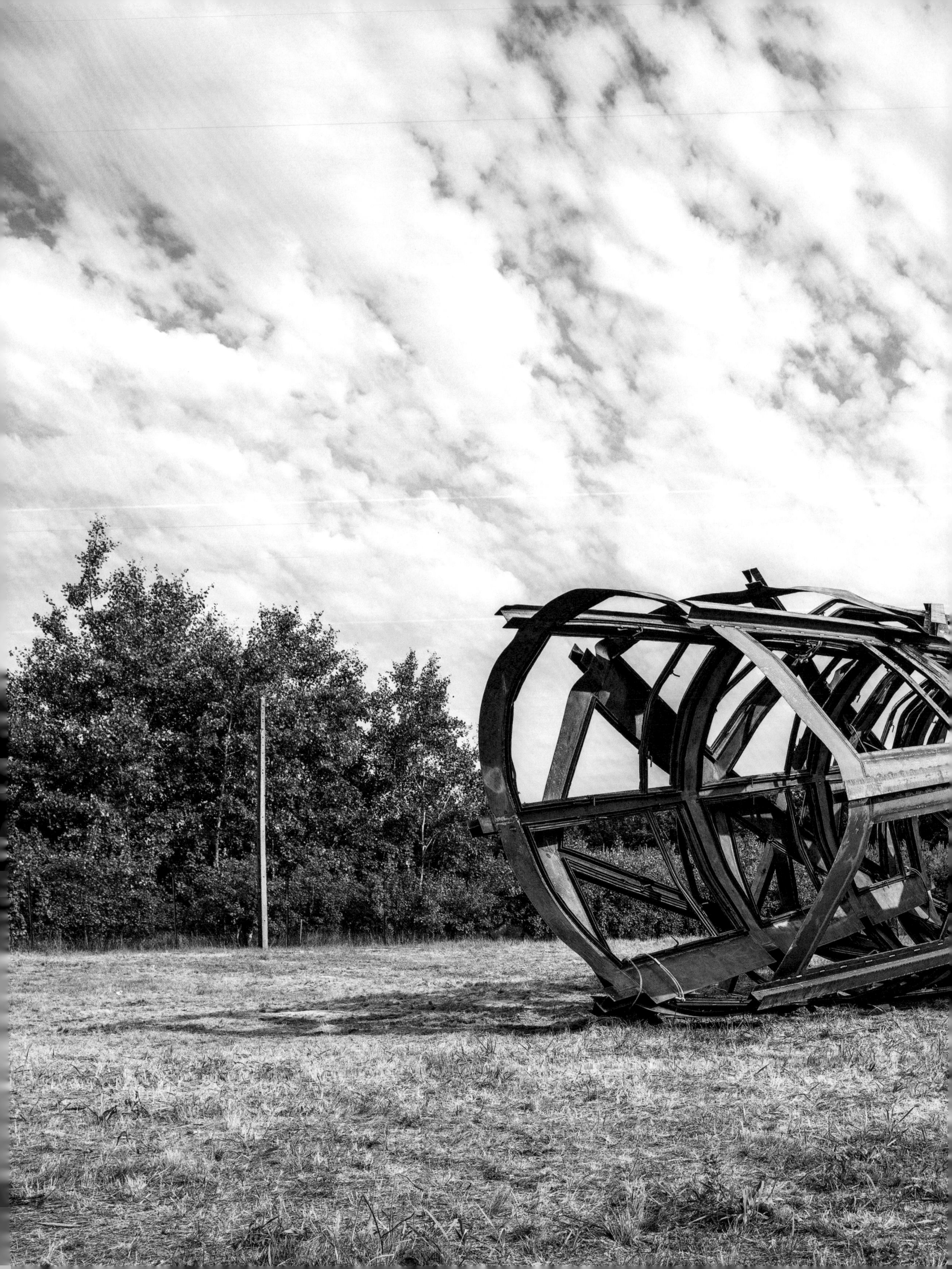

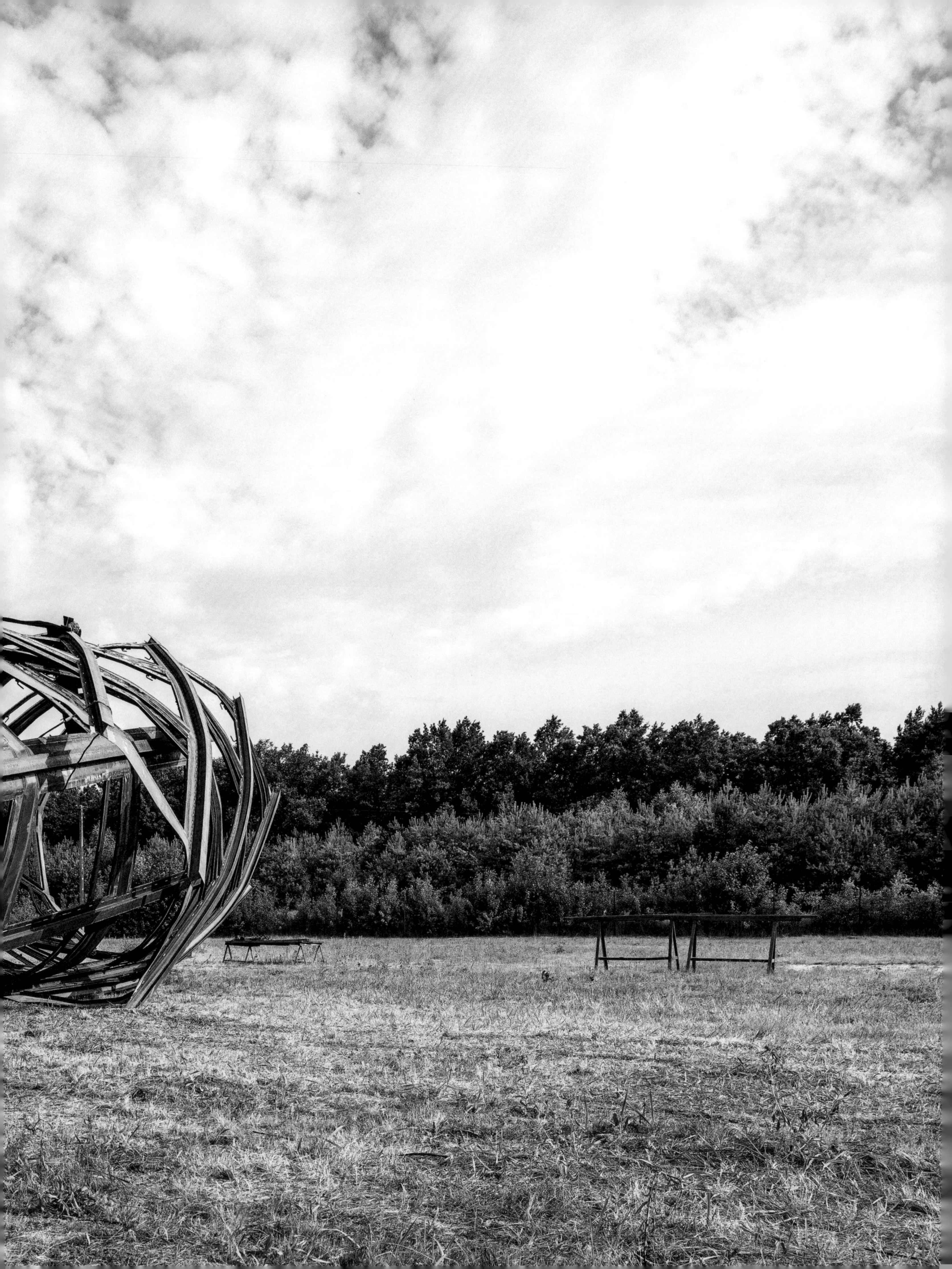

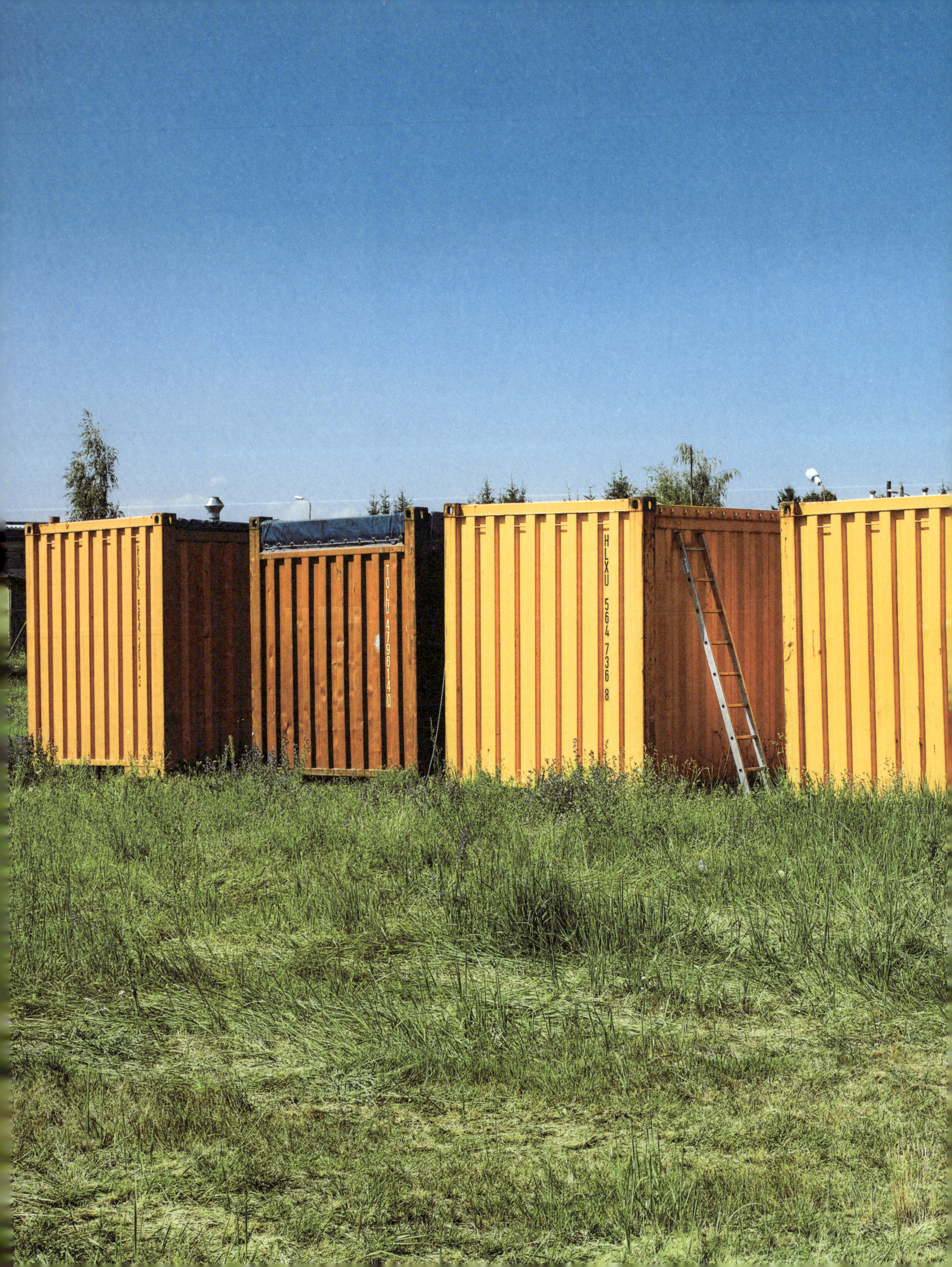
TOLU 479614 0
HLXU 564 736 8

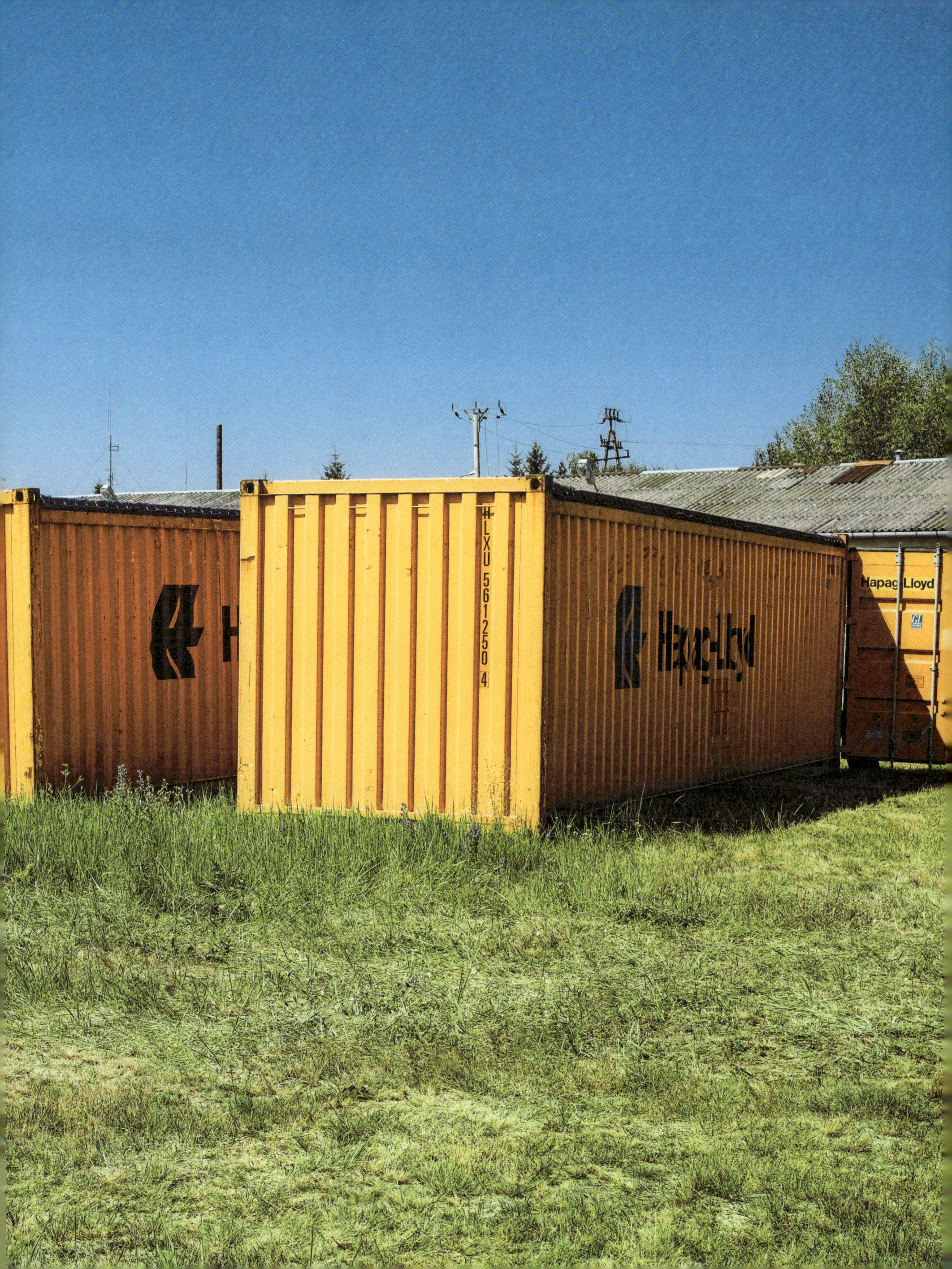
HLXU 561250 4
Hapag-Lloyd
Hapag Lloyd

The Tower

Andrzej Turowski

The significance of Monika Sosnowska's work lies in the tension between the individual, emotion-filled experience of seeing one's closest surroundings, notably the architectural landscape that is accessible "within arm's reach," and the generalizing, order-imposing concepts of art and architectural history, social mythology, the vagaries of collective memory, the utopias of art, and the ideologies of power. This allows the artist to confront, ironically or critically, the contradictions of an industrial and mental landscape in which every figure assuming an articulated and finished form is subject to dissolution in the spatial entropy of today's cities, and the anarchic fiction of contemporary history [fig. 1]. The dialectic of the construction/destruction process, which clearly interests the artist, arises from the very essence of architectural metaphor present in her sculptural projects. On the one hand, she links them to a "foundation," from which human construction rises toward the heavens, a symbol of the modernist metropolis with its uncompromising order of lines and right angles, the glitter of steel and the transparency of glass, and the uniformity of elementary blocks and modular spaces. On the other hand, with the irony of a cool observer, the artist notes the intimation, embedded in the structure, of the destruction of this "solid foundation," and the downfall of the subtle construction, which expresses the end of the modern dream along with the chaotic crumbling of the postmodern world, and that is captured in an image of ruins.

In Sosnowska's art, however, this is neither a romantic ruin infused with nostalgia for the past, nor the surrealist formlessness that was the dark desire of the former avant garde, nor a social anomie resulting from total catastrophe. Sosnowska's ruin is the very essence of the process of deconstruction, in which the disassembly of the whole allows the structuralist order of rising upward to metamorphose into a metonymic game of horizontal approaches and differences. In this sense, too, the ruin is a building—only of a different kind; the kind that embraces the ephemerality of the human condition, the shapelessness of the folded form, and the aesthetic of spontaneity and the ethic of contradiction. Metaphysics, wrote Jacques Derrida, constitutes itself with the help of the architectural metaphor of all thought having a well-grounded basis. Art, Sosnowska would say, is closer to the image of a ruin, the source of all unease. "Architecture arranges, introduces order, reflects political and social systems," Sosnowska once said in an interview. "My works are more about introducing chaos and uncertainty. They make reality stop being obvious."[1]

[fig. 1] Mieczysław Choynowski, *America*, 1932.

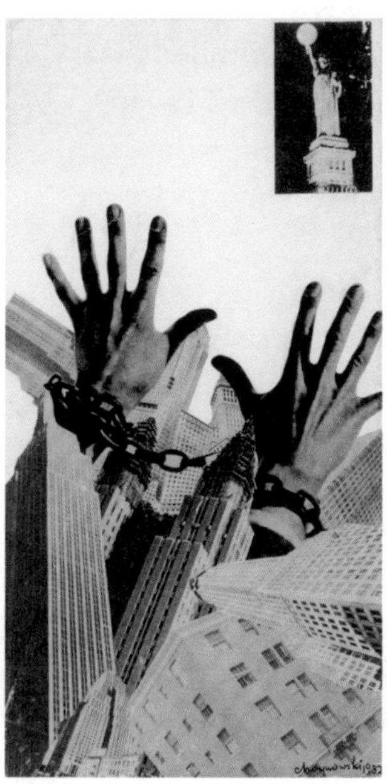

1

History

In her first works, Sosnowska utilized pseudo-labyrinths: connected spaces of varying scale, long corridors lined with doors leading to nowhere, impassable passageways, unenterable interiors, surfaces covered with colors borrowed from who knows where, angles losing their precision, lines serving only to create illusions; it was an architecture of destabilized forms and nonexistent symmetry. Her art from that time was something of a chaotic dance among the apartment blocks of late modernism, in the atmosphere of Eastern European communism on the verge of collapse. Its seeming pointlessness contained a premonition of the end, of cleaning up a littered landscape, of destroying its specific monotony, of the decline of faux stabilization, of turning doubtful utopias into rubble. The independent trade union Solidarity, the collapse of the communist political economy, the fall of the Berlin Wall, the victory of democracy: this changed everything. The apartment blocks were quickly replaced with market stalls, which created new, entirely unregulated arteries of the creeping, unsupervised city. Cut-off pipes, discarded bricks, ferro-concrete fragments dug up from under the rubble: these were the frameworks of the portable architecture of ambitious small retailers. A low, earthly architecture that replaced the uniformity of prefabricated panel structures with cultural colorfulness. Sosnowska's work featured absurd structures, which in denying modernist functionalism, created a world of forms that were perfectly useful, but deprived of their primary form. Discarded elements, a sort of refuse, bent plates, elements of former constructions that nobody needed, entered the sphere of sculptural production. But the world was changing fast. The liberal capitalism of the "transformation period" proudly entrenched its authority, buttressing the city with glass towers that heralded the future. They sprang up, replacing the symbols of the bygone modernity; former constructions demolished by bulldozers, whose only asset was their framework, briefly exposed during demolition—a framework that had once been such an innovation. With a documentary scrupulousness, the artist noted images of destruction in her photographs: fallen floors of buildings, interiors exposed to the world, broken doors, shattered windows, metal bars hanging every which way, and mountains of rubble.

Sosnowska's sculptural projects, which appeared alongside her photographs, filled in the places that appeared in the photographs, or rather the non-places—the ruins and wastelands hiding between the past and the future. An abandoned factory that had produced prefabricated housing elements became Sosnowska's sculpture workshop; the bent T-squares of a non-supporting construction became her chosen form. Such was the deconstructed construction shown at the 2007 Venice Biennale. The architecture of the Polish Pavilion, weighed down by the nation's history, was forced to confront the constructive "style" of communist modernism, disassembled as aggressive capitalism arose. A steel skeleton of construction engineering, "too big to fit," was placed in the empty space of the pavilion. The construction engaged in a test of strength with the walls. It submitted to, and resisted, imagined pressures. The iron beams bent, the connections stretched to the edge of endurance. The forms grappled. "The project isn't utopian," the artist said, "but in a certain sense it concerns utopia. In this project the utopias of different epochs confront each other, represented by two different architectural styles. The title of one such work is *One to One.* It can be understood in various ways, it can apply to the scale, but it can also be the result of a match, a bout, in which there is no winner."[2]

The lack of a winner, even though it applied to architectural material as the basis for modern construction, was a questioning of the power structure that was contained in each of the structures. From this point of view it seems logical to me that Sosnowska's next great question would concern *Tower.* For the mythology of the tower, by making current the constructive questions of architecture, has brought up the fundamental conflict between the will to dominate and the recognition of multiplicity, between the power of hieratic order and the spatial synchrony of differences, and between the infinity of construction and the unease of ruin [fig. 2]. As in the history of the artistic avant garde, and as in the contemporary political history of Central and Eastern Europe, the tower was and is a constant presence.

[fig. 2] Drawing by Erich Kettelhut for Fritz Lang's film *Metropolis*, 1927.

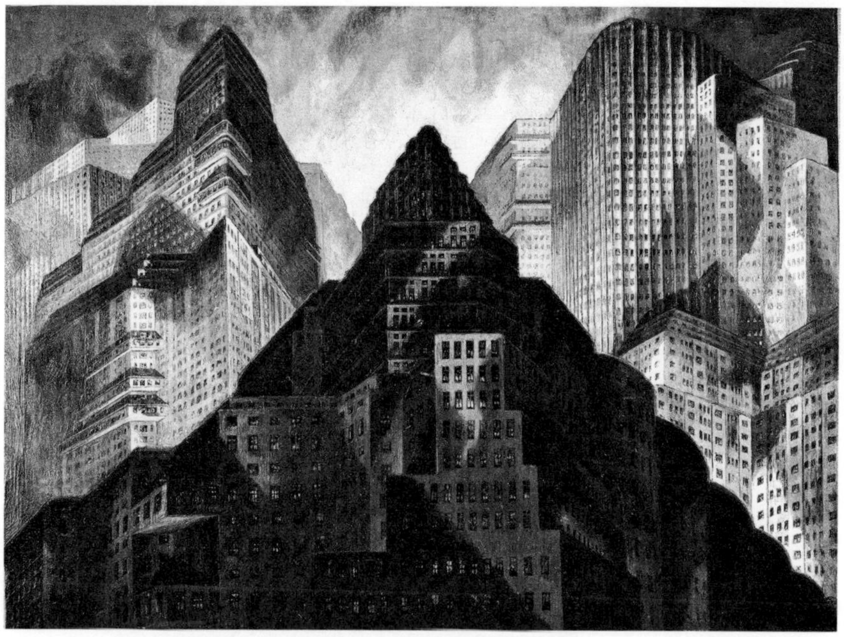

2

The Idea

[fig. 3] Lev Rudnev, Palace of Culture and Science, 1951–55.

[fig. 4] Plan for buildings around the Palace of Culture and Science, Warsaw, 2009.

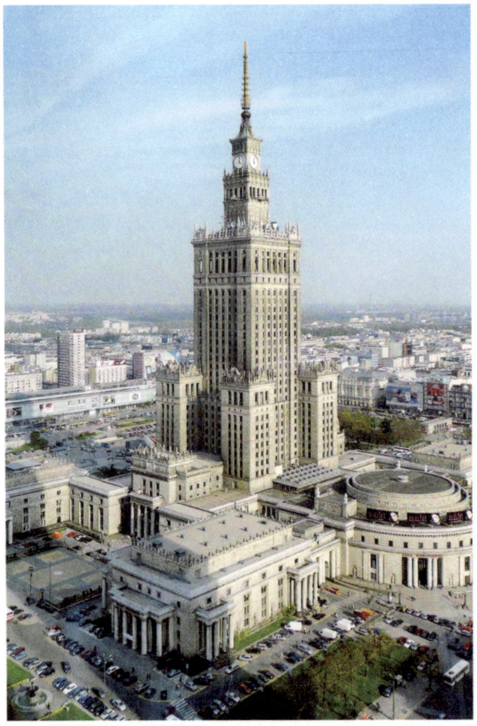

3

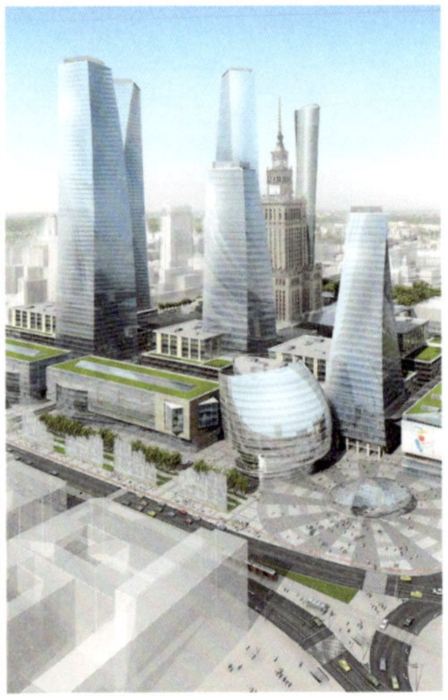

4

The exhibition catalogue accompanying the exhibition held at the Australian Centre for Contemporary Art from August to September in 2013, included a text titled "Regional Modernities," Sosnowska described it as an exposition on the history of her art.[3] Surprisingly, she began by presenting Warsaw's Palace of Culture and Science, whose emblematic silhouette, the most obvious heritage from the times of Social Realism, came to dominate downtown Warsaw. Looking further, at how the palace is today being surrounded by skyscrapers that are rising up somewhat chaotically, she underscored the opposition that the Stalinist architecture presents to the postmodernist poetry of glass and steel. Apparently, outside the definition of context, this selection didn't have a lot in common with the rest of her argument. Nonetheless, in devoting her first paragraphs to the skyscraper, the artist somehow subconsciously made the Warsaw tower and its rivals the basis for her artistic references; and so it's no surprise that here I would see the birth of an idea, not yet fully formed, of "Tower Building," and simultaneously of the deconstruction of its ideological form.

The Palace of Culture and Science in Warsaw (at one time known as the Josef Stalin Palace of Culture and Science) was built by Russian workers between 1952 and 1955—as a "gift from the Soviet comrades" to the Polish nation [fig. 3]. "The wonderful, soaring silhouette of the palace," the press wrote at the time, "will be an eloquent symbol of the ideological content of our socialist capital." It was to be, they declared, an expression of international cooperation, although it was an obvious sign of de facto Soviet rule. The palace is rooted, as Sosnowska stresses, in the middle of a gigantic square, a place for ceremonial parades, creating a new urban order for the communist city, in which the domination of the landscape by a political creation gave birth to a feeling of alienating emptiness in the center of the capital city. There was no true dialogue between the party authorities and society, just as in the relationships of the cityscape. The architect was Lev Rudnev, known earlier for the construction of one of Moscow's most famous Socialist Realism buildings, the main building of Moscow State University (1952), inspired by the façade and form of the Manhattan Municipal Building (1909–14, William M. Kendall). Warsaw's palace was to be the tallest building in Poland, whose height was indicated by a balloon raised over the construction site while design work was underway. The Russians, led by Rudnev, decided that one hundred and twenty meters was sufficient for the highest point in the city. One story is that a group of Poles led by Józef Sigalin, the chief architect of Warsaw, who was in charge of the construction of the palace, began to shout, "Higher!," each time the balloon was raised another ten meters. In the end, the main tower was set at one hundred and twenty meters, reaching one hundred and sixty meters with the upper central tower, and two hundred and thirty meters with the mast.[4] Today, the palace is slightly more than one hundred and eighty-five meters tall.

After 1989, during the period of social and economic transformation, the palace was to be razed to the ground, as it was seen as an evil symbol representing years of enslavement. This never happened, and the palace, inscribed on the list of historic buildings, became a monument of architectural tradition. Simultaneously, the land around the palace, left open to free-market speculation, saw prices rise, along with the soaring towers of the postmodern high-rises of Poland's Manhattan [fig. 4]. The blue sky and the twinkling of the stars reflected in their glass surfaces, their vigor and wonder was to be no match for the Stalinist construction. In hemming in the communist tower, they wanted to cover up the compromised ideology along with the city's shame—the embarrassing lump with a phallic mast protruding from the top.

This strange game of "hide and seek," which at the beginning had all the elements of post-conceptual architectural criticism and an irony-filled game between totalitarian Stalinism and late-capitalist consumerism, suggested to Sosnowska—in line with her earlier adopted strategy of confrontation—the thought of building a new tower from a specific type of material, which would be able to conceptually demolish both of the political-architectural orders. Still, it wasn't about a simple operation of compromising a piece of architecture that was already the butt of jokes, but about placing the emblematic constructions of communism and capitalism within the perspective of the entirety of modernism. For that was where both types of Warsaw tower had their historical roots. Thus, it was necessary to build such a tower from a specific kind of material, which would question the dominant force of the existing towers but not supplant them. Thus, the tower would be able to, through a process of self-destruction, reveal the ideological ambiguity of the optimistic construct of the world as something to be built and consumed.

Unable to turn the Warsaw buildings, which were holding up well, into ruins, it was instead possible to build a ruin out of modernist forms and materials, which in the name of the Polish transformation were indeed ridiculed, actually demolished, and subsequently pushed into historical oblivion. Here I'm not thinking of a historic preservationist's care for monuments, which is foreign to the artist, but of struggling with the very heart of dialectical history, undermining the stability of successive orders. Sosnowska meant to critically connect the phenomenon seen so clearly in the perspective of regional modernism ("regional modernities") with the universal problems of how the ideologies of artistic, social, and political modernity function. In turning to the beginning, she inquired into the end. In inquiring into Poland, she inquired into the world. Intellectually and technically, the operation was very difficult.

For here it's not about "overcoming" history (or metaphysics), a concept typical of modernity: in Sosnowska's framework this could not be a category allowing an exit from modernism; she was rather thinking of the artistic radicalization of the tendencies embedded in modernism, to use a range of metonymizations, among which the tower seemed to be the most useful, to fasten history to time and to see the alternatives it contains therein. The ruin, which has much in common with the Tower of Babel, was the most obvious construction towards this end. It fit with Nietzschean nihilism, in whose thought the words "God is dead," killed by the will to truth that His followers cultivated, led to the discovery that He too was a mistake that is now no longer necessary. According to Nietzsche, this ". . . nihilistic conclusion offers us a way out of modernity. Since the notion of truth no longer exists, and foundation no longer functions (insofar as there is no longer a foundation for the belief in foundation, that is, in the fact that thought must be 'found'), there can be no way out of modernity through a critical overcoming, for the latter is a part of modernity itself. It thus becomes clear that an alternative means must be sought. . . ."[5]

It wasn't simple. The interpretive key to modernism, which was also the construction material for her ruin, was supplied to Sosnowska by Ludwig Mies van der Rohe, the most representative example of architectural formalism in the first half of the twentieth century. Mies van der Rohe was an architect who hailed from Europe's Bauhaus milieu and who, after World War II, constructed the largest buildings in the United States. His unrealized architectural plans for glass towers, sketched between 1919 and 1921, fired the imaginations of modernist architects around the world. They were also the basis for all of his later work. Cleansed of the expressionist dream of the Cathedrals of Socialism, they aroused admiration by their pure form, which was uninfected by ideology. In 1949, thirty years after he first studied the form of the skyscraper, Mies van der Rohe built high-rise apartment blocks along the shore of Lake Michigan in Chicago. The view from the expansive windows over the endless space of the lake is stunning, wrote Sigfried Giedion, author of the seminal treatise on the birth of the modernist tradition, who was delighted by the architecture of this classic of modernism. When a creative architect is able to master playing on the colossal keyboard of mechanization, we need not fear for the future of architecture, he wrote of Mies van der Rohe. None of the architect's other buildings had such a direct influence on contemporary American architecture as his two biggest and most radical residential buildings on Lake Shore Drive in Chicago, which were constructed between 1949 and 1951 [fig. 5]. Here the purity of form became the highest law, to which everything else was subjected. With uncompromising strength, the architect didn't allow even the smallest deviation from the cleanly cut smooth glass surfaces of the prisms and glass boxes. Every detail, Giedion went on to stress, reminds the viewer: architecture is discipline.[6]

Sosnowska began her work on *Tower* by studying Mies van der Rohe's rich architecture archive.

[fig. 5] Ludwig Mies van der Rohe, 860–880 Lake Shore Drive, Chicago, Illinois, 1949–51.

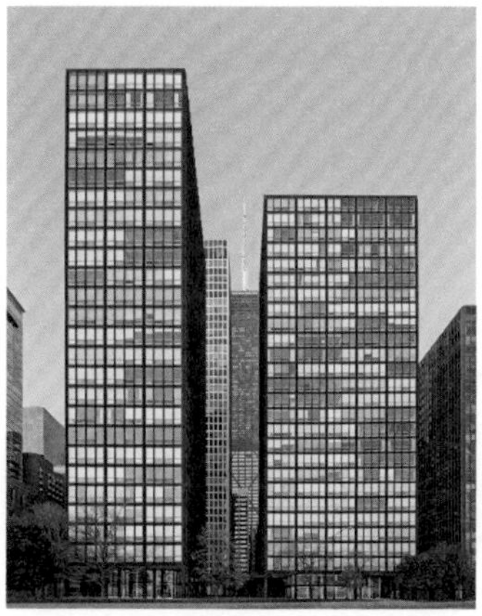

5

The Workshop

"The work is divided into stages," Sosnowska once said about the process of how her projects are carried out. "At the beginning, working with the engineer, I designed the structure. I knew what effect I wanted to achieve, and he made sure everything was in line with the logic of construction. When the design was ready, we made a 1:10 scale model, which we used for flexibility tests . . . The engineer built a machine to do the bending, which allowed us to achieve the right shape for the structure. Later we started to build the original in a 1:1 scale. The hardest part was still ahead of us: repeating on a large scale what we had done with the model. It's also interesting that our building will have to be sent on a trip. . . . First it will go by land, then by water. In this project, the very process by which the work takes shape is important. It's significant that we're building it in a defunct factory . . . and that the work is in a sense a collective effort."[7]

Today, the process has not changed all that much. First, the construction work in a factory hall or industrial workshop is accompanied by the search for the right materials and the equipment to manipulate them (both the workshop and the materials); then the materials are used in accordance with the principles of the mechanization and rational organization of the work (mass scale, modularity); later the reconstructed forms are given their proper shape by bending, squeezing, tensioning, and creasing (downfall); and finally the transportation from the workshop to the location chosen for the reinstallation (travel and reconstruction). "I often say," the artist says, "that my works are produced, and this must be understood very literally. Most of them aren't made by me. They take shape in carpentry or metalworking shops, they're produced by groups of people with specialized roles. Recently I've been working more and more with architects, engineers—specialists in various techniques. In my works there's no trace of 'the artist's hand.' My role is limited to the concept, the choice of the proper means, and checking the final stage—seeing to what degree the product is in line with what I imagined."

In other words, the successive stages by which the sculpture comes to be are significant because of the physical process of constructing the form. But they also sustain the conceptual work that determines the entirety of the oscillating and interconnected meanings. Observing Sosnowska's work, I can readily say that it is a process of deconstruction. The process of deconstruction that I'm writing about here is not a one-time act of will, or a critical operation, but rather a chain of events. In contrast to the economy of a material production process, in a process of deconstruction the sequence doesn't result from a logical or linear arrangement, but rather from complex references to places and the topoi that explain them, to histories of the utopias that are inherent within them, and to the people and the myths that sustain them. In this sense deconstruction is a series of substitutions, which can be called its discursive context.[8]

It's a process of displacing, moving, substituting, distinguishing, marginalizing, and metaphorizing, under the reign of the uncertainty resulting from the lack of the unequivocality of references, and from successive translations and the indefinability of the end. The form that intermeshes with such thought ultimately leads to formlessness (ruin). The aesthetic that defines Sosnowska's sculpture is the aesthetic of unease.[9]

To understand the productive metaphor of Sosnowska's art, let us appeal to history, and first of all to the evolution of Russian and Central European Constructivism, together with its myth of mechanization, and more broadly of technique, industry, and production; the foundations of avant-garde modernism. Constructivism was tightly connected with the concept of building, and it applied broadly to the issues of production work, developed technologies, the shaping of materials, mass production, and finally the rational organization of labor. The art of the Constructivists built a world that heralded, with pathos, the approaching future. The "worker-giant" took the place of the artist [fig. 6]. "Look," wrote the proletarian poet Aleksei Gastev in one of his poems, "I stand among them: workshops, hammers, blacksmiths' flames and among hundreds of comrades / With my shoulders I burst all bonds . . . / Still I lose my breath among these superhuman efforts; now I cry: / 'Hear my voice, comrades, hear me!' / The iron echo absorbs my words, in expectation the whole building shakes. I climb even higher, to chimney height / Not a tale, nor a speech do I shout out, but the iron words / We shall win."

The place of the alienated man had been taken over by the victorious new man, his city was to be a new Babylon: "What a wonderful city!" Anatoly Lunacharsky, commissar for art in the Bolshevik government, sang of this Babylon's towers. In his *Italian Letters,* he commented enthusiastically on Benozzo Gozzoli's *The Tower of Babel*: "All architectural fantasies, full of refinement and sparkle, crowd together, as if fighting for every scrap of ground, growing up one over the other, intoning this hymn in stone in honor of man the constructor."[10]

[fig. 6] Sergey Chekhonin, illustration for the Anatoly Lunacharsky play *Faust and the City*, Petrograd, 1918.

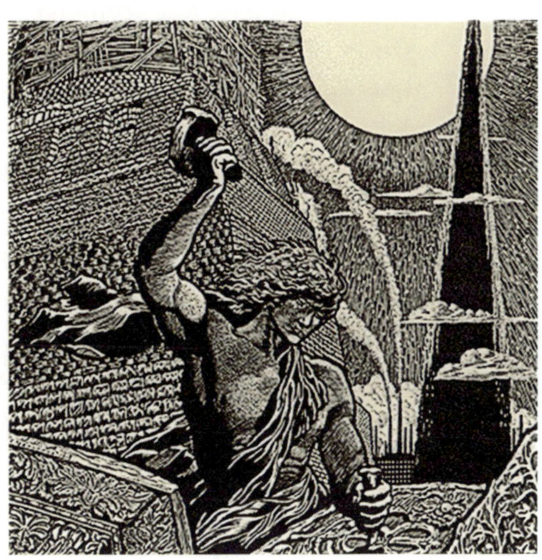

6

[fig. 7] Production facilities (a locomotive factory) in the Sormovsky district of Nizhny Novgorod, USSR, 1922.

[fig. 8] Biomechanical laboratory of the Central Institute of Labor run by Aleksei Gastev, Moscow, 1923.

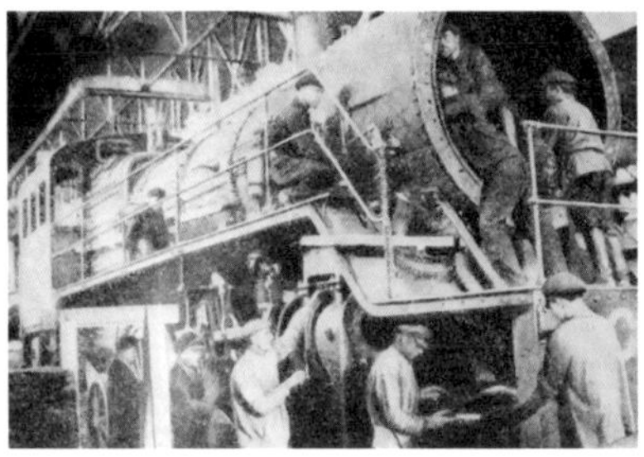

7

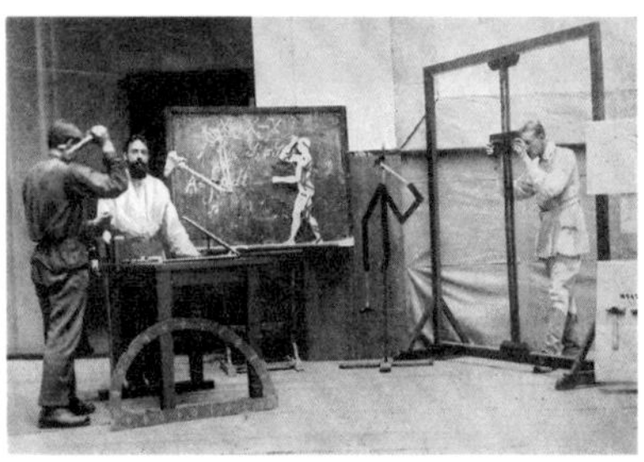

8

A new era was approaching. The artists who heralded its arrival were producers engaged in production—not imitating the creative world, but producers forging the future reality [fig. 7]. The world appeared to be an infinitely large industrial hall; a workshop pulsing with the banging of hammers, the hiss of steam, and plumes of sparks. Every factory was a laboratory for scientific management. From Constructivism arose Productivism. In Russia, from 1920–21, it was precisely this line of artistic thinking that gained popularity, and its adherents adopted the slogan, "Artists to Production, to Industry" with complete conviction [fig. 8]. The Constructivist "I" became the Productivist "We." "The red banner is the symbol of the new Adam, whose principle is collectivism," wrote Lunacharsky, "the collectivism of this truly colossal cooperation of labor, labor subduing nature with the help of a gigantic mechanism—the great production machine of the entire world. The machines draw themselves toward one another in mutual attraction, along all their tracks and cables, through the walls of factories and across the borders of states, they unite, they seek out a mighty steward. And this steward now arises: 'Workers of the world, unite!'"[11]

The man of Productivism arose in the historical process from the mass of workers standing at their machines, and was transformed into the "spiritual proletarian," the laboring Anthropos, freeing himself from class obligations to embody the new artist—the great constructor. The absolutism characteristic of such thinking, tearing the idea of the artist and creation from the material (formal) base led—in the nineteen-thirties—to the reimagining of the Productivist artist no longer as a producer of objects, but as an organizer of "human consciousness." The production process was clearly increasingly losing its material character and the consciousness that outgrew everything, henceforth most readily identified with ideology. Artists, incapable of monopolizing industrial material production, which in the Soviet Union's limping industry didn't belong to them, made an effort to gain control over the entire mental sphere, creating a Productivist utopia.

It's understandable that the communist authorities in Russia didn't want to agree to this takeover of ideology, giving up control over it. Between 1925 and 1928, attacks on Productivism grew in strength. Simultaneously, the administration granted ever-greater support to a group of artists that emerged with great intensity starting in the mid-nineteen-twenties, whose concept of art was completely foreign to the avant garde and which related art to reality on entirely different principles. Rooted in mimetic aesthetics, they usually treated art as a reflection of social ideology (and not as its production or organization). The basic task of the artist was no longer "to create life," but "to present reality ideologically," and to do so at the behest of the political leaders.

At the beginning of the nineteen-thirties, as a result of the process of monopolization of communist authority by Stalin and his Politburo, art was subjected to a uniform organizational-administrative system connected with the doctrine of Socialist Realism. The ethos of Productivist collectivism, its particular holism and, simultaneously, its form, alien to the avant garde, led, in this new context, to renewed appeals to culture steered by "inevitable historical processes." However, this concept, now embedded in the slogans of centralized authority, signified something completely different from what it once did—when the Constructivists spoke of the development of artistic form. Productivism appeared not as a utopia of art, but as a "Socialist Realist" principle for subordinating culture; subordinating in effect the political-party organization and its leader, who in the nineteen-fifties, assigned to the artist the ambiguous role of "engineering human souls" [fig. 9]. One of them was Lev Rudnev, the Muscovite builder of Warsaw's palace.

From this history, which at its origins is both Constructivist and utopian, and later Productivist and material, Warsaw's Palace of Culture and Science was founded—and it was saturated in politics and ideology. The Productivist metaphor, in which the story of the palace could be read, created the critical context for the construction of Sosnowska's monumental *Tower,* namely in a defunct factory near the Warsaw suburb of Legionowo, which after all was taking shape "in the shadow of Yalta." She created a discursive context and, simultaneously, she was dangerously duplicating the engineering construction forged by the Warsaw workers. The acts of the Productivist avant garde and the defeat of the social-artistic utopia that emerged from it—events so characteristic for revolutionary Russian art and the related geopolitical trends of modern art in Central Europe—left their mark on the form of Sosnowska's *Tower,* and allowed no claim to innocence.

[fig. 9] Aleksandr Rodchenko, *Male Pyramid, Sports Parade on the Red Square*, 1936.

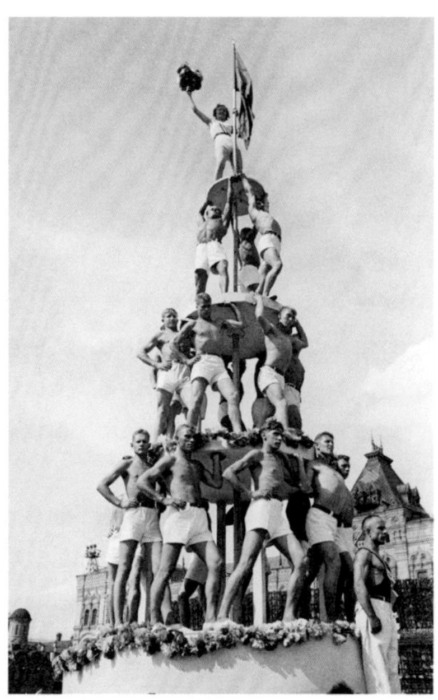

9

The Material

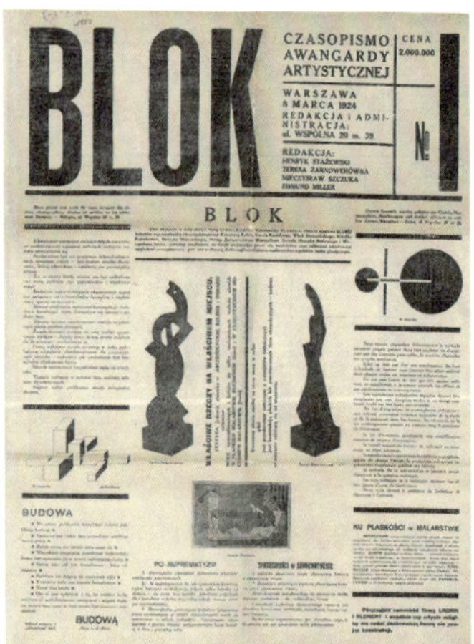
BLOK

CZASOPISMO AWANGARDY ARTYSTYCZNEJ

CENA 2.000.000

WARSZAWA 8 MARCA 1924

REDAKCJA I ADMINISTRACJA:

REDAKCJA:

№ I

BLOK

10

[fig. 10] *Blok* magazine, no. 1, p. 1, 1924.

The material from which Sosnowska built her *Tower* is a fragment of the curtain wall from the façade of Mies van der Rohe's building on Lake Shore Drive in Chicago. It was no accident that Sosnowska chose this architect and this building.

Mies van der Rohe, as I have already written, was one of the most rigorous architects of European and American modernism, who starting in the nineteen-twenties, upheld the formal purity of geometric constructions in his designs and implementations, thereby eliminating all pollution of architecture by means of ideology. In 1933 he was criticized for accepting the commission for the Reichsbank in Berlin, but, despite this, he maintained that form is independent from political authority. "There is no place for a mistake in his absolute universe," wrote Charles Jencks, "because extreme simplicity makes one hypersensitive to each inch of a structure and the Platonic form, with its transcendental pretension, demands utter perfection."[12] According to Mies van der Rohe, the mission of the architect—like that of every scholar and theologian—is the principle of simplifying, explaining, and arranging. The desire for order, which gives each thing its proper place and that which is appropriate to it, in accordance with its nature.

Those in the Polish avant garde regarded Mies van der Rohe's work with a certain degree of interest. A position statement from the architect, reprinted from the German periodical *Gestaltung,* appeared in the first edition of *Blok* magazine in 1924; the story of Polish Constructivism begins with this periodical [fig. 10]. "We do not know the problems of form," wrote Mies van der Rohe, "but only the problems of construction. Form is not the goal, but the natural result of our work. No form exists in and of itself. The condition for the achievement of true perfection of form is its expression in the most elemental form. . . . We seek only to free construction from aesthetic speculation and make the building again that which in its essence it should be—that is, a BUILDING."[13]

Mies van der Rohe's high-rises were supported by steel skeletons, which by moving the iron structure into the interior of the building allowed the architect to eliminate load-bearing walls. The use of curtain walls, which were not limited by material or thickness, allowed Mies van der Rohe to introduce expansive glass-enclosed spaces, opening the structure to the outside. The broad, continuous bands of windows allowed light to flood in and reflected the sun's rays, and shone from every side when lit up at night. The buildings gave an impression of lightness, of a structure somehow rising into the air. There was a reason why people called them buildings deprived of architecture. The enduring and strong steel skeleton didn't restrict the height, and the standard element of the windows placed in the walls, which appeared to be suspended, rhythmicized the great surfaces.

The use of the iron skeleton and glass was one of the greatest achievements of modernist architecture, whose beginnings date back to the commercial passages in the capitals of nineteenth-century Europe, the first spectacles of consumption, and the architecture of the great universal exhibitions symbolizing the new era of technology, industry, and progress; an era that moved to the rhythm of the machine. The constructive myth rising toward the top of the iron structure was what grounded the Eiffel Tower [fig. 11], built in 1889 on the occasion of the World's Fair and as a monument to the centennial of the French Revolution. It was simultaneously a preview of the twentieth century and an "empty symbol," as Roland Barthes wrote, open to all meanings. It was a package, which like a bag could be filled up with anything, to create a legend. It was a phenomenon, whose existence is hard to doubt, and whose significance could be asked about for an eternity. Although it was visible to all, the tower remains hidden—in a certain sense, it slips away; it is always itself, and simultaneously something else. It's an object exhibited for viewing, and, at the same time, it is the center of an optical system that is unaware of its own gaze, however it constantly "peeks out from hiding." But above all, the Eiffel Tower is a structure suffering from a "Babel complex."[14]

The Eiffel Tower began the story of modern and postmodern towers, which—taking on various forms and various contents, quickly became the image of the contemporary city, the metropolis packed with high-rises, inspiring delight and terror. Towers overgrew the showpiece downtown districts like scaffolding, drawing attention away from the labyrinth of shameful alleyways and dime-novel gangsters. Visible from everywhere, high-rises established a new visual system, which gave pure visuality of structure and form precedence over any meaning at the center of artistic awareness. The boldness of the construction arose from the strength of the creation. The formalism of modernism [fig. 12], even though it had political roots, was read as a pure creative plan, the constructive essence of the subordinated world of progress and reason.

Just such an idea guided the construction of the high-rises surrounding the Palace of Culture in Warsaw after 1989. We will return to this problem a bit later, but for now let us pause to examine the well-known example of Tatlin's Tower, which was

[fig. 11] Eiffel Tower and Fountain Coutan, looking toward Trocadéro Palace, Paris Exposition, 1889.

[fig. 12] Kazimir Malevich, *Architekton in Front of a Skyscraper* (Suprematist transformation of New York), 1924.

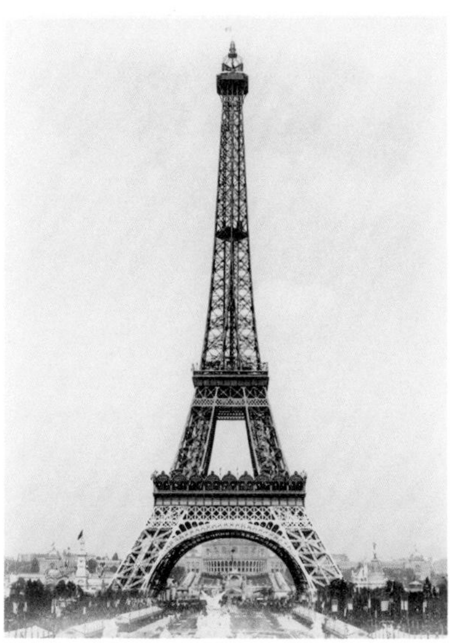

11

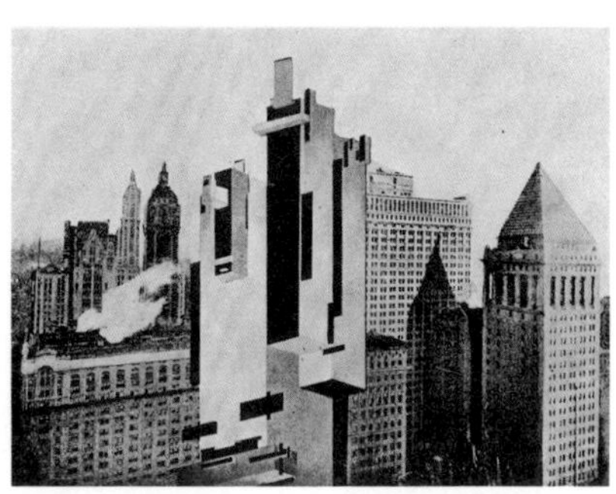

12

constructed between 1919 and 1921. Taking its cues from the Eiffel Tower, it quickly became an architectural-sculptural icon of international Constructivism, and its Eastern European version born in revolutionary Russia. Tatlin's Tower, let us recall, was intended as a monument to the Third International, and in the final model it expressed pure form [fig. 13]. The giant, almost four-hundred-meter steel structure created a gigantic, tilted spiral that formed the skeleton for three glass blocks located inside it, which rotated around a vertical axis. The lowest of them, in the shape of a cube, made one full rotation per year. Above it was a cylinder, making one rotation per month. Highest was a cone, rotating every day. Above them were heaped radio antennas with a network of wires, and giant screens that came to life at night. Fast elevators, escalators, and all other kinds of installations were located in the steel construction of the tower. The double glass walls filled with water were to play the role of a thermos, allowing the maintenance of a uniform interior temperature. Ilya Ehrenburg, the author of the Constructivist adventures of Julio Jurenito, gazing upon Tatlin's Tower, looked with a certain reserve on the functionally absurd shapes of the glass meeting rooms spinning inside it, and showed an attitude of well-intentioned distance toward its iron construction, in which, as he wrote, the twenty-first century spoke in a dream language. But he unreservedly admired the creative potential and new order of pure forms, of "resurrected shapes," arising from the demiurgic creation

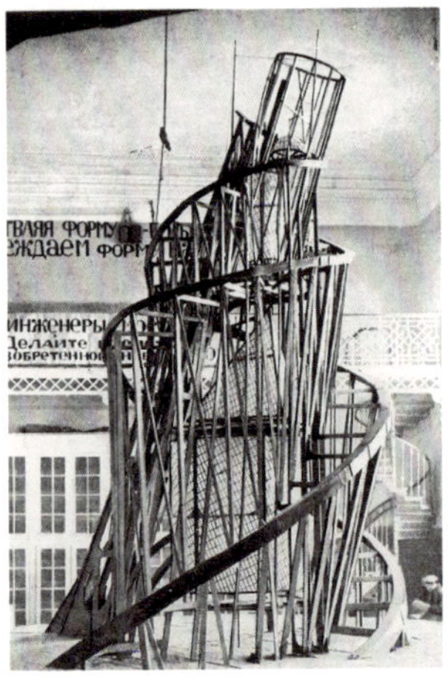

13

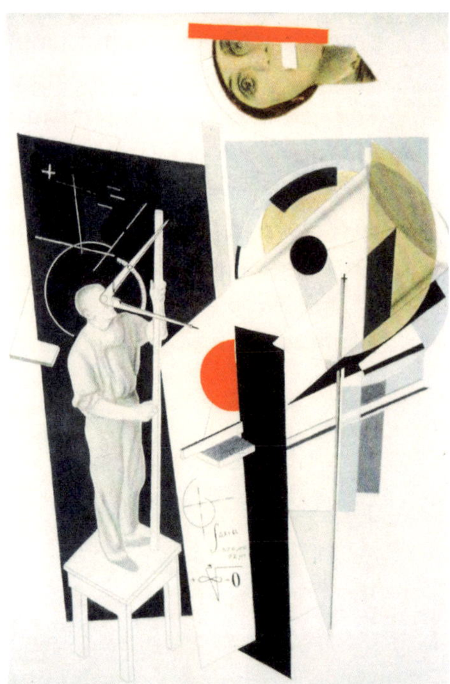

14

[fig. 13] Vladimir Tatlin, *Model of the Monument to the Third International*, 1920.

[fig. 14] El Lissitzky, *Tatlin at Work*, 1922.

of the artist, that were present in the upward-thrusting tower.[15] A well-known photomontage of the time by El Lissitzky presented Tatlin against the backdrop of a blackboard, next to a white screen, on which mathematical symbols were written [fig. 14]. Tatlin held a measuring rod in his hand, while observing—"through a compass"—the rotating, interpenetrating stereometric figures with their clean, colorful surfaces. It was the Ehrenburgian Tatlin of modernist mythology.

It's no surprise that the Tatlin of Ehrenburg and Lissitzky, and not the Tatlin of the Bolshevik International, most resembled Mies van der Rohe's building art, the art of the most consistent Constructivist formalist in Western European architecture, as we now know. Precisely in the same years, when in the East the model of Tatlin's Tower was being created in Germany, the plans for Mies van der Rohe's towers were being sketched. The first was an expressive high-rise on Friedrichstrasse in Berlin, from 1921 [fig. 15]. The plan, on a triangular plane, gave the impression of slicing into the cellular structure of construction in the city's tissue. The structure consisted of three separate residential spaces, which spread out like the leaves of a palm, and was supported by a common ferro-concrete core, creating the central, common axis of the building. The glass façades, articulated by the regular rhythm of the windows, and the sharply cut corners of the structure increased the illusion that the entire structure was pushing upwards. Mies van der Rohe also produced (in around 1922) another well-known design for a Berlin skyscraper that was never built [fig. 16].

Its slim silhouette of soft, rounded shapes was composed, like the earlier one, of three wings built around a ferro-concrete, two-cylinder structural core. The crystalline structure of the all-glass curtain walls was to reflect the natural and artificial light of the city, creating an effect of reflective radiance. Both designs are seen today as some of the earliest suggestions of International Style, and in Mies van der Rohe's work they begin the trend, characteristic of his entire oeuvre, of architectural building structures striving for the most extreme elementarization and standardization of form. There is a direct line from them to Mies van der Rohe's architecture in the United States after World War II. This includes, first and foremost, the Chicago buildings on Lake Shore Drive and the crowning achievement of his minimalist accomplishments, the Seagram Building at 375 Park Avenue in New York (1954–58).

The building in Chicago that concerns us here, as material for Sosnowska's sculpture, was a twenty-six-story pair of twin apartment buildings, laid out in an L-shape: two eighty-meter towers standing at right angles to each other and connected by an interior hall. All-glass façades were combined with an exposed iron structural skeleton supported by steel columns, which simultaneously offered a frame for the network of windows that constituted the curtain wall.

The structural-formal visual purity of Lake Shore Drive that resulted from this, as an architectural "thing in itself" in the emptiness of space (the infinite view of the giant lake), which was the basis of Mies van der Rohe's modernist thinking, created an optical illusion of distance and the upward ascent of the buildings, giving it an almost transcendental and timeless character. On the one hand, this fact caused delight in the lightness of abstract form; on the other, it was the object of criticism that noted a conservative streak in striving toward architectural autonomy of construction closed off from the social context, and the abstraction of the pure visuality of its structure [fig. 17].

The tension here quite obviously reflects the dispute that engaged modernist and postmodernist architects in the nineteen-eighties and nineties. This is of interest to Sosnowska, not only because of the constructive use of unconstructive grids in her own tower, which I will discuss later, but also because of the ideological context, which interests us here (and to which I have already alluded), of the plans for building up the center of the capital around the Palace of Culture and Science with high-rises.

This idea has been around for a long time, and its implementation began with the construction of the Elektrim Building (Intraco II, or the Oxford Tower, 1975–78), along with the neighboring Marriott Hotel (the LIM Center, 1980–89), and later, the Warsaw Financial Center (1997–98), the Intercontinental Hotel (2001–04), Rondo 1 (2003–06) [fig. 18], Złote Tarasy with its Skylight Tower (2002–07), et cetera. The idea to surround the palace with a crown of skyscrapers dates back to 1992 (Białyszew, Skopiński). They were to stand along an elliptical boulevard, called the Corso, overshadowing the palace with their modernity and vigor. It was even attempted, albeit unsuccessfully, to convince Christian Kerez, then

[fig. 15] Ludwig Mies van der Rohe, *Friedrichstrasse Skyscraper Project, Berlin-Mitte, Germany, Exterior Perspective from North*, 1921.

[fig. 16] Ludwig Mies van der Rohe, *Glass Skyscraper Project, View of Lost Model, No Intended Site Known*, 1922.

[fig. 17] Ludwig Mies van der Rohe, 860–880 Lake Shore Drive, Chicago, Illinois, 1949–51.

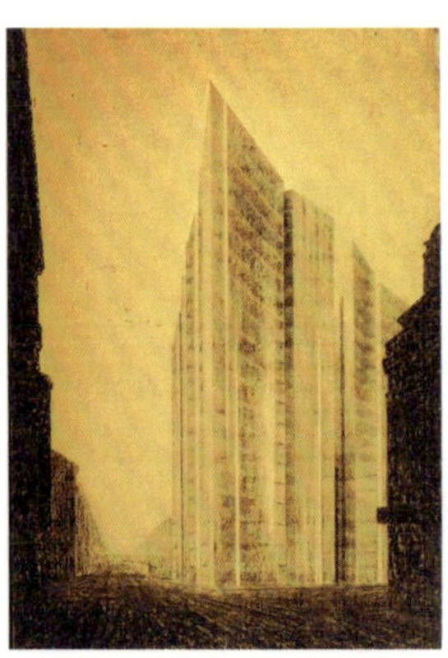

15

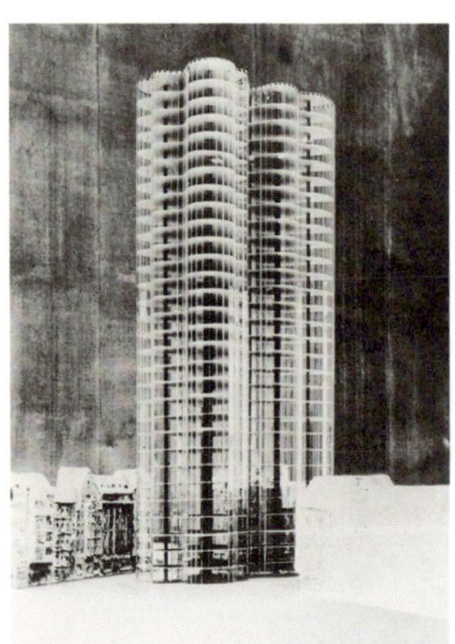

16

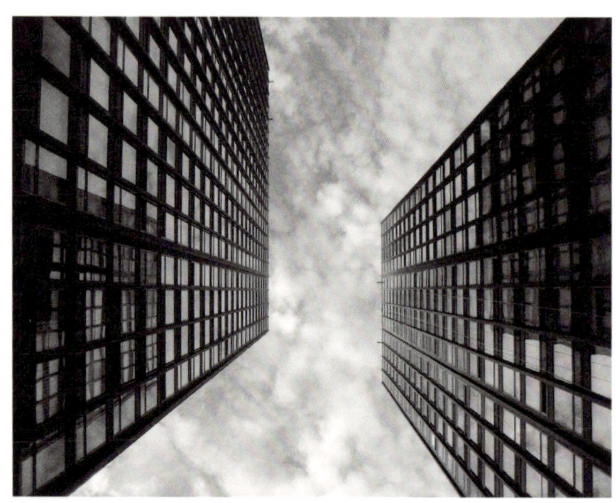

17

the designer of the Museum of Contemporary Art's low building on Defilad Square, which is situated in front of the palace, to stretch his building upward. The plan for a uniform set of high-rises quickly failed, but as a result of the city's neoliberal plan, towers rose anyway. Individual initiatives of corporate investors multiplied, with popular architects invited to build in the surrounding areas. Among the best-known are Daniel Libeskind's tower on Złota Street (2008–13), in the form of a sail with a sparkling, patterned façade, broadening out as it ascends as if inverted [fig. 19]; the Cosmopolitan Tower on Grzybowska Square (2010–13), designed by Helmut Jahn, and finally the design, thus far unrealized, for Zaha Hadid's Lilium Tower (2007), whose rounded forms could call to mind the form of a cigar.

Aside from these last plans and projects, which exhibited distinct postmodernist ambitions, all the earlier ones borrowed liberally from modernist concepts of construction, referring to the purist architecture derived from Mies van der Rohe. Chicago was the center of this type of architecture, sometimes called neo-modernist, and towers built in Poland owed much to that city's Aon Center (Amoco Tower, 1973), the office and commercial building at 333 Wacker Drive (1983), and the reinforced-concrete tower Two Prudential Plaza (1990). All the buildings of this type, competing with each other in height and slenderness, had glass surfaces, sometimes taking on the character of slightly curved façades, whose simple sections, using aluminum, were lost among the colorful and flowing reflections of the living city. But all that connected them, beyond the International Style, was their purpose. They were most often built to order for huge corporations, trading companies, and developers. All of them, whether office buildings, retail centers, or luxury apartment houses—and most often combining all three of

[fig. 18] Skidmore, Owings and Merrill, Rondo 1 Office Tower, Warsaw, 2003–06.

[fig. 19] Daniel Libeskind, Złota 44 Tower, Warsaw, 2008–13.

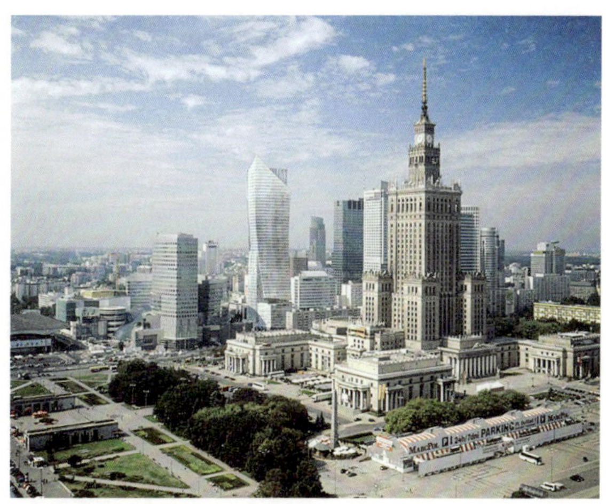

19

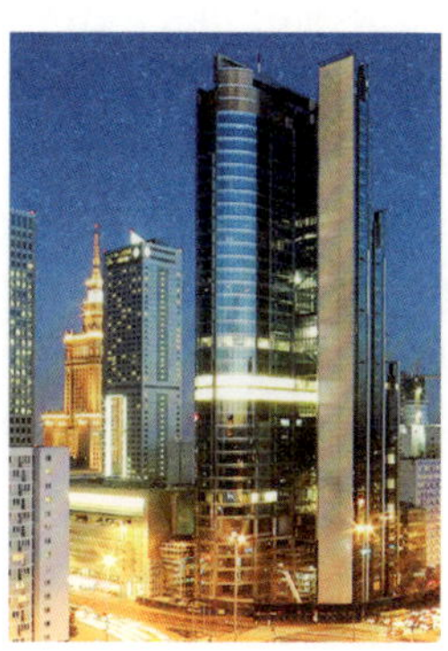

18

[fig. 20] Ludwig Mies van der Rohe, 860–880 Lake Shore Drive, Chicago, Illinois, 1949–51.

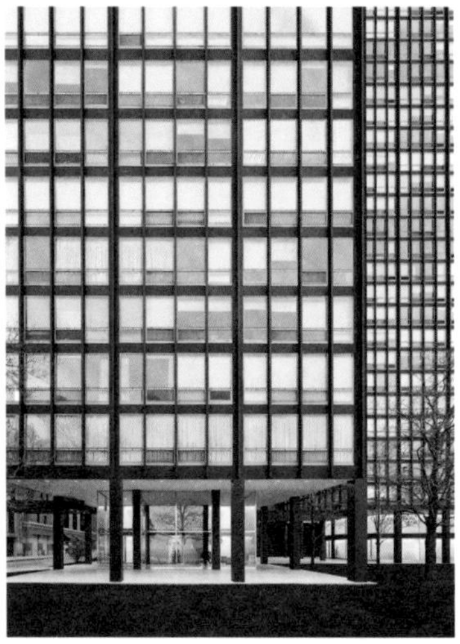

20

these functions—became symbols of the postmodern city, its order and affluence, progress and success, and its extravagant spectacle and technological perfection. They created a boundless world of business and consumption. Surrounding Warsaw's Palace of Culture and Science, they made sport of its puerile structure, bashfully covering up its primitivism and naïve symbolism. In opposition to the losing ideology, they established a triumphant consumerism.

Neoliberal politics announced "the end of ideology" (Fukuyama) in a world where history was ending, creating an illusory hope of eternal freedom and economic prosperity, in an atmosphere where market rules reigned supreme. The structural metaphor of this world—understood to be without history—was the polished surface of the high-rises, which reflected the lights of the advertisements and of each other. Towers that were erected on the seemingly solid basis of commercial ground floors, containing the stately, marble-lined, spreading halls of banks and consumer lenders, and the mobile and unending shelves of abundance in the shopping centers, beguiling with an orgy of colors and the lightness of aluminum.

The vision of the postmodern world, thus understood, personified by the Warsaw high-rise architecture surrounding the palace, created a second critical frame, alongside the Productivist metaphor, for the tower being built by Sosnowska, whose material was a huge grid of iron I-beams borrowed from Mies van der Rohe. In this light, the choice of this architect and his buildings as the material for *Tower* resulted from the discovery of an interesting gap between the Productivist past and the consumerist future. Her point, after all, was to pose a critical question, on a basis that was formally the most neutral, and simultaneously the most entangled with modern history: What was modernism? What message and what threats for the contemporary world does it hold?

Does it result in any form other than the one that disassembles itself? And if not, shouldn't criticisms of reality be replaced by deconstruction of the form that defined reality? This last question was key to Sosnowska's work, because it allowed her to break from the practice of postmodern critical art and engaged form, and subsequently move onto the ground which can be described with a term borrowed from Gombrowicz: "struggling with immature form." These struggles were not about giving form to political meanings, but bringing form into crisis. It was about perceiving its performative frailty, to make this immaturity and imperfection an anarchy-producing force that provoked unease; like a dream, it allowed one to touch the emptiness of reality. I stress that art will not generate knowledge about reality; rather, it brings us face to face with the discomfiting political and social crisis that surrounds us. This conviction haunts the newest generation of artists. Their procedure is a strategy of resistant form, whose democratic egalitarianism, in light of the intended indifference of the work, relies on the suspension of all preferences and hierarchies in its deconstruction, and its subversiveness on the radical deepening of contradiction to the point at which is brought to light the repressed "dissonance of capitalist production, separating work from pleasure. Such art is politics on the condition that it refrains from any political intervention,"[16] whether in the form of representation or of agitation.

The disassembly of the material that the artist used began at the moment when she laid the vertically hanging grid surrounding the windows of Mies van der Rohe's tower [fig. 20] on the flat surface of the production hall, and when the modularly spreading forms ran out of space there too, she spread their iron grid out over a vast construction site. The change in orientation from vertical to horizontal was significant. First and foremost, this lessened the power it had derived from its earlier place in a rising structure, making the supine grid defenseless. Now it could be walked on, its pieces could be moved around at will, it no longer was in danger of collapsing, it covered nothing, it was neither a wall nor a mock-up, it was somehow unneeded. There was no place for it in a structure that could live its own life, even in the way the one in the Venice Biennale pavilion did. The horizontal orientation opened up a range of possibilities. The artist had anticipated these possibilities long before, photographing the flat geometry of Warsaw shopping pavilions, their low forms fitting into the streetscape, or their ruins, when they were knocked down to make room for high-rises. She was interested in the architectural work of Christian Kerez, when, against the expectations of the day, he designed the low building of the Museum of Modern Art, modeled on the architecture of the pavilions, not even attempting to compete on height with the adjacent Palace of Culture and Science. She also engaged in a dialogue with Kerez, in their joint exhibition in Vaduz, Lichtenstein.

In Sosnowska's work, Mies van der Rohe's grid attained autonomy, as pure material, which could be spread out, multiplied, connected and divided, shaped and reshaped. It was also the beginning of the constructive work of building *Tower,* as well as a procedure allowing the deconstruction of its construction utopia.

The Grid

The standardization of building and construction elements was a result of modern industrial production and the technical properties of materials. At their foundation lay processes of elementarization and modularization, meaning the furthest-reaching simplification and uniformization of both work and product. This usually led to the definition of the basic parameters of each shape, whose multiplication created a structure. The rational organization of work, known as Fordism (and Taylorism), demanded the granular division of labor. A worker on the assembly line repeated one and the same action many times, approaching automatic perfection. The adoption of defined modules of products facilitated their mechanical production and assembly. Due to the sturdy and malleable building materials, the basic units could be replicated in any quantity. The principle of standardization, governing all of modern construction and its technology, led to the prefabrication of particular architectural elements outside the construction site, and construction became the assembly of these elements. This is how prefabricated panel construction worked. The final consequence of this method, which allowed for cheap and fast construction, was "house factories," producing entire residential units from prefabricated panels. Panel construction gained great popularity and was applied on a large scale in the construction of modular blocks in the great housing estates of Soviet Russia and its satellite states.

These panels were prefabricated construction elements used on a mass scale in Poland in the nineteen-sixties and seventies [fig. 21]. They quickly became propaganda synonymous with communist construction, which was to ensure free housing, of a unified standard, for all. The standardization characteristic of panel construction included the entirety of construction and functional

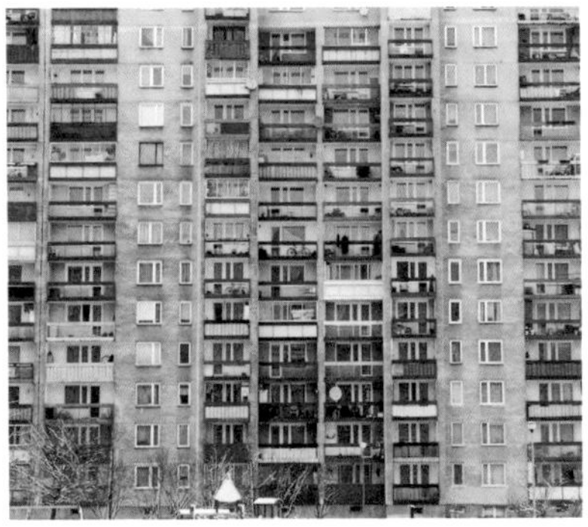

21

[fig. 21] Apartment blocks, rhythm of prefabricated panels and windows, 1970s.

[fig. 22] Construction of apartment blocks from prefabricated panels, 1950s.

[fig. 23] Warsaw apartment blocks, 1970s.

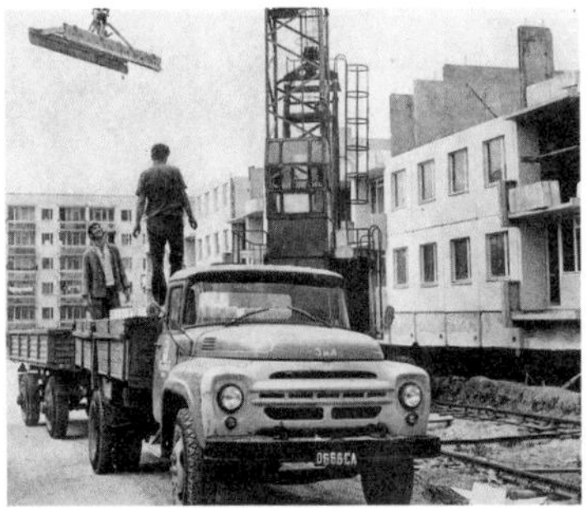

22

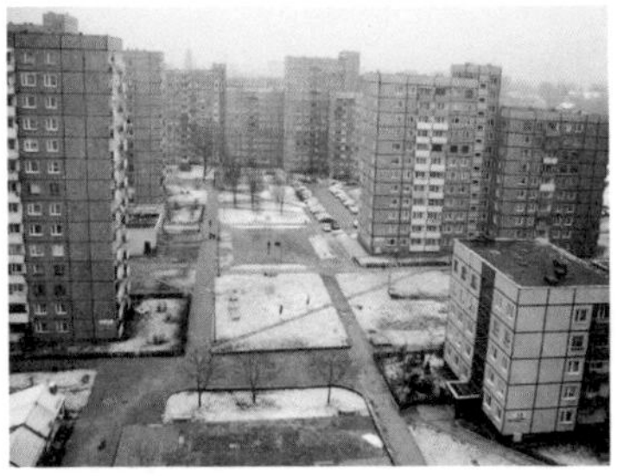

23

[fig. 24] Helena and Szymon Syrkus, House in Saska Kępa, Warsaw, 1937.

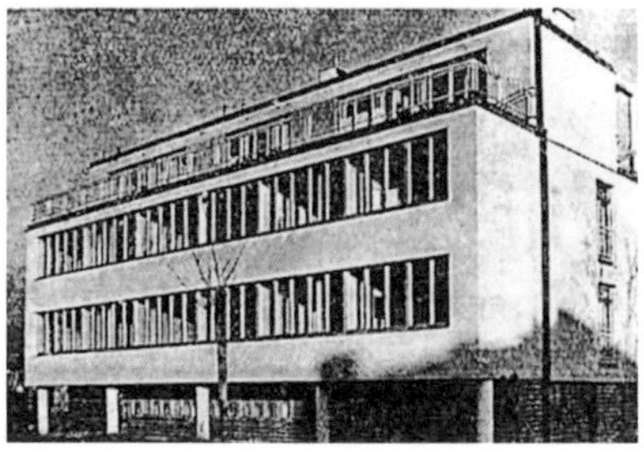

24

methods. It applied equally to basic concrete façades, thin dividing walls, suspended ceilings, premade stairwells and hallways, windows and balconies that repeated the same forms, and finally to all details, from similarly painted doors to the shapes of hinges and locks.

In the construction of housing estates from prefabricated panels, the transportation of the elements from the factory to the place of assembly played an important role. Trucks floundering in the mud, rusting earthmovers leveling the ground, high cranes with dangling sections of walls—all these created a well-known landscape of seemingly endless construction [fig. 22]. The myth of sterility and precision was somewhere far away. The forgotten elements of iron and concrete construction, like now-meaningless monuments, as well as the spreading joints of the panels and their fissures hastily covered with tar, for many years afterward, formed landmarks and lent variety to the geometric regularity of the network of streets that wound among the blocks, to the horizontal lines of windows and the vertical rhythms of stairwells and elevators, and ultimately to the grid of the giant panels [fig. 23]. Even though an apartment in a prefabricated block, including analogous wall-unit furniture and identical kitchen fittings, was an object of universal desire and a sign of stabilization, it didn't enjoy a good reputation, symbolizing as it did the monotony, anonymity, and shoddiness of life in the countries of "real socialism."

Studies on systems of standardized elements in construction interested almost all modern architects, even before 1914. Still, the pressing construction needs after the destruction experienced during World War I accelerated work on these questions. Le Corbusier is seen as the precursor; he was the first in the twentieth century to develop the contemporary architectural module defining the functions of architecture, utilizing serial production of prefabricated materials. An architectural program announced in 1920 (on the pages of *L'Esprit Nouveau*) announced future "residential machines," which were to be made possible by the production of houses according to strictly applied and reproduced standards.

In Poland one of the architects who worked closely with Le Corbusier was Szymon Syrkus (1891–1964), creator of the Praesens group (1926), initiator of cooperative architecture (Warsaw's WSM housing cooperative), an activist of the International Congresses of Modern Architecture (CIAM) in 1929–1959, a signer of the Athens Charter in 1933, a theorist and practitioner of the furthest-reaching standardization in residential construction. In 1927 Syrkus took part in the residential exhibition at the Weissenhof Estate in Stuttgart.[17] There he saw Le Corbusier's buildings with garden terraces on their roofs, and a Mies van der Rohe residential building, in which the architect for the first time used the form of a grid made from a steel skeleton and a curtain façade of glass, applying it to the new needs of residential construction—foreshadowing the postwar Chicago apartments. The Le Corbusier and Mies van der Rohe buildings shown in Stuttgart relied on the standardization of structural and functional elements.

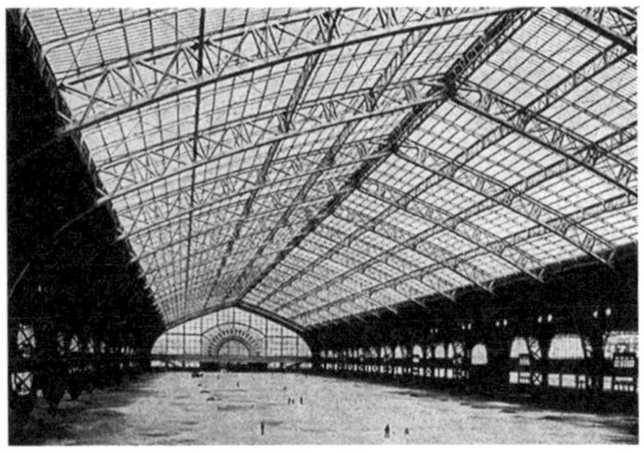

25

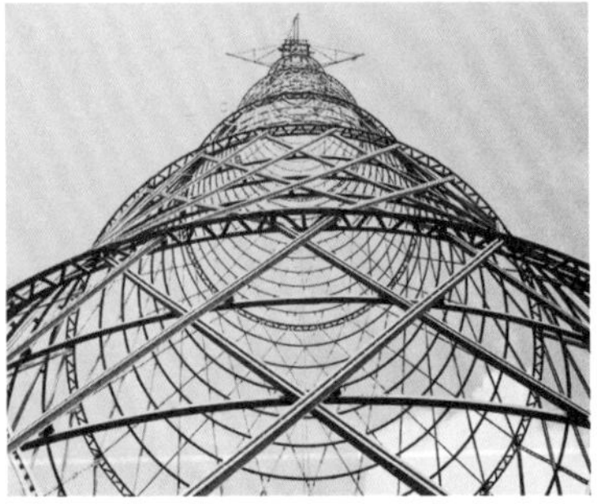

26

[fig. 25] Ferdinand Dutert, Galerie des machines, Paris, 1889.

[fig. 26] Aleksandr Rodchenko, *Shuchov Transmission Tower*, 1929.

From that moment, the guiding thought of all designs, including those of Syrkus [fig. 24], was the problem of mass prefabrication. In reflecting on the Weissenhof Estate he paid particular attention to the significance of the normalization of architectural forms and plans. He stressed the importance of the idea of finding a pattern "that has the ability to scale up and down, while simultaneously multiplying itself in various combinations through mechanical duplication."[18]

For the modernist architects, this pattern was the grid. Giedion, in describing the beginnings of modern architecture, pointed out the aesthetic significance of structural latticework in the Galerie des machines at the Universal Exposition of 1889, in Paris [fig. 25]. He was convinced that the gridwork, used there for the first time, allowed for the interpenetration of interior and exterior spaces, creating a completely new feeling of boundlessness and endlessness, which thus far had been the basis for architectural forms that dematerialized in spatial rhythms. "Each arched truss is made up of two segments. A pin unites them at a pivotal point high above the centerline of the hall. Moving downward, the trusses become increasingly attenuated until they appear scarcely to touch the ground; mobbing upward, they spread and gain weight and power. The usual proportions seem to be exactly reversed. These triply articulated arches disturb, or rather disrupt, traditional static feelings with regard to the rational relations of support and load. Elongated like immensely drawn-out cantilevers, the trusses embody movement in all their parts . . . In addition these girders were unusually light, since this was the first time steel framework had been used to such an extent."[19]

The grid, often known as the regular net or the geometric skeleton, and sometimes the elemental structure, came to dominate the constructive imagination of modern thinking, lying at the heart of the new world order that was built on it. Rosalind Krauss, taking on the myths of modernity at the end of the nineteen-seventies, referred to the form of the net, which she called, and not without reason, "the emblematic structure of modernist ambitions." In the space of contemporary art—around which a cult has grown, she stressed—the net is not only a symbol, but also a myth [fig. 26]. Like every myth, it deals with paradox or contradiction, while not resolving either. The mythical power of the net depends on our capability to think that we are dealing with materialism (sometimes with science or logic), while at the same time we are granted access to faith (or illusion or fiction). The net, by nature ambiguous, is a locus in which the modernist contradictions of space and time both complete and cancel each other, in which knowledge fights with spirit, the rational with the spiritual, the material with the transcendental, the completed with the continuous, the closed with the open, the disclosed with the displaced, the joyful with the tragic. The net is a place seemingly autonomous and neutral, and in fact tangled and conflicted.

Because of its bivalent structure (and history), the net is joyfully schizophrenic, writes Rosalind Krauss:

> Logically speaking, the grid extends, in all directions, to infinity. Any boundaries imposed upon it by a given painting or sculpture can only be seen—according to this logic—as arbitrary. By virtue of the grid, the given work of art is presented as a mere fragment, a tiny piece arbitrarily cropped from an infinitely larger fabric. Thus the grid operates from the work of art outward, compelling our acknowledgement of a world beyond the frame. This is the centrifugal reading. The centripetal one works, naturally enough, from the outer limits of the aesthetic object inward. The grid is, in relation to *this* reading a *re*-presentation of everything that separates the work of art from the world, from ambient space, and from other objects. The grid is an introjection of the boundaries of the world into the interior of the work; it is a mapping of the space inside the frame onto itself. It is a mode of repetition, the content of which is the conventional nature of art itself.
> The work of Mondrian, taken together with its various and conflicting readings, is a perfect example of this dispute. Is what we see in a particular painting merely a section of an implied continuity, or is the painting structured as an autonomous, organic whole? . . . There are certain paintings that are overwhelmingly centrifugal, particularly the vertical and horizontal grids seen within diamond-shaped canvases—the contrast between frame and grid enforcing the sense of fragmentation, as though we were looking at a landscape through a window, the frame of the window arbitrarily truncating our view but never shaking our certainty that the landscape continues beyond the limits of what we can, at that moment, see. But other works, even from the same years, are just as explicitly centripetal. In these, the black lines forming the grid are never allowed actually to reach the outer margins of the work, and this caesura between the outer limits of the grid and the outer limits of the painting forces us to read the one as completely contained within the other."[20]
> [fig. 27]

[fig. 27] Henryk Stażewski, *Textural Composition*, 1930–31.

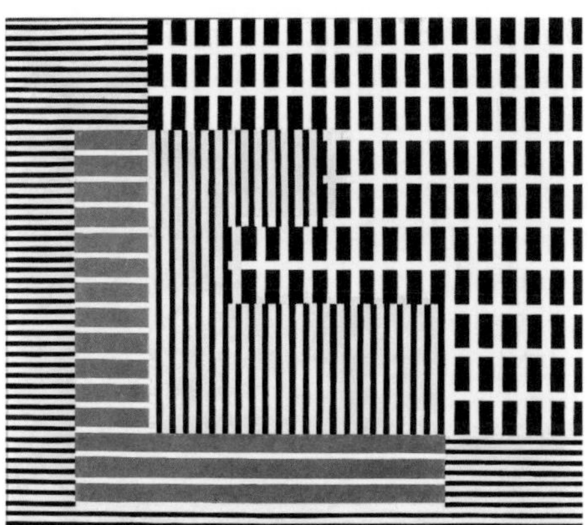

Despite its monumental scope, Sosnowska's grid is a small fragment of a much larger whole, a frame cut out of a plane, a series of windows from the curtain-wall façade. Something of a prefabricated panel delivered to the building site and waiting to be joined with other, analogous prefabs. It creates an independent structure of identical elements inscribed in their own context, which do not at all differ from the whole, i.e. a modular series of rectangles, a regular rhythm of horizontals and verticals, a geometry of shapes stretching upward, downward, and outward. Sosnowska's grid is barred, and itself bars off the surrounding space.

The standard unit of Sosnowska's grid is a metal window frame, mounted on hinges and closed with a latch, placed between the structure's I-beams. All of the windows and their details are made with the same mechanical precision—ruling out coincidence—and foreshadow the solidity of a particular construction, as well as the visual order of abstract space. For Sosnowska this is very important. The window is the boundary of the plane, that which makes it transparent; it simultaneously opens and negates, and dematerializes and construes. We can say that windows, and specifically grids of windows, are the symbolic essence of modernist sculpture, allowing concentration on the sculpture itself, as a formal matrix; but also, functioning by their openings as a denial of any kind of shape, a representation of the endlessness of spatial rhythms, grids of windows build the world. The basic modernist construction unit was the grid.

The Constructivist avant garde believed that the path "from plane to space" was the only one on which an autonomic planar structure could achieve its social utopia; a path where the visual order of the world can take up the challenge of engagement. But that's not how it turned out. The functionalism of modernist architecture, for which the starting point was the search for primary structures and modular units and their usage on a mass scale, was to be a response to the omnipresent need for apartments for everyone; in construction practice it quickly failed, and that did not make life any more fair. Architectural functionalism, tangled up in the political slogans of great construction in Poland, in the nineteen-sixties and seventies, led to the "small stabilization" based on propagandistic falsehood. The ordered world, in accordance with Mies van der Rohe's grid—even though it aroused admiration with its initial resistance against ideological capture and the temptations of consumption—did not, in the context of Warsaw architecture, open alternative windows. The Mies van der Rohe grid, assembled with such care by Sosnowska, had to be disassembled. Subjected to stress tests: tests of bending, stretching, pressure, elongation, creasing, crushing, and cutting. Another illusion, says Sosnowska, an illusion to be deconstructed.

Construction/ Destruction

The tower being built by Sosnowska, like the Eiffel Tower, suffered from a "Babel complex." The joy of building it up was accompanied by the stigma of downfall, as in a Greek tragedy—love is accompanied by death. This time it wasn't about the areas hidden or repressed by the avant-garde experience in Polish art and architecture in the second half of the twentieth century, but the broad fields of modernist discourse, for which catastrophe, as an ingredient of philosophical doctrine, cultural practice, and political ideology, constituted a fundamental underpinning for bold artistic projects. "The stone Colossus 'Cosmopolis' stands at the end of the life's course of every great Culture," wrote Oswald Spengler in *The Decline of the West.*

> The culture-man whom the land has spiritually formed is seized and possessed by his own creation, the city, and is made into its creature, its executive organ, and finally its victim [fig. 28]. This stony mass is the absolute city. Its image, as it appears with all its grandiose beauty in the light-world of the human eye, contains the whole noble death-symbolism of the definitive thing-become. The spirit-pervaded stone of gothic buildings, after a millennium of style-evolution, has become the soulless material of this daemonic stone-desert. . . . This, then, is the conclusion of the city's history; growing from primitive barter-center to culture-city and at last to world-city, it sacrifices first the blood and soul of its creators to the needs of its majestic evolution, and then the last flower of that growth to the spirit of civilization—and so, doomed—moves on to final self-destruction.[21]

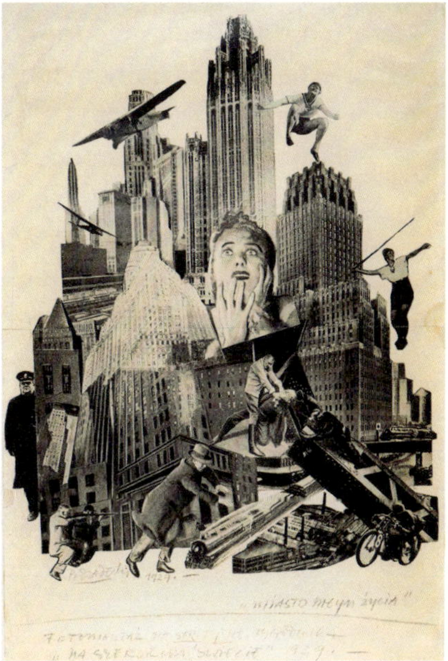

28

[fig. 28] Kazimierz Podsadecki, *City, Mill of Life*, 1929.

The biblical story of the Tower of Babel, found in chapter eleven of Genesis, reaches to the very foundations of the myth of human construction of the world, whose boldness and perfection would rival the divine act of creation. It's also a story about divine punishment on humanity for the pride embodied in a structure that man had no right to build. The perfection of construction was to remain an attribute of God, and the tower was to be destroyed. According to the apocryphal tradition (*Speculum Humanae Salvationis,* early fourteenth century) the construction of the tower was directed by the giant Nimrod (Nemroth, Nemrod, Niemrod, Nebrod). He was the great-grandson of Ham—a hunter dressed in the skins of Adam, the first man. The story of the building of the tower was borrowed from Mesopotamian civilization, specifically from the Chaldean tradition. From there it entered the Hebrew tradition, where it was a reminder of the buildings of Babylon and of Babylonian cosmopolitanism. The city of Babylon was the capital of Akkadian civilization, and later that of the Kassites and the Chaldeans. Alexander the Great planned to make Babylon the capital of his empire. The final fall of Babylon came in the third century CE. For more than fifteen hundred years the city had been a strong, multilingual center of culture and trade, it was seen as the center of the world. In this sense, too, the etymology of the word "Babel" and the construction of the ziggurat were directly connected with the history of the divine city, and simultaneously with the linguistic chaos that reigned within it.

In the iconography of the Tower of Babel we are dealing with several, sometimes conflicting, narrative threads, which at different times and in different ways have renewed the relevance of the problems of its meaning. In the first meaning, Babylonian iconography was connected with the process of building the tower, as a human construction rising upward [fig. 29]. This structure belonged to man, who in praise of God or from human pride put up a house connecting earth with heaven. Depending on the specific version, this construction was presented in the surroundings of working masons and their tools, or of a master designer and his plan. In each case, the particular iconographic version of the tower was connected with the idea of human construction. Here, man repeated the divine act of creation [fig. 30].

In the second meaning, the iconography of the tower was connected with a range of presentations of structures as ruins. The structure, unfinished or falling down, portrayed divine wrath and punishment. Usually these were dramatic occurrences—catastrophes, misfortunes, and disasters that met the builders. People fell from scaffoldings, and the top of the teetering building was left forever unfinished. This time the iconography stressed the divine act of destruction. The structure that arose lost its structural transparency, transforming instead into a sort of dark, unknown labyrinth.

In drawing out the fundamental contradiction written into the progressive topos of construction, well known in Western culture,

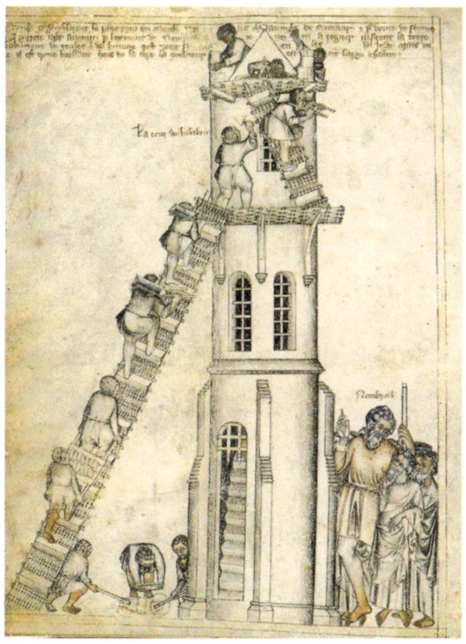

29

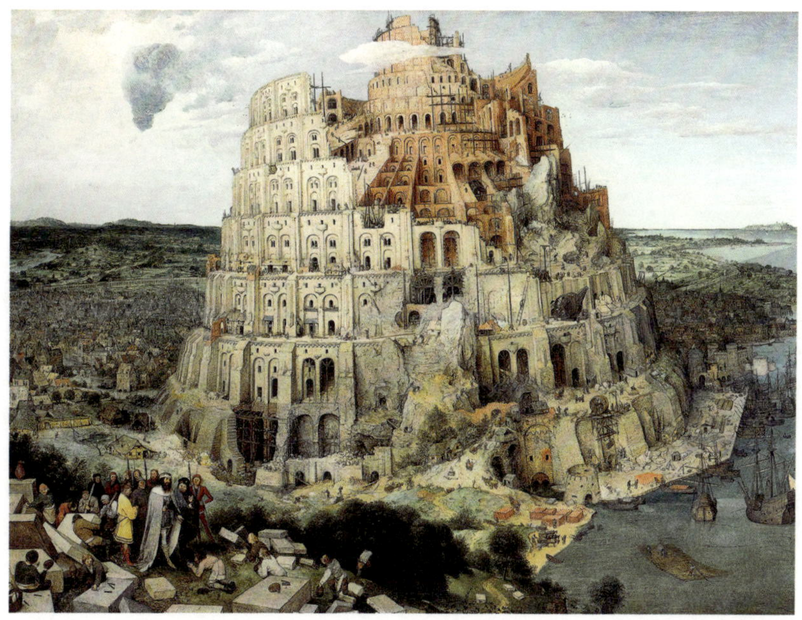

30

[fig. 29] “Building the Tower of Babel,” *Egerton Genesis Picture Book*, circa 1360.

[fig. 30] Pieter Bruegel the Elder, *Tower of Babel*, 1563.

[fig. 31] Cornelis Anthonisz, *Fall of the Tower of Babel*, 1549.

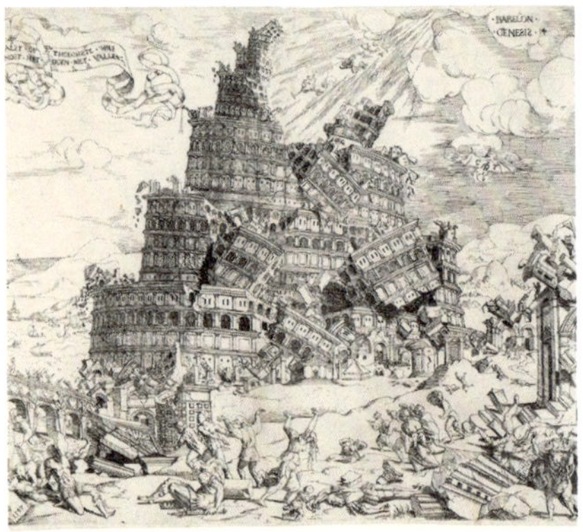

31

I would like to stress its ambiguity. In this sense construction and destruction, just like structure and ruin, do not form opposing pairs expressing themselves in the concepts of a modernist utopia and anti-utopia; rather, they are part of the same process of creation in which the Apocalypse is already present. The connection between construction and destruction in the sense proposed here does not contain either history or time; it does not apply to geography, or space, but it is derived from the project itself, as its internal criticism. The critical relation connects, more than it divides, the construction of the world with its catastrophic end. Both concepts function within the same field of meaning, intermeshing with each other [fig. 31]. In considering the art of the modernists who sought to set up their Towers of Babel, it is difficult not to notice the fissures etching their way across the buildings, not to see the ruins surrounding the structure, not to hear the voices predicting its collapse [fig. 32]. The dark labyrinth was not the antithesis of the joyful structure: it lay within the structure—it was the dark side of the same body. It threatened the body's structural coherence, its rational wholeness, and its universal unity. Sosnowska has noticed this ambiguity of the modernist Tower of Babel, and this has become the meaning of its construction and destruction, a metaphor for the process of deconstruction. When designing *Tower,* Sosnowska made many models of it, on various scales, from a Mies van der Rohe grid.

With a certain irony, in one interview she stresses that she was astounded from the very beginning, that despite the structural concept and the engineering calculations, the tower didn't want to stand up vertically. It wasn't tilted like the one in Pisa; it simply fell over. It was a horizontal tower, similar from this point on to a labyrinth of bent forms, girders lying flat, twisted windows. The process on the sculpture recalled the project that had preceded it. Copied precisely in a 1:1 scale, the horizontal grid "taken down" from the building, now the material of the tower under construction, was laid flat during the reconstruction, which allowed her to capture and recreate the serial regularity of forms and details. Further work on the grid, which subjected it to forces that deformed the flat construction, to shape a tower with volume, led to an amorphous chaos of somehow jammed-together steel trusses—the creeping structure of a metal snake. The structure was incapable of being erected, stood up, or held vertical. The prone colossus mocked its engineering prototype, and as a work of art was more suitable for transport and display in the closed space of a gallery. Cutting the "body, being reborn" of the tower-snake into pieces (a return to modularity), which could be packed into containers, didn't threaten to collapse, and changed this creature once again into something artistically functional. This process of re-repeating (or translation) of form and meaning in Sosnowska's *Tower* was being carried out, similarly to the Tower of Babel, within this same construction; its growth and collapse became part of the initiating project.

They were a translation, a transposition of one onto the other: a process of deconstruction.

Deconstruction "inhabits" (construction) within a structure, in order to peel apart, shift, reshape, retranslate. It inhabits the tower (of Babel) in order to show that it always remains an unfinished construction, which is no surprise, as every intervention of deconstruction, Derrida says, uncovers a new figure of the untranslatable. "The Tower of Babel, being an architectural figure of translation (but also of untranslatability) thus points not only to the mixing of languages, but also to incompletion: the impossibility of merging, totality, creating a coherent and universal system," says Cembrzyńska. "Thus it is a challenge thrown down to the structural order, to the coherence of structure. But simultaneously with the architectural figure of translation (but also of untranslatability) one must escape, 'translating' deconstruction. For the Tower of Babel is a metaphor of deconstruction itself, its possibility (something without which deconstruction cannot take place), not only representation."[22]

The strategy of deconstruction in Sosnowska's sculpture, thus understood, is a rhetorical process shaping the internal mechanism of the statement, which I would call "setting narration in motion." The neo-formalism that characterizes such a statement requires that we discover, in the internal dynamic of deforming, successive events allowing us to view, through their metamorphosis, the movement that finally shatters the order that once belonged to the formal structure. The artist discards final effect (the meaning of meanings), and dramatizes every event in its own way. Sosnowska's form thus enters into narrative threads, operating by their characteristic literary tricks, among which it privileges the synecdoche (operating by a part in place of the whole).

[fig. 32] Yang Yongliang, *Heavenly City-05*, 2008.

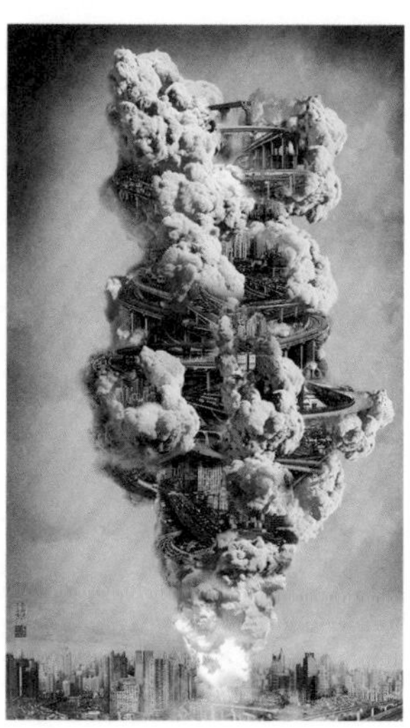

32

The first formalists from the nineteen-twenties, born with the avant-garde, and their second, nineteen-fifties, mutation, often called Greenbergian, sought to deprive form of meaning, neutralizing its expression or closing it up in its own autonomy. They were seeking the complete silence of form. Out of opposition to formalisms, thus understood, American postmodernism arose. Out of it also came critical art, seeking social application of form and engaged activism. There too, the return of reality, shattered into an agonistic multiplicity of voices, had an ideological character, implicating art in power relationships. The return of the formal in Sosnowska's sculpture places her in a successive generation of postmodernist Deconstructivists, because her art is not about realism, but "a realistic style of form": documentary work, prosaic speech, metonymic rhetoric. Together they create the sculpture and its self-commentary. It's not a theoretical text, nor an artistic manifesto, but a visual story, deprived of words, about metamorphosis, material, production, and context. It is a photographic documentation included in the project and depriving the sculpture's final meaning of form. It is a deconstruction of sculpture.

The Vastness and the Vortex

Jacques Derrida, commenting on Emanuel Kant's aesthetic of the sublime, connects it to words and concepts such as colossus, colossal, colossality, whose synonyms are giant, powerful, total, as well as absolute, skyrocketing, limitless, immeasurable, and also unimaginable, mad, vertiginous. "*Erhaben*, the sublime, is not only high, elevated, nor even very elevated. Very high, absolutely high, higher than any comparable height, more than comparative, a size not measurable in height, the sublime is *superelevation* beyond itself."[23] (Kant, in his *Critique of Judgment,* says that, "The mere presentation of a concept is called colossal, which is almost too great for any presentation.") Colossality is connected with the philosophical category of lack of real reference, "the emptiness of the real." In this sense, the colossality that is the very heart of the sublime belongs to the order neither of nature (as, for example, a tall mountain or tree does), nor of architecture (such as, for example, a strictly measurable column); the colossus of sublimity is unrepresentable (incapable of being presented), it is a pure concept. It escapes the relationship between the object and its representation, it escapes description, it escapes language, it escapes meaning. To capture meaning, not in its conceptual essence but in the dialectic of discourses and contexts, the sublime (the absolute) needs to be transformed into the monstrous (to deform, lay down, reshape the elevated), making the giant something real and representable. That which has a monstrous appearance is strange, irregular, and clumsy, like the sublime transformed into the earthly. In the monstrous, the real returns.

Franz Kafka once wrote in a note the well-known words: "What are you building? I want to dig a passage. A progress has to happen. My position is too elevated. We are digging the pit of Babel." (The well of Babel, according to Herling-Grudziński [fig. 33].) The exchange of words in Kafka's note transforms the metaphor of the Tower of Babel into the image of a hole in the ground, a bottomless

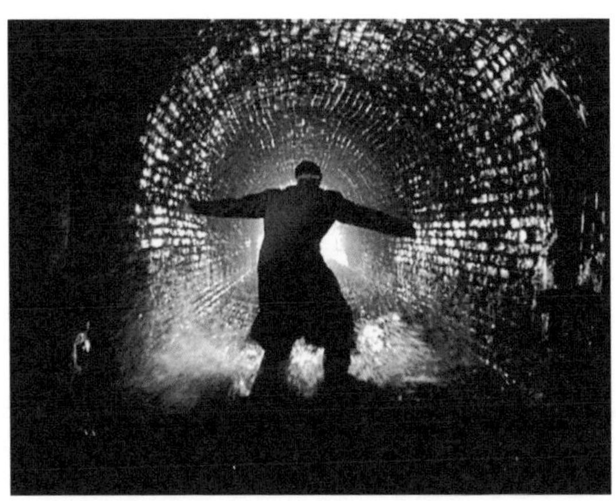

33

[fig. 33] Scene from the underground labyrinth in the film *The Third Man*, directed by Carol Reed, screenplay by Graham Greene, filmed in 1948 in the ruins of Vienna, and released in 1949.

well. The gigantic excess of constructing a tower that aroused divine wrath is replaced by the writer with the image of a gigantic absence. The hole expresses the absence, which should find compensation in being filled in. According to Pliny and Sigmund Freud, all art is born from compensation for things that are absent, and artistic activity results from the desire for representation.[24] Instead of constructing sublimity, which in any case remains in the hands of an alien authority, Kafka proposes the creation of monstrosity, which astounds and imprisons. In *The Metamorphosis,* the hero Gregor Samsa is transformed one morning into a giant insect, lying supine ("he lay on his armor-hard back") who, locked in his room as if in a kind of dungeon (a labyrinth of opening and closing doors), attempted to divine the source of the alien emptiness that surrounded him, which is the source of the burdensome reality in whose form he was clothed.

Sosnowska's toppled *Tower* resembles a monster, is monstrous. Like some kind of creature devouring itself, which, having lost the foundation of the structure, the roots of the tree, the backbone of the human, is sentenced to crawl; an octopus, whose tentacles bind each other; a crustacean whose shell seems to have been cracked; a lizard, whose moving body can only undergo transformation. The lying *Tower* contains the vastness of a labyrinth, but it is not sublime, it doesn't rise up like a victory monument. In its recumbence it is defenseless; it fills up space, yet it is internally empty; it speaks, but its voice bounces back hollowly with the echo of grinders and scrapers, lathes and hammers. The sound of construction is replaced by the rumble of a collapsing building and the piercing silence of a ruin. It takes on meanings only to lose them immediately; it creates metonymies, only to apply them to others; it fills a hole, but can't extract itself. It asks about reality, it asks about representation, looking in terror at its own powerlessness. It is not an abstraction, but an emptiness waiting to be utilized, a sublimation of absence seeking rejuvenation, a well to be drawn from and a net to be scooped with.

The net of the avant garde that is deconstructed by Sosnowska in *Tower,* like a modular grid, a matrix of art and the world, now in the sculpture spread out on the ground, it has taken on a new meaning. The regular net, multiplied in endless repetitions, allowed the modernists to describe the very source of art and the world, erecting a utopian structure of unity, presence, and wholeness: in Sosnowska's sculpture, that net has been replaced by a netting. A netting that is slightly used, pulled from the depths, but all the time still used for fishing. A netting with different-sized holes, threads broken up by knots, and frayed edges. A netting that is not a copy of the being concealed on the bottom, but a successful entangling. In Sosnowska's sculpture the netting is a lying tower entangling the world, and simultaneously it is a netting that entangles the lying tower. Using this double ploy the artist attempts to catch the one guilty of the downfall, the one who causes all the problems, for at the bottom of it all, as Umberto Eco says, the basic question of philosophy (like that of psychoanalysis) is the same as that of a crime story: "Who is the guilty party? To know this (to think you know this), you have to conjecture that all the events have a logic, the logic that the guilty party has imposed on them. Every story of investigation and of conjecture tells us something that we have always been close to knowing . . ."[25]

The logic of the netting is the labyrinth. The labyrinth is the antithesis of the tower; it is, as a rule, down below; its organizational structure is horizontal. In Kafka's *The Trial,* K lives and moves as if in a labyrinth, knowing neither the way nor the goal. In Schulz the labyrinth is a wandering to the depths of the psyche through a complicated system of rooms and corridors. In Georges Bataille's essay "The Labyrinth," the human world has the form of a labyrinth; it is a labyrinth of language and simultaneously of incomprehension, of the crisis of social communication, and of a searching for a way out. There are many labyrinths. One of them is the Greek labyrinth of Theseus. As Umberto Eco says:

> This kind does not allow anyone to get lost: you go in, arrive at the center, and then from the center you reach the exit. This is why in the center there is the Minotaur; if he were not there the story would have no zest, it would be a mere stroll. Terror is born, if it is born, from the fact that you do not know where you will arrive or what the Minotaur will do. But if you unravel the classical labyrinth, you find a thread in your hand, the thread of Ariadne. The classical labyrinth is the Ariadne's-thread of itself.
>
> Then there is the mannerist maze: if you unravel it, you find in your hands a kind of tree, a structure with roots, with many blind alleys. There is only one exit, but you can get it wrong. You need an Ariadne's-thread to keep from getting lost. This labyrinth is a model of the trial-and-error process.
>
> And finally there is the net, or rather, what Deleuze and Guattari call "rhizome." The rhizome is so constructed that every path connected with every other one. It has no center, no periphery, no exit, because it is potentially infinite.[26]

The space of conjecture, like the space of Sosnowska's lying tower, is a space resembling a rhizome [fig. 34]. Rhizomes, Gilles Deleuze and Félix Guattari assert, have the structure of "a map, not a tracing." A tracing is always a reproduction. Behind the tracing stands the hierarchy of the original; a map is absolutely flat. A tracing, like a tree, is rooted, while rhizomes remain tangles of regrowth. A tracing always "leads to the same thing;" a map is made from measurements and moving points, successive twists. A rhizome, like a map, does not reflect any reality, it draws it. It is a space of creation. A map "can be torn, reversed, adapted to any kind of mounting, reworked by an individual, group, or social formation." A map can be brought to a workshop, "drawn on a wall, conceived as a work of art, construed as a political act."[27]

The vastness (monstrous) and the vortex (rhizomial) make up the two sides of what is formal in Sosnowska's *Tower.* The first sneers at perfection of form (lack of fulfillment); the second alarms (by its lack of rootedness); still, both result from historically defined reality, they are the context of the reality returning in postmodernism. The deconstructed vastness lays bare the otherness of Warsaw's monstrous constructions from the era of communism (the Palace of Culture and Science) and the times of consumerism (the high-rises in the center of the capital), it creates distance from the purist architecture of modernism (Mies van der Rohe) and its Polish version from the years of "real socialism" (tower blocks). The loss of modernist utopias (lack of fulfillment) changes the vastness into a ruin, into a huge rubble heap of shapes and ideologies. Arising on the rubble of the vortex, like a rhizome it is deprived of foundations, deprived of grounding in the deconstructed history of monstrous forms and concepts. Postmodernity is unrooted, and no tree grows from it, no tower arises. Sosnowska, refraining from constructing a vision of the future, an illusion of utopia, experiences the world traumatically.

In Sosnowska's *Tower,* and possibly in all of her art, which belongs to the times of political transformation, there is a distinct shift "from reality as an effect of representation to the real as a thing of trauma."[28] This process, seen in the broad perspective of the avant garde and the neo- (post-) avant garde at the turn of the twentieth and twenty-first centuries, has numerous connections and references to psychoanalytic and feminist theory. Reflection on these questions requires a separate essay. Here, in conclusion, I will be interested, to put it very briefly, only in the degree to which the shift toward art built on trauma, in Sosnowska's work, is a reflection of her historical experience. The experiences of the post-communist era, the period of fundamental changes: structural and ideological, social and cultural, regional and generational.

[fig. 34] Rhizome.

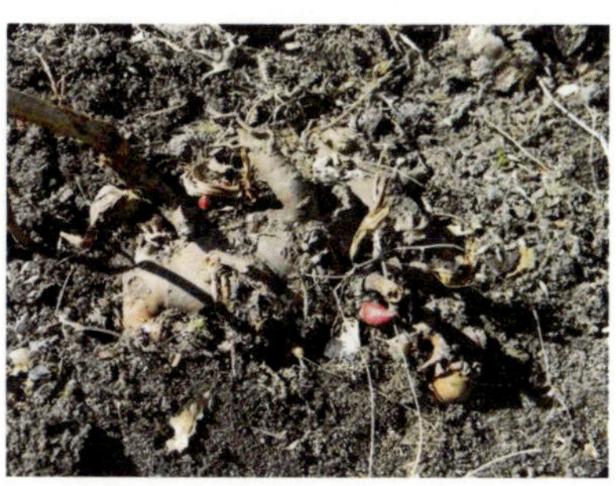

34

Among the basic categories describing the "era of transition" in Poland and the rest of Central Europe is the concept of a society without foundations. This is one of the observations of contemporary political philosophy, which assumes that postmodern society cannot be said to have any positive basis, identified in communist ideologies with the economic base, in others with language, nation, or faith. Yet this does not mean that in times of crisis, tension, or change, all of the foundations for political communities have disappeared, never to return. They still exist, as caricatures, traces of the once-solid foundations on which during "times of transformation" there arise doubtful social hegemonies, characterized first of all by political (neo-liberalism), cultural (Catholicism), propagandistic (populism), or ideological (nationalism) fanaticism and imagined or real authority. The "post-foundational condition" that characterizes young democracies does not assume the discouraging of the search for a social basis, but rather sees it from the point of view of social practice as being in vain, and from the point of view of democracy, as dangerous. In this way, it throws down a challenge to traditional political theory, and lays bare the social insufficiency of contemporary conventional politics. It is a pondering of its own time, which "stand[s] among is born out of the ruins of that what which was once considered society's unshakable foundations."[29]

During the historic transition from 1989–90, Boris Buden, the Croatian philosopher of post-communist society, writes, "It is easy to recognize the historical turning point of 1989–90 also as a post-foundational one: the political event as an experience of a radically dissolving society. Thus if post-communism actually constitutes an epochal 'situation,' it is such in the sense of a post-foundational situation, in which the 'dispute with the foundation' in a decisive way describes not only the public political life of a particular society, but also the *condition humaine* of man as a social entity."[30]

Life in a community that has lost its foundation, and has decided that the search for one is in vain or dangerous, and has all the characteristics of a traumatic experience, whose existential fear and alienation transforms into a fear of the future. Such is the cultural and generational experience of Sosnowska, who stands uncertainly between two eras, of which the past, in the process of deconstruction, has lost its meaning, and the future has not taken them on. The supine *Tower* deprived of foundations has changed into an eerie, ominous vortex, from which no utopia will spring. Welcome to the desert of the present! The guilty party is among us.

Notes

1 Krzysztof Pijarski, "Jeden do jednego. Rozmowa z Moniką Sosnowską i Sebastianem Cichockim o polskim pawilonie na 52. Biennale Sztuki w Wenecji" (One to one: a conversation with Monika Sosnowska and Sebastian Cichocki on the Polish Pavilion at the 52nd Venice Art Biennale), *Obieg,* www.obieg.pl, July 15, 2014, http://www.obieg.pl/rozmowy/1442 (accessed September 9, 2014).
2 Ibid.
3 Monika Sosnowska, "Regional Modernities," in *Regional Modernities,* exh. cat. Australian Centre for Contemporary Art (Southbank, 2013), p. 22.
4 *Pałac Kultury i Nauki* (The Palace of Culture and Science), *Wikipedia,* last modified September 6, 2014, http://pl.wikipedia.org/wiki/Pałac_Kultury_i_Nauki (accessed September 9, 2014).
5 Gianni Vattimo, *The End of Modernity: Nihilism and Hermeneutics in Postmodern Culture,* trans. Jon R. Snyder (Cambridge, 1988), p. 167.
6 Siegfried Giedion, Space, *Time and Architecture: The Growth of a New Tradition,* 5th ed. (Cambridge, 1967), pp. 603–07.
7 Pijarski, 2014 (see note 1).
8 Jacques Derrida, "Letter to a Japanese Friend, (Prof. Izutsu)," in *Derrida and Différance,* Robert Bernasconi and David Wood eds. (Coventry, 1985), pp. 1–5.
9 Andrzej Turowski, *Sztuka, która wznieca niepokój. Art That Sparks Unrest: The Artistic-Political Manifesto of Particular Art* (Warsaw, 2012).
10 Anatoly Lunacharsky, "Campo Santo w Pizie. Wieża Babel" (Campo Santo in Pisa: The Tower of Babel), trans. into Polish by Maria Okołów-Podhorska, in *Selected Works,* vol. 2. (Warsaw, 1964), p. 418.
11 Ibid.
12 Charles Jencks, *Modern Movements in Architecture* (Harmondsworth, 1973), pp. 95–96.
13 Mies van der Rohe, "Budowa" ("Construction"), *Blok* 1 (1924).
14 Patrycja Cembrzyńska, *Wieża Babel: Nowoczesny projekt porządkowania świata i jego dekonstrukcja* (The Tower of Babel: The Modern Project of Order-Making and Its Deconstruction) (Kraków, 2012), pp. 5–6. Cf. Roland Barthes, *Oeuvres complètes,* vol. 2: *1962–1967* (Paris, 2002).
15 Ilya Ehrenburg, *People, Years, Lives: The Revolution of 1918–1921,* trans. into Polish by Wacława Komarnicka (Warsaw, 1963), p. 174.
16 Jacques Rancière, *Estetyka jako polityka,* (Aesthetics as Politics), trans. into Polish by Julian Kutyła i Paweł Mościcki (Warsaw, 2007), p. 36.
17 Szymon Syrkus, "Fabrykacja Osiedli" (The fabrication of housing estates), *Architektura i Budownictwo* 8 (1928).
18 Szymon Syrkus, "Masowa produkcja mieszkań" (Mass production of apartments), *Dom, Osiedle, Mieszkanie* 9 (1931).
19 Giedion 1967 (see note 6), p. 271.

20 Rosalind E. Krauss, *The Originality of the Avant-Garde and Other Modernist Myths* (Cambridge, 1985), pp. 18–21.

21 Oswald Spengler, *The Decline of the West*, trans. Charles Francis Atkinson (London, 1934), vol. 2, pp. 99, 107.

22 Cembrzyńska 2012 (see note 14), p. 66. The entire paragraph refers to two books that are fundamental from this point of view: Michał Paweł Markowski, *Efekt inskrypcji: Jacques Derrida i literatura* (The effect of inscription: Jacques Derrida and literature), (Bydgoszcz, 1997), pp. 306–07; Mark Wiglay, *The Architecture of Deconstruction: Derrida's Haunt* (Cambridge, MA and London, 1993), pp. 31–32.

23 Jacques Derrida, *The Truth in Painting,* trans. Geoff Bennington and Ian McLeod (Chicago, 1987), p. 122.

24 Hito Steyerl, "Dziura Babel" (The (W)hole of Babel), *Magazyn sztuki* 23 (1999).

25 Umberto Eco, "Postscript," in *The Name of the Rose,* trans. William Weaver (New York, 1984), p. 564.

26 Ibid., pp. 564–65.

27 Gilles Deleuze and Félix Guattari, A *Thousand Palteaus: Capitalism and Schizophrenia,* trans. Brian Massumi (London, 2004), pp. 13–15.

28 Hal Foster, *The Return of the Real: The Avant-Garde at the End of the Century* (Cambridge, 1996), p. 146.

29 Oliver Marchart, *Post-Foundational Political Thought: Political Difference in Nancy, Lefort, Badiou and Laclau* (Edinburgh, 2007), p. 155.

30 Boris Buden, *Zone des Übergangs: vom Ende des Postkommunismus* (Frankfurt am Main, 2009), p. 83.

Source Notes and Photo Credits

[1] Mieczysław Choynowski, *America,* 1932. Photomontage. Muzeum Narodowe w Warszawie (National Museum, Warsaw). [2] Drawing by Erich Kettelhut for Fritz Lang's film *Metropolis,* 1927. Deutsche Kinemathek Museum für Film und Fernsehen. [3] Lev Rudnev, Palace of Culture and Science, Warsaw, 1951–55. "Palace of Culture and Science," *Wikipedia,* created April 26, 2008, http://en.wikipedia.org/wiki/Palace_of_Culture_and_Science#media. [4] Plan for buildings around the Palace of Culture and Science, Warsaw, 2009. © Urząd m.st. Warszawy. [5] Ludwig Mies van der Rohe, 860–880 Lake Shore Drive, Chicago, Illinois, 1949–51. Photograph by William Zbaren. © 2014 ProLitteris, Zurich. [6] Sergey Chekhonin, illustration for the Anatoly Lunacharsky play *Faust and the City,* Petrograd, 1918. "FAUST I GOROD (*Faust and the City*)," http://lunacharsky.newgod.su/lib/dramaticheskie-proizvedenia/faust-i-gorod. [7] Production facilities (a locomotive factory) in the Sormovsky district of Nizhny Novgorod, USSR, 1922. Photographer unknown. "Istoriya Rossii (History of Russia)," http://www.history-at-russia.ru/foto-30-x-godov-xx-veka. [8] Biomechanical laboratory of the Central Institute of Labor run by Aleksei Gastev, Moscow, 1923. Photographer unknown. "The Charnel-House: From Bauhaus to Beinhaus," http://thecharnelhouse.org/2011/12/07/the-ultra-taylorist-soviet-utopianism-of-aleksei-gastev-including-gastevs-landmark-book-how-to-work/. [9] Aleksandr Rodchenko, *Male Pyramid, Sports parade on the Red Square,* 1936. A. Rodchenko & V. Stepanova Archive. © 2014 ProLitteris, Zurich. [10] *Blok* magazine, no. 1, p. 1, 1924. Instytut Sztuki Polskiej Akademii Nauk (The Institute of Art of the Polish Academy of Sciences, Warsaw). [11] Eiffel Tower and Fountain Coutan, looking toward Trocadéro Palace, Paris Exposition, 1889. Albumen photoprint, photographer unknown. Library of Congress, LC-USZ62-102660. [12] Kazimir Malevich, *Architekton in Front of a Skyscraper* (Suprematist transformation of New York), 1924. Originally published in *Praesens* magazine, no. 1, 1926. Muzeum Sztuki (Museum of Art, Łódź). [13] Vladimir Tatlin, *Model of the Monument to the Third International,* 1920. Originally published in *Veshch. Gegenstand. Objet* magazine, nos. 1–2, p. 22, 1924. Digital Image © 2014 The Museum of Modern Art, New York/Scala, Florence. [14] El Lissitzky, *Tatlin at Work,* 1922. Collage. Plate 73 in: Sophie Lissitzky-Küppers, ed., *El Lissitzky; Life, Letters, Texts,* trans. Helene Aldwinckle and Mary Whittall (Greenwich, 1968). © G&B Fine Arts Press Verlag GmbH. [15] Ludwig Mies van der Rohe, *Friedrichstrasse Skyscraper Project, Berlin-Mitte, Germany, Exterior Perspective from North,* 1921. Charcoal and graphite on brown paper, mounted on board, 173.4 x 121.9 cm. Mies van der Rohe Archive, gift of the architect. Acc. no.: 1005.1965. Digital image © The Museum of Modern Art, New York/ Scala, Florence. © 2014 ProLitteris, Zurich. [16] Ludwig Mies van der Rohe, *Glass Skyscraper Project, View of Lost Model, No Intended Site Known,* 1922.

Airbrushed gelatin silver print, 22.9 x 15.9 cm. Mies Van der Rohe Archive, gift of the architect. Acc. no.: MMA9208. Digital image © The Museum of Modern Art, New York/Scala, Florence. © 2014 ProLitteris, Zurich. [17] Ludwig Mies van der Rohe, 860–880 Lake Shore Drive, Chicago, Illinois, 1949–51. Photograph © Gunny Harboe, Harboe Architects. © 2014 ProLitteris, Zurich. [18] Skidmore, Owings and Merrill, Rondo 1 Office Tower, Warsaw, 2003–06. [19] Daniel Libeskind, Złota 44 Tower, Warsaw, 2008–13. Rendering by Aldinger+Wolf. [20] Ludwig Mies van der Rohe, 860–880 Lake Shore Drive, Chicago, Illinois, 1949–51. Photograph by William Zbaren. © 2014 ProLitteris, Zurich. [21] Apartment blocks, rhythm of prefabricated panels and windows, 1970s. Photographer unknown. "FILOSSSOGRAFIA," May 18, 2008, http://www.filosss.fotolog.pl/5,2008,archiwum.html. [22] Construction of apartment blocks from prefabricated panels, 1950s. Photographer unknown. "Co dalej z wielką płytą?" *Co za Dzień,* August 8, 2012, http://www.cozadzien.pl/wiadomosci/radom/11432.html. [23] Warsaw apartment blocks, 1970s. Photographer unknown. "Dlaczego blok z wielkiej płyty to zła inwestycja?" *iFin24* (blog), March 24, 2010, http://blogi.ifin24.pl/leszek-maruszczyk/2010/03/24/dlaczego-blok-z-wielkiej-plyty-to-zla-inwestycja/. [24] Helena and Szymon Syrkus, House in Saska Kepa, Warsaw, 1937. Photographer unknown. Andrzej Niezabietowski, "Polish avant-garde architecture of 1918-39 in relation to contemporary trends in Europe," *ELISAVA,* 1995, http://tdd.elisava.net/coleccion/12/niezabietowski-en. [25] Ferdinand Dutert, Galerie des machines, Paris Exposition, 1889. Photographer unknown. "Favourite Works of Architecture," andymalanowski.com, last modified December 28, 2005, http://www.andymalanowski.com/Favorites/favorites.htm. [26] Aleksandr Rodchenko, *Shuchov Transmission Tower,* 1929. A. Rodchenko & V. Stepanova Archive. © 2014 ProLitteris, Zurich. [27] Henryk Stażewski, *Textural Composition,* 1930–31. Oil on canvas, 70 x 80 cm. Muzeum Sztuki (Museum of Art, Łódź). [28] Kazimierz Podsądecki, *City, Mill of Life,* 1929. Photomontage, 43 x 29 cm. Muzeum Sztuki (Museum of Art, Łódź). [29] "Building the Tower of Babel," *Egerton Genesis Picture Book,* circa 1360. © The British Library Board, Egerton 1894, f5.v. [30] Pieter Bruegel the Elder, *Tower of Babel,* 1563. Oil on canvas, 114 x 155 cm. Kunsthistorisches Museum, Vienna. © De Agostini/ The British Library Board, 11064662. [31] Cornelis Anthonisz, *Fall of the Tower of Babel*, 1549. Etching, 32.2 x 37.8 cm. Inv. 461-22. © bpk/ Kupferstichkabinett, SMB/ Volker-H. Schneider. [32] Yang Yongliang, *Heavenly City—05, 2008.* Collection Philippe Gilbert. Courtesy of Galerie Paris-Beijing. [33] Scene from the underground labyrinth in the film *The Third Man,* directed by Carol Reed, screenplay by Graham Greene, filmed in 1948 in the ruins of Vienna, and released in 1949. © 1949 STUDIOCANAL Films Ltd. [34] Rhizome. Photographer unknown. "Ogrodniczo Działkowe Forum," photograph posted April 3, 2012, http://forumogrodnicze.info/viewtopic.php?f=32&t=10342&start=364.

Tower

New York, September/October 2014
Photographs by Genevieve Hanson and Gustav Hoiland

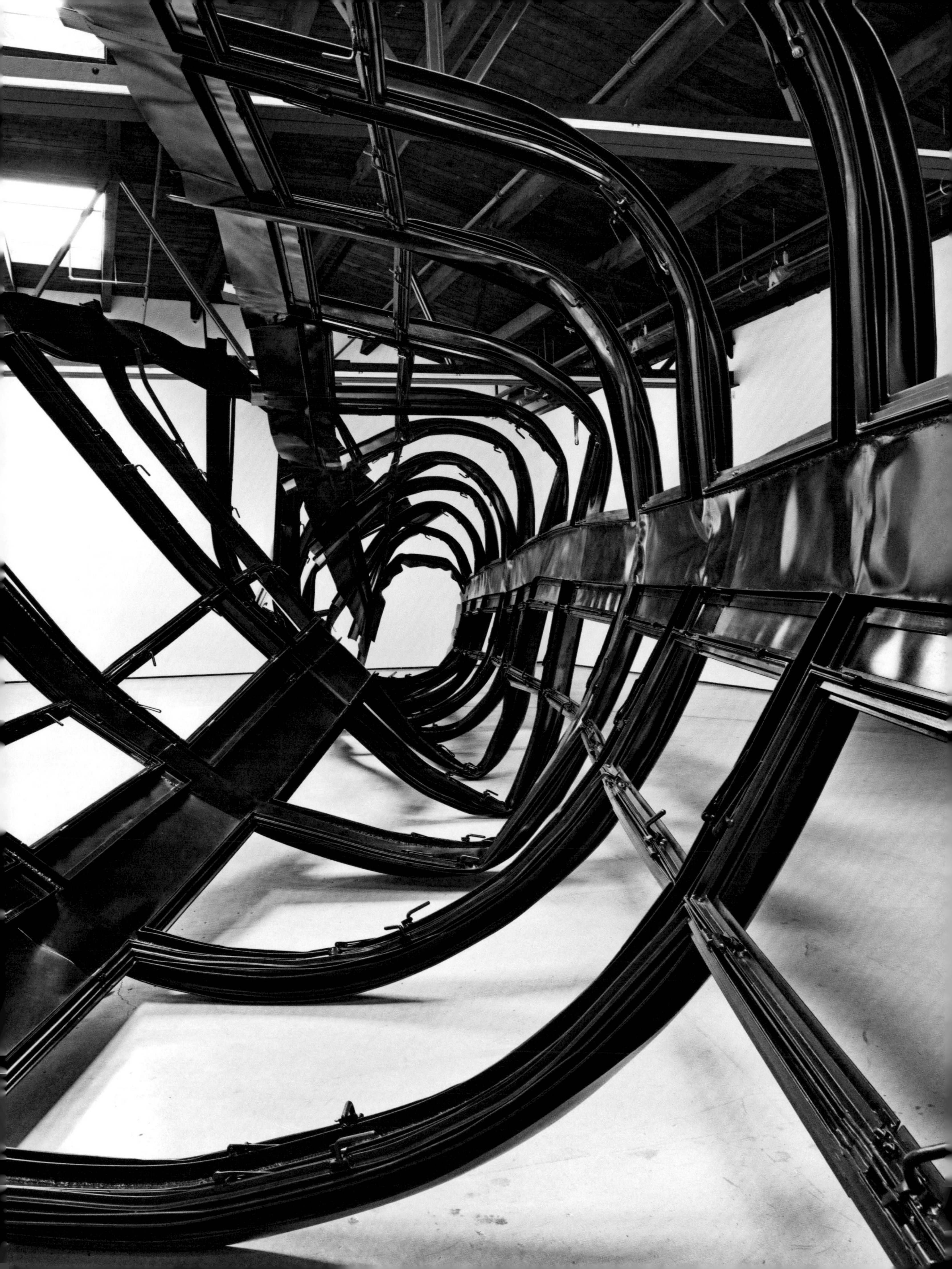

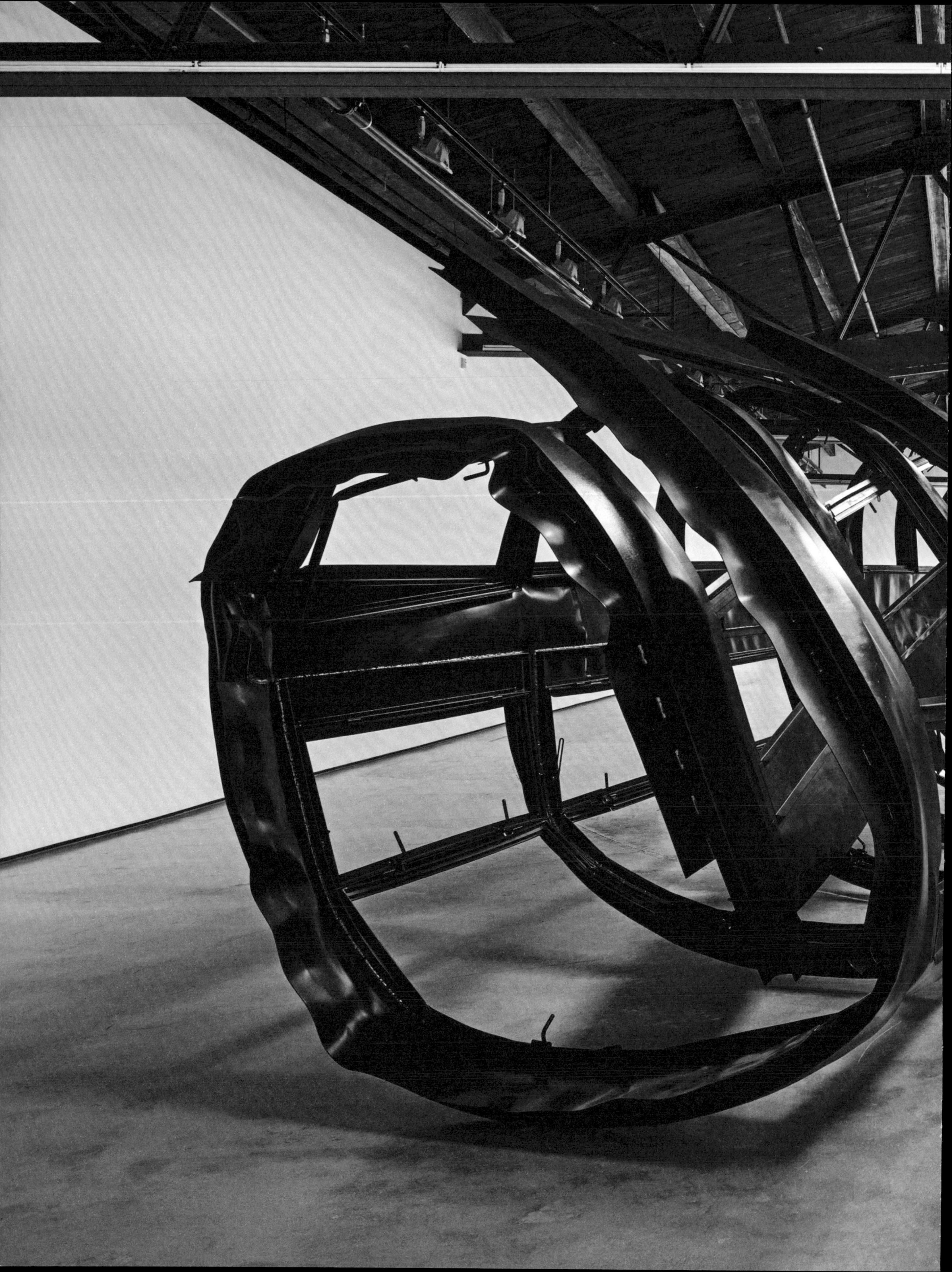

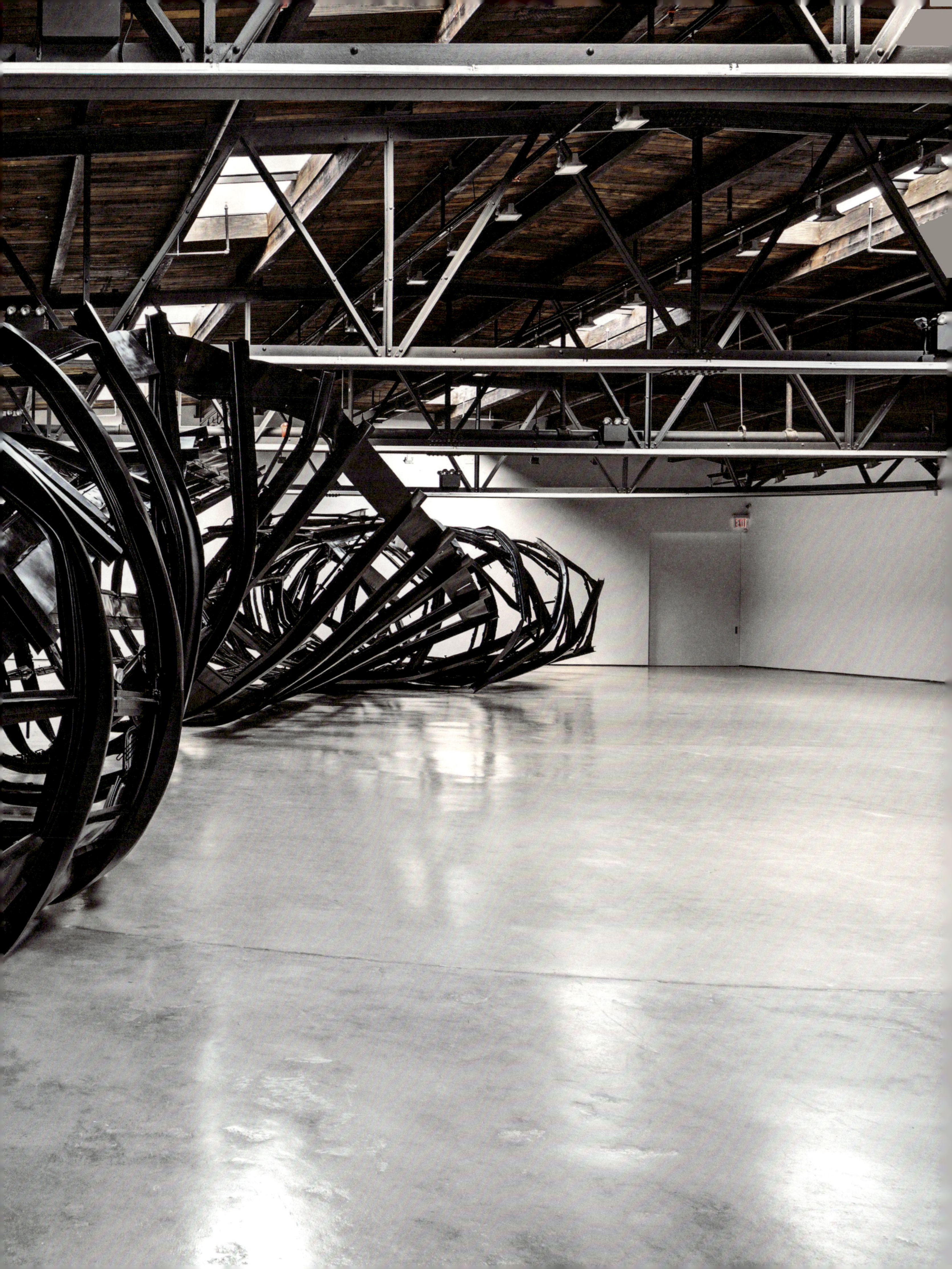

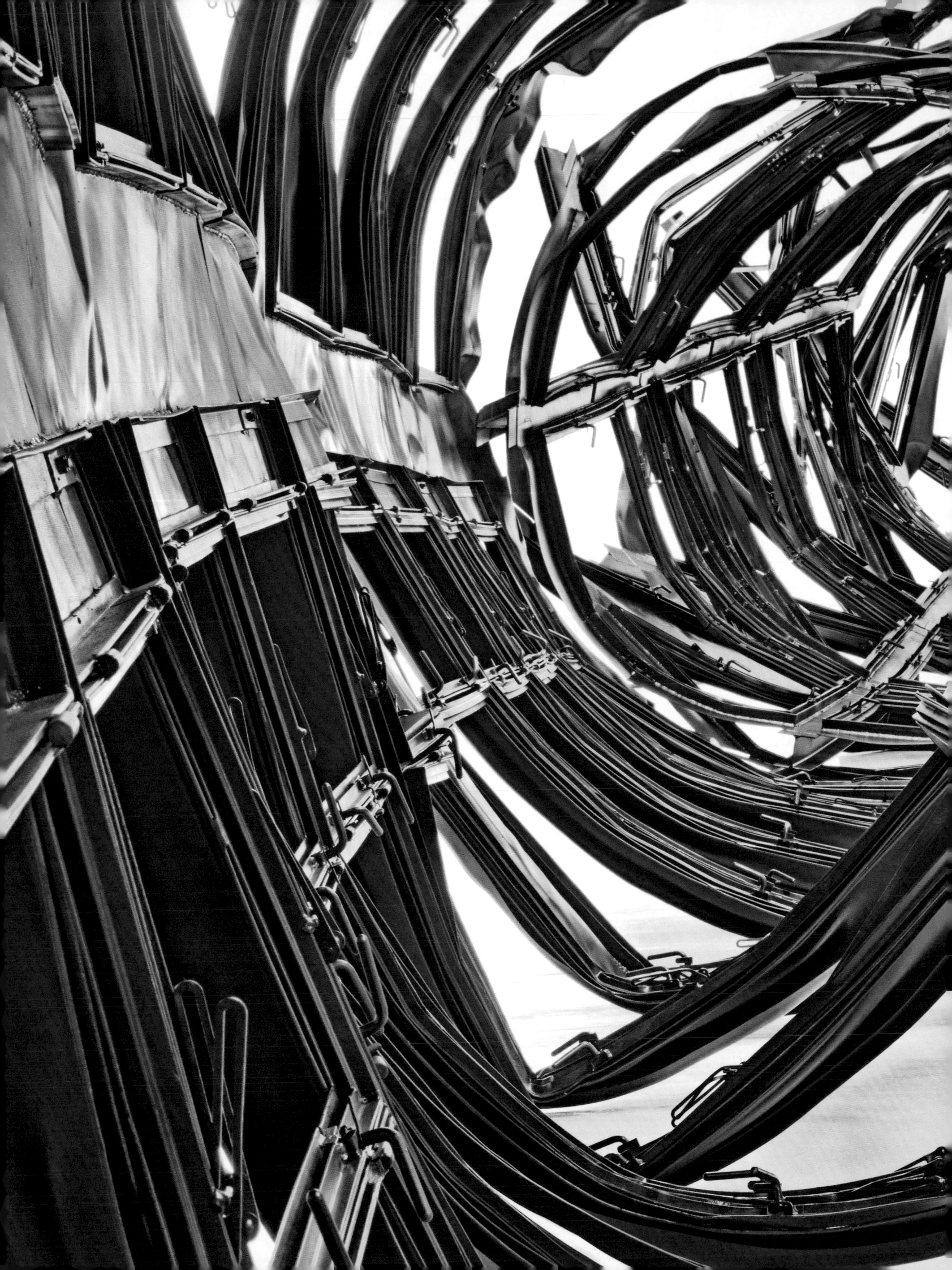

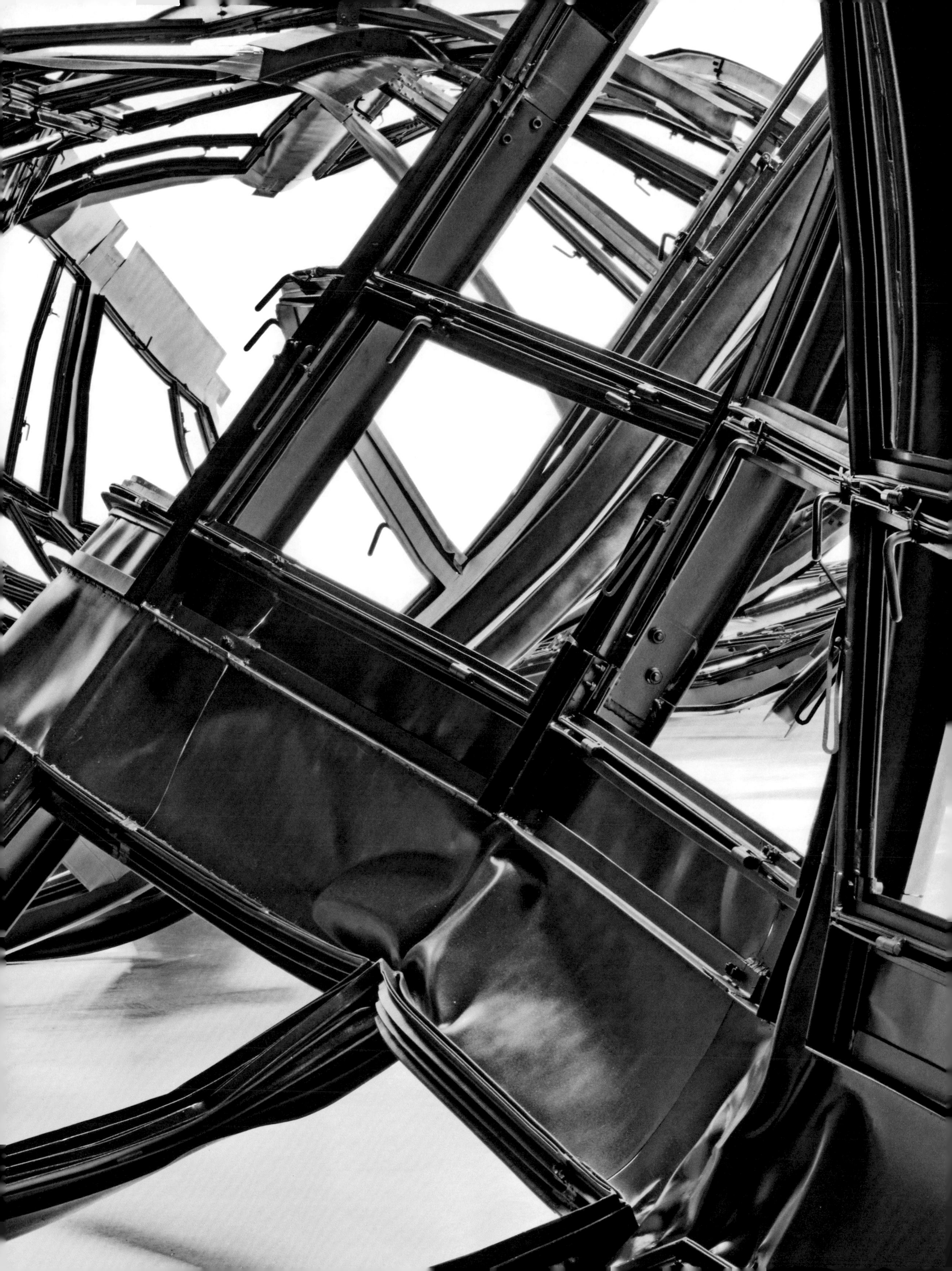

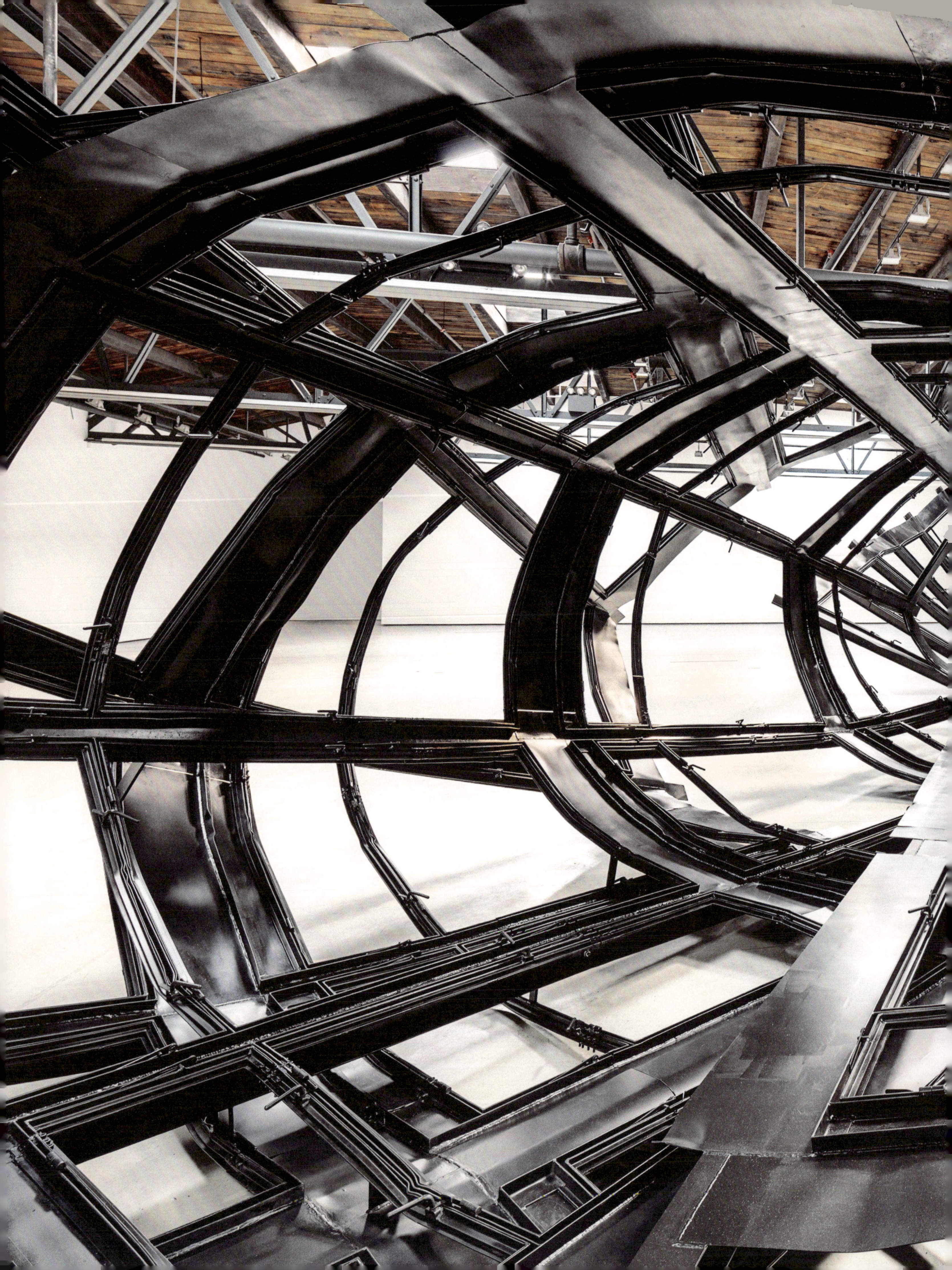

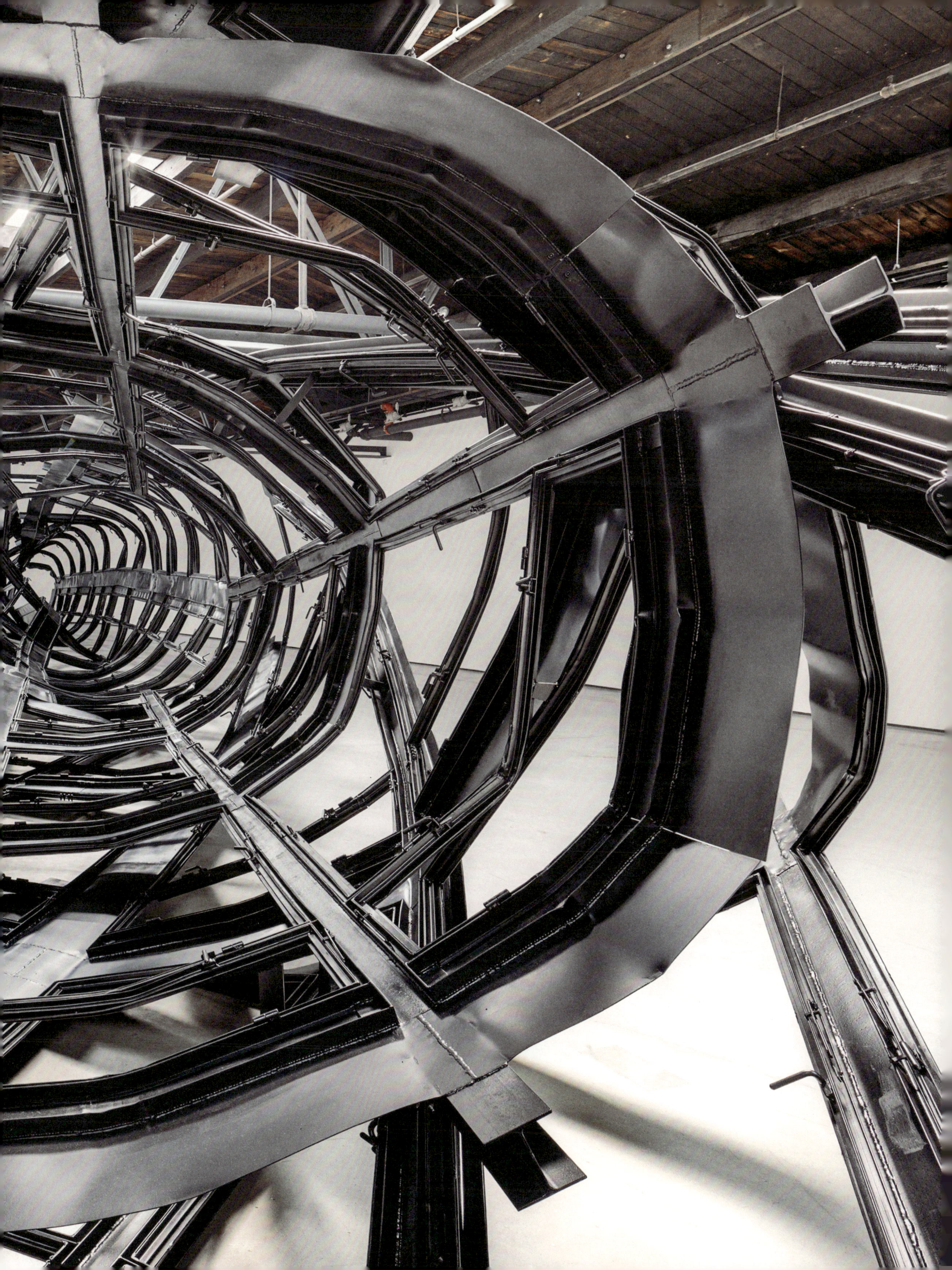

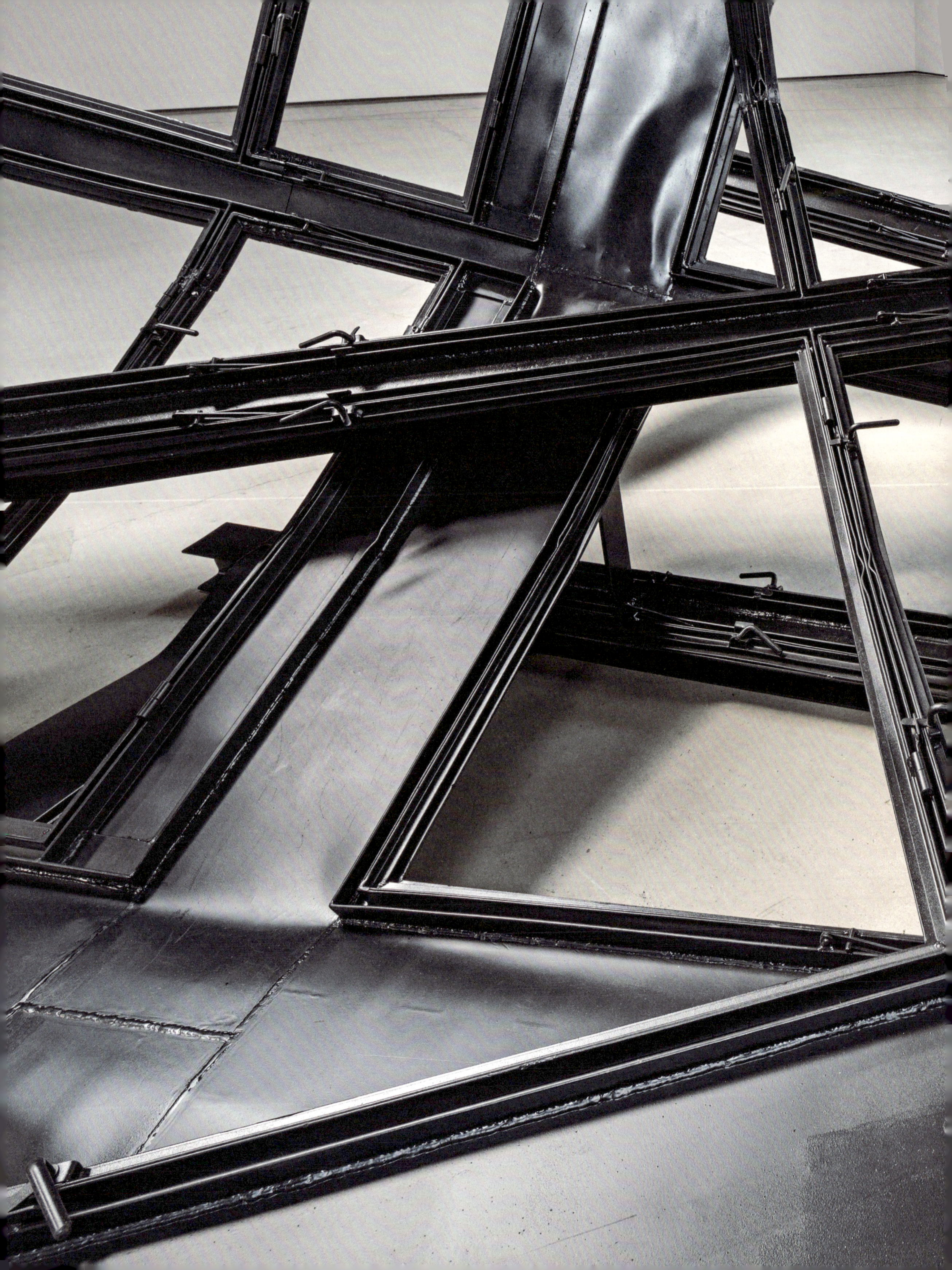

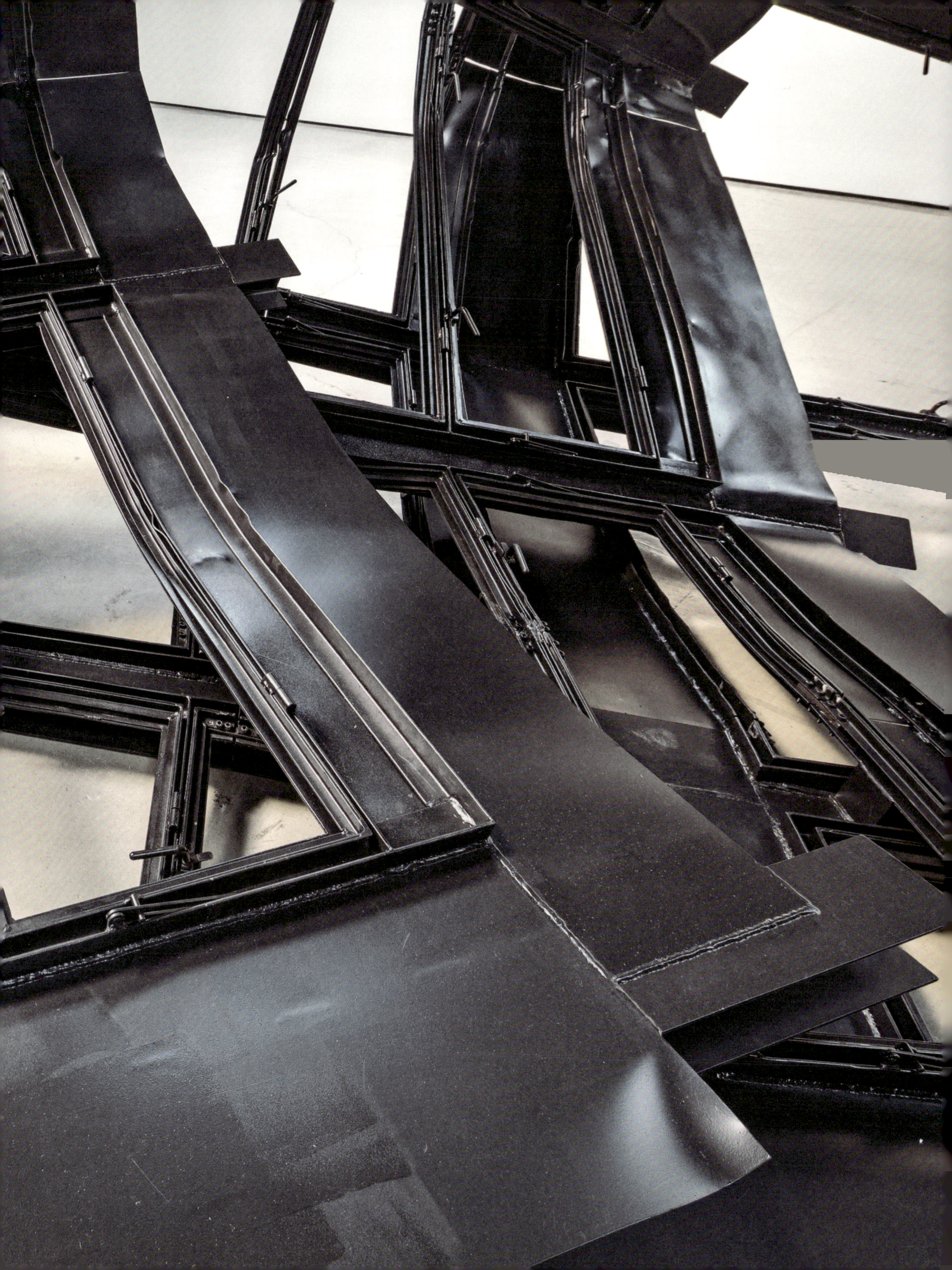

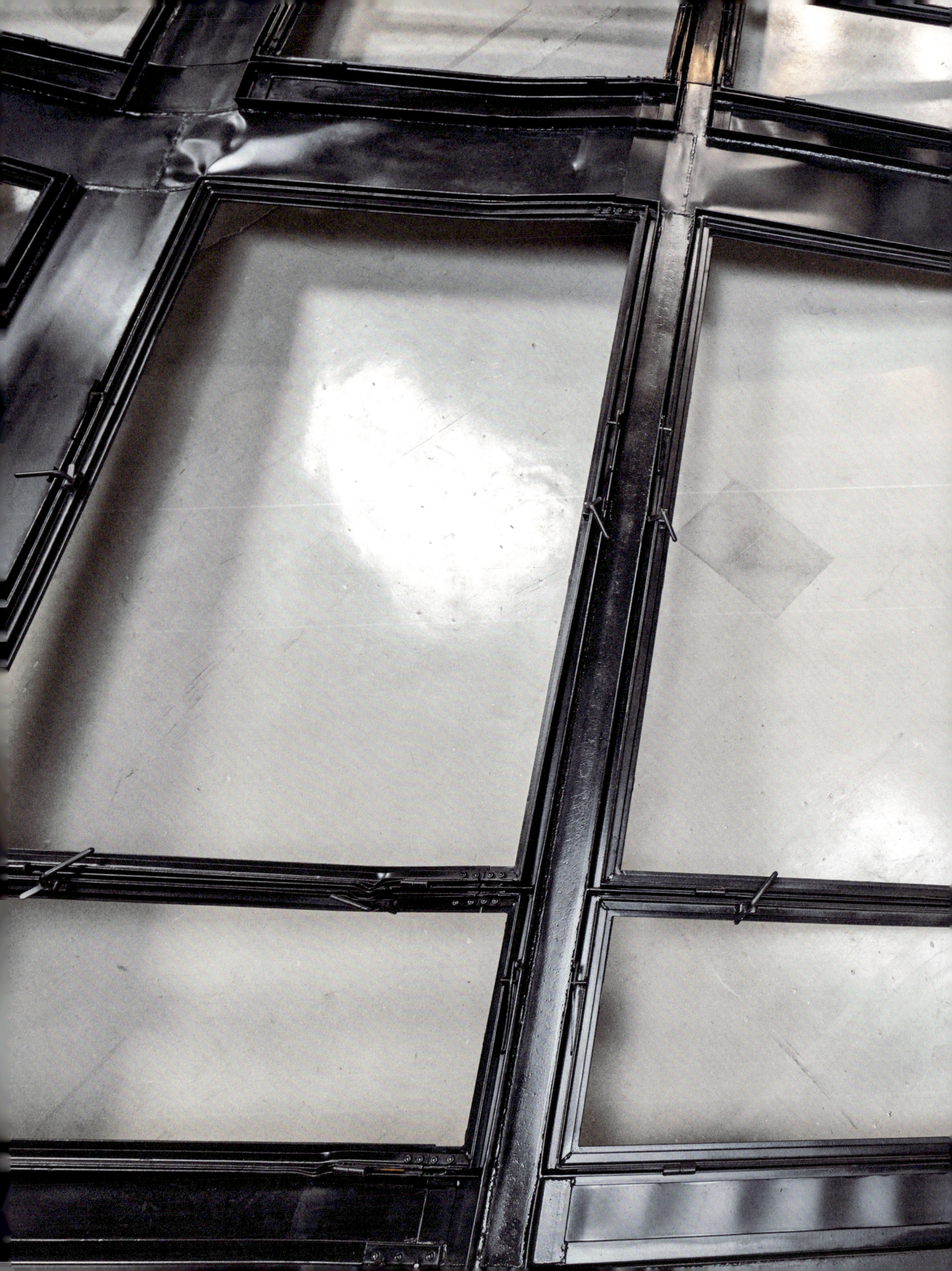

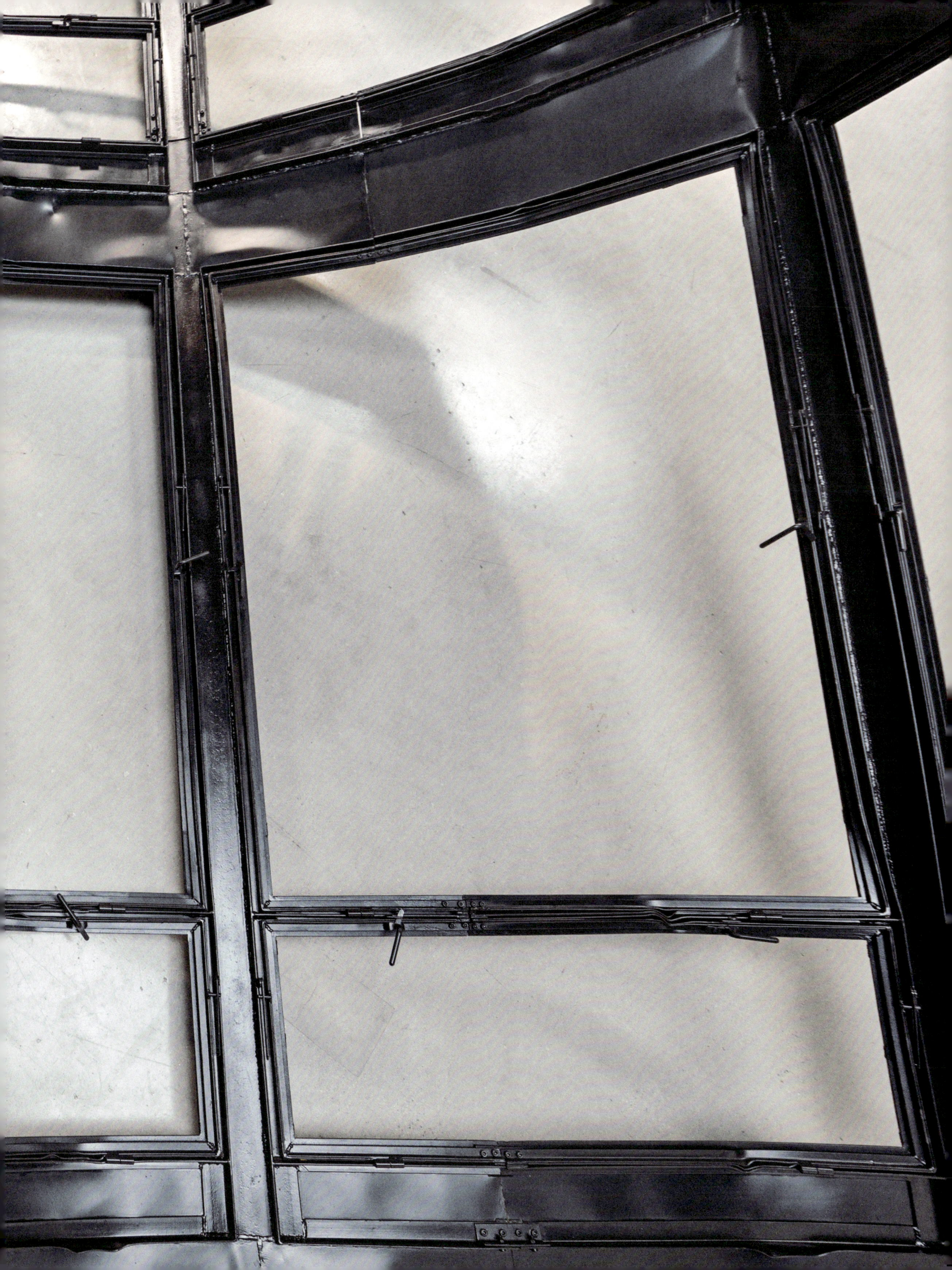

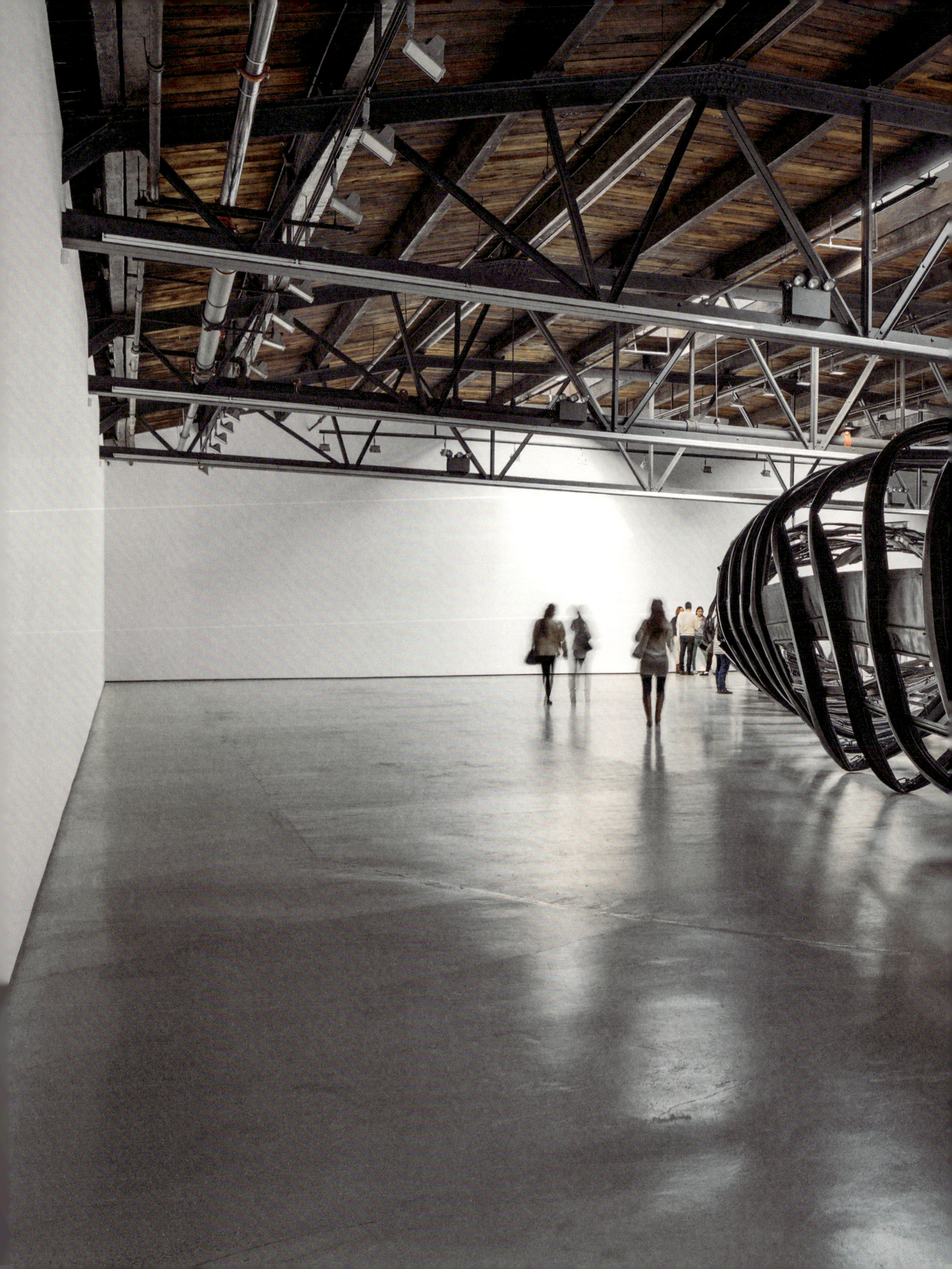

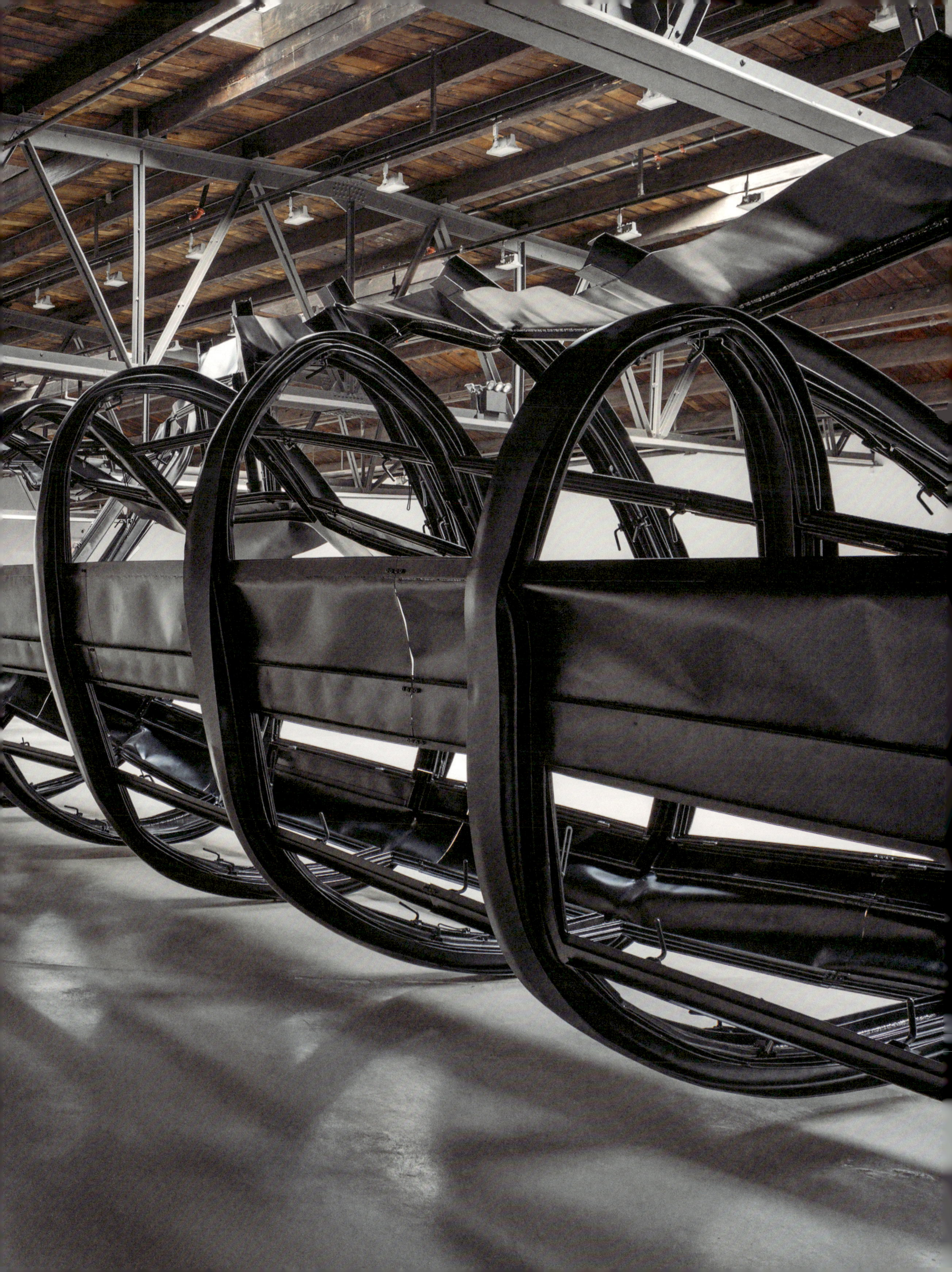

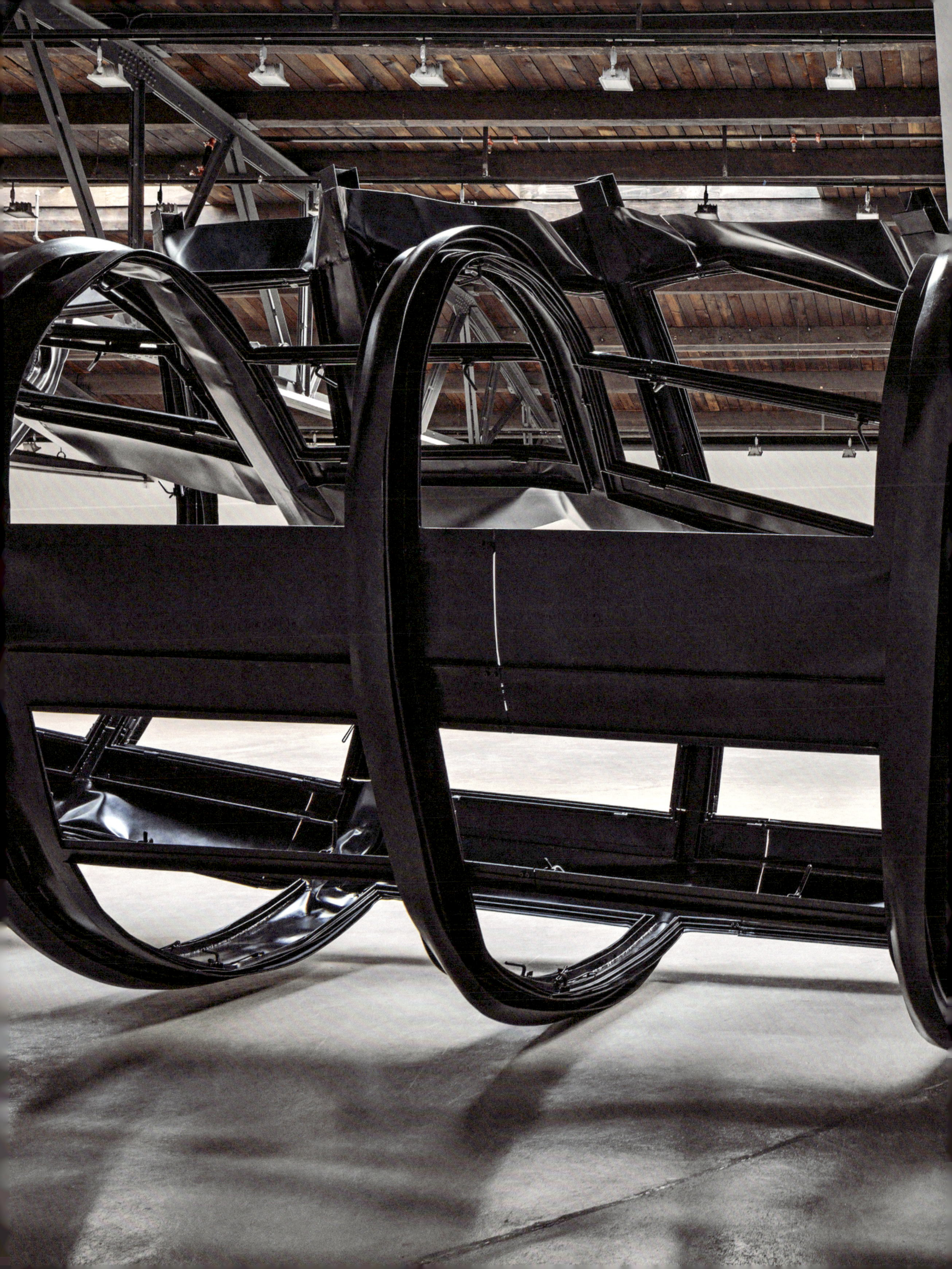

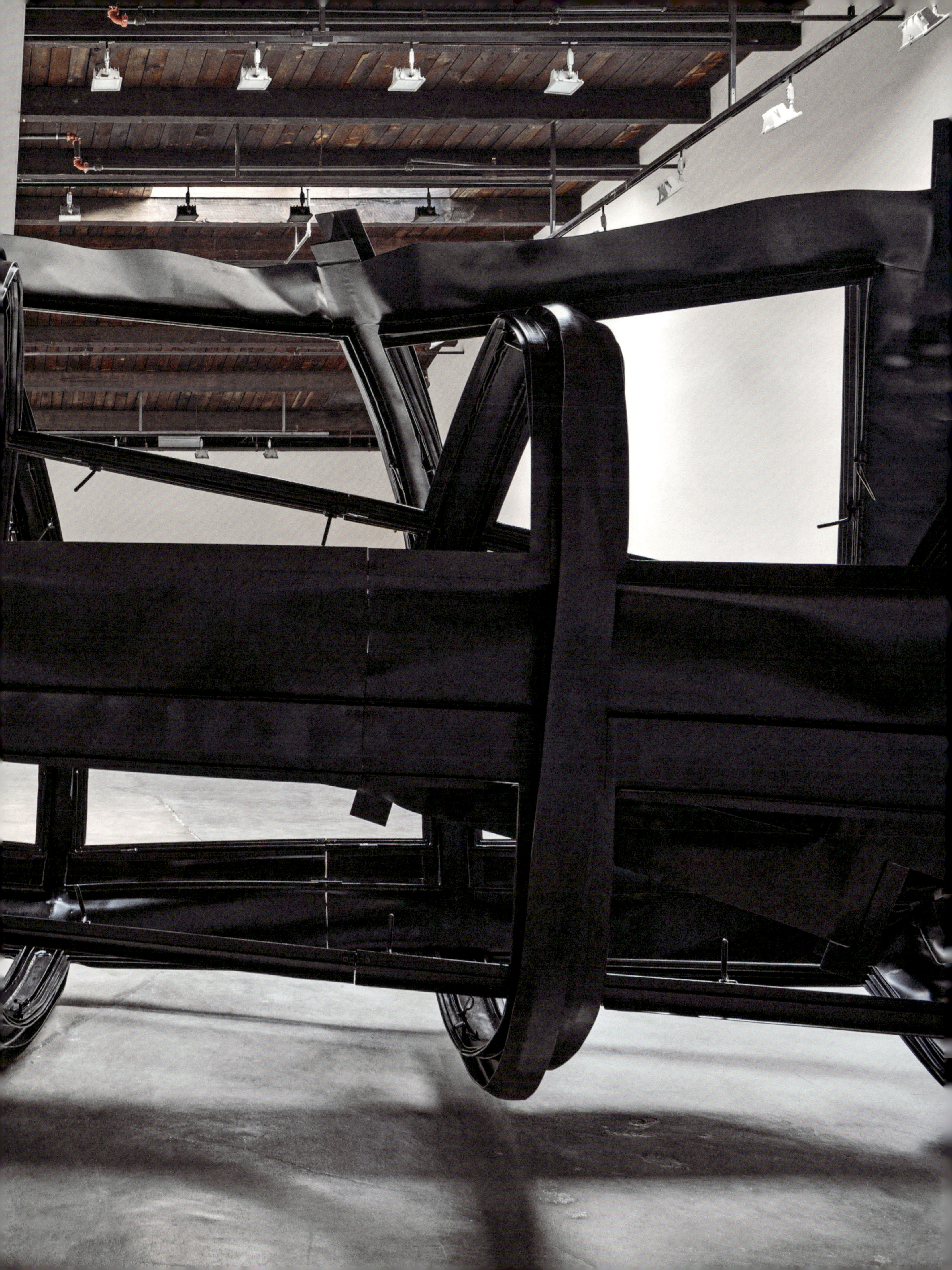

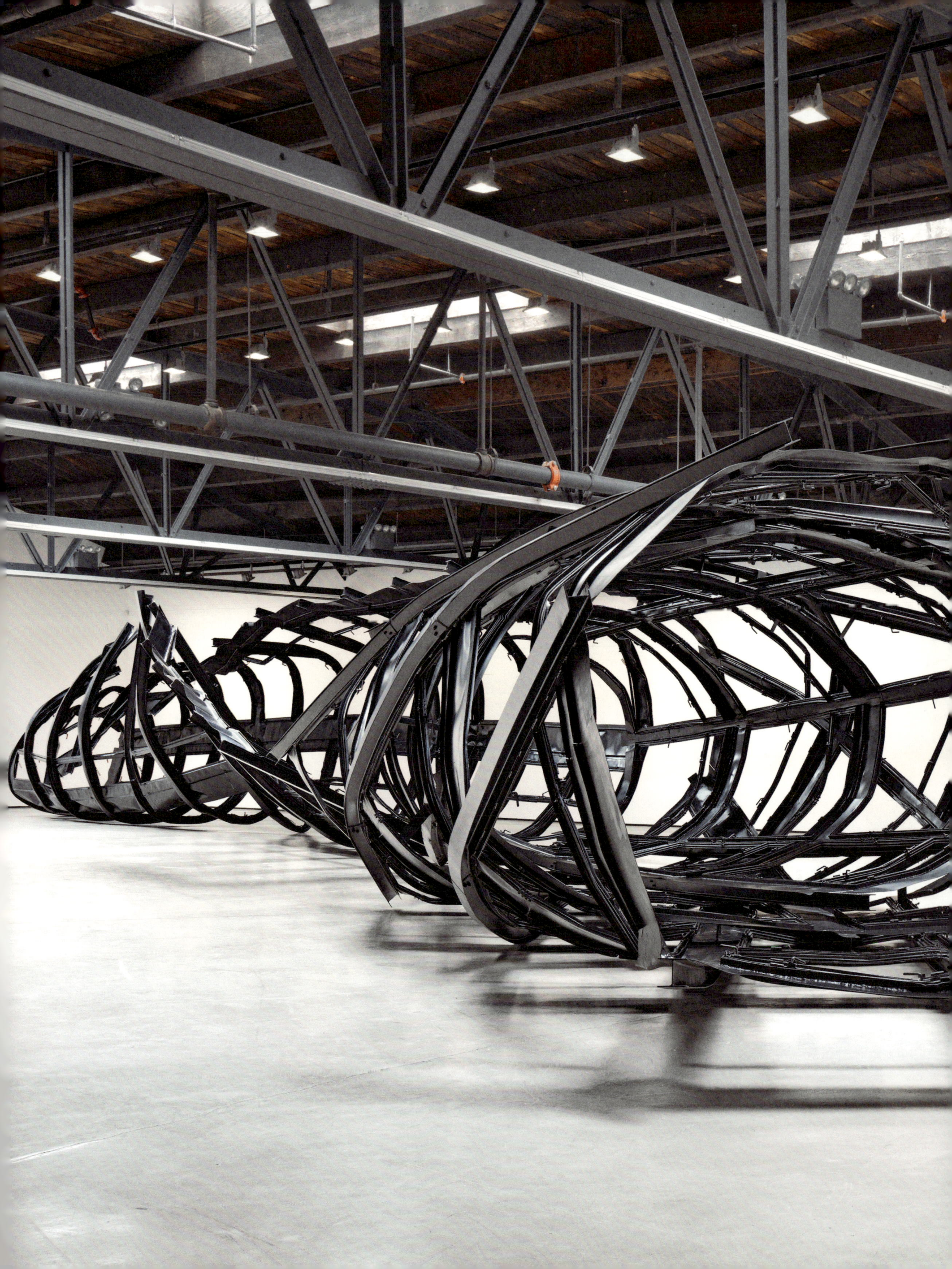

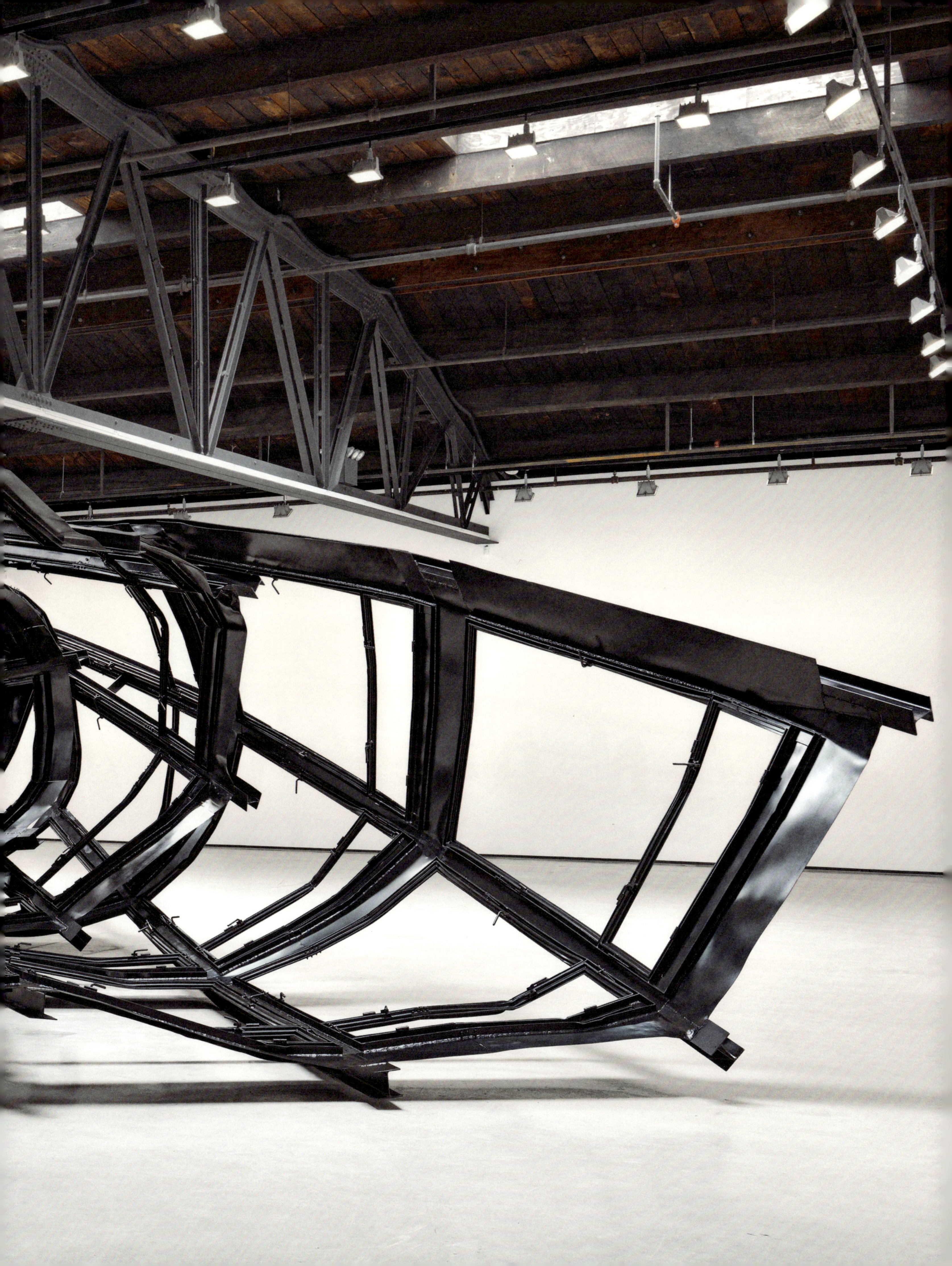

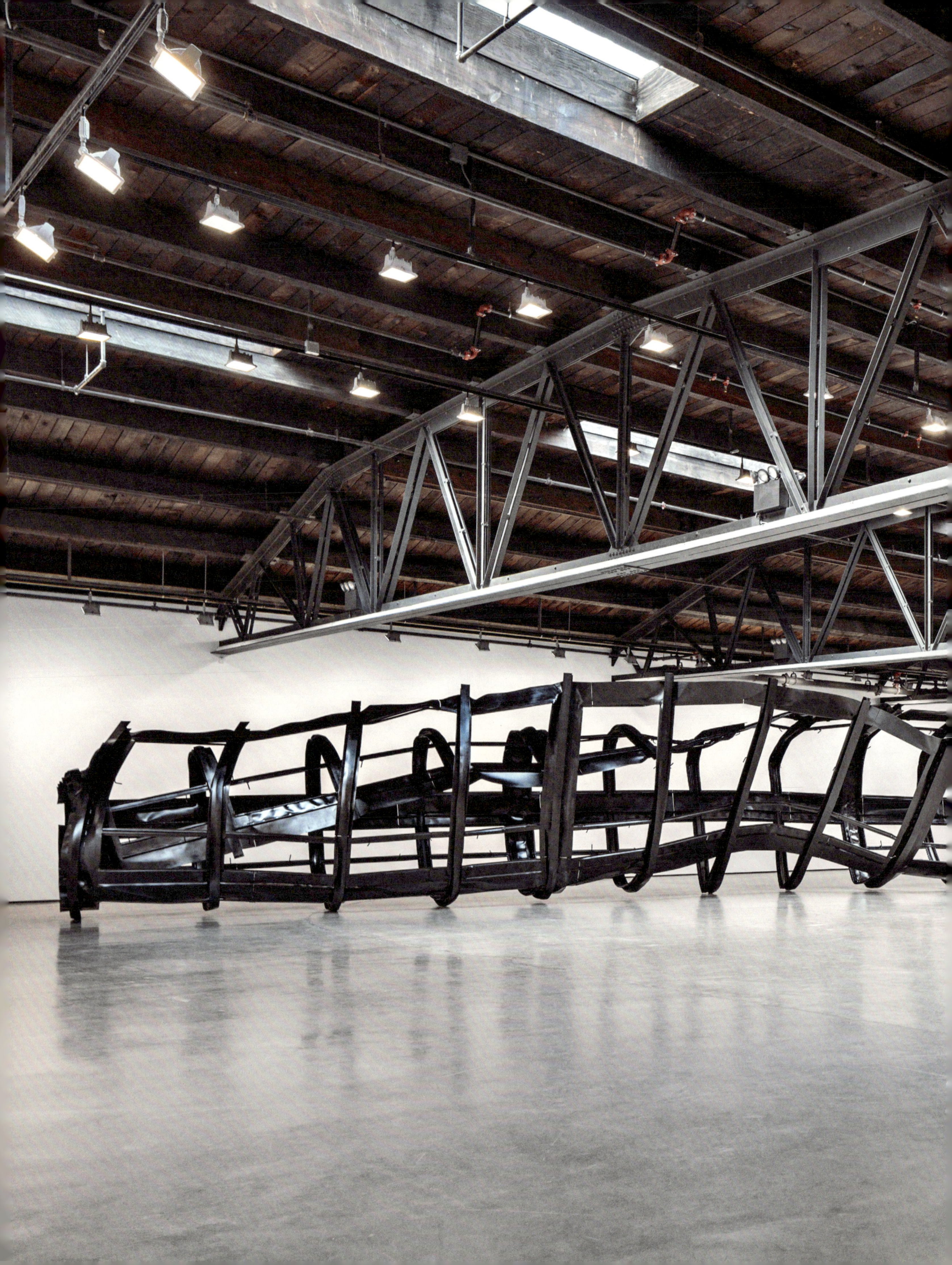

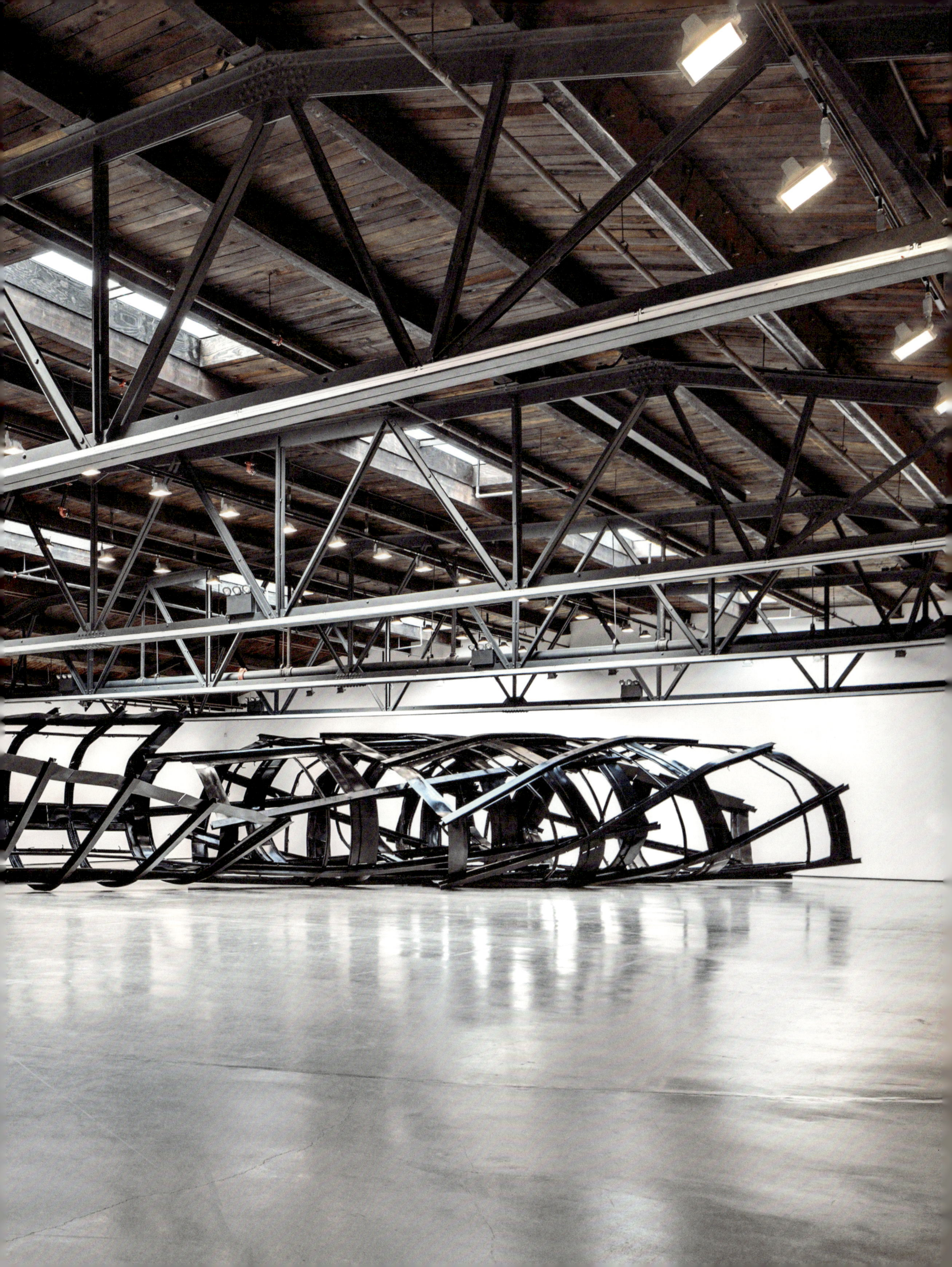

Artist Biography

Monika Sosnowska (*1972, Poland) lives and works in Warsaw. She studied at the Rijksakademie van beeldende kunsten in Amsterdam and the Academy of Fine Arts in Poznań, Poland. In addition to representing Poland at the 52nd Venice Biennale in 2007, Sosnowska has had solo exhibitions at institutions including: Serpentine Gallery, London (2004); Museum of Modern Art, New York (2006); Kunstmuseum Liechtenstein, Vaduz (2007); Schaulager, Basel (2008); Herzliya Museum of Contemporary Art, Israel (2010); K21 Ständehaus, Düsseldorf (2010); Public Art Fund, New York (2012); Aspen Art Museum, Colorado (2013); and Australian Centre for Contemporary Art, Melbourne (2013).

This book is published on the occasion of the exhibition

Monika Sosnowska Tower
September 5 – October 25, 2014

Hauser & Wirth New York
511 West 18th Street
New York, NY 10011
www.hauserwirth.com

Editorial coordination and production: Michaela Unterdörfer
Project coordination: Rowena Chiu, Stefan Zebrowski-Rubin
Copyediting: Leina González
Translation from Polish to English: Nathaniel Espino, Artur Zapałowski
Book design and typesetting: Marek Knap
Production: Nadine Schmidt, Hatje Cantz
Typeface: Maax by Editions deux-cent-cinq
Paper: Munken Lynx Rough, 120 g/m²
Color separations: Jan Scheffler, prints professional; Juliusz Sokołowski
Printing: Offsetdruckerei Karl Grammlich GmbH, Pliezhausen
Binding: Josef Spinner Grossbuchbinderei GmbH, Ottersweier

Published by
Hatje Cantz Verlag
Zeppelinstrasse 32
73760 Ostfildern
Germany
Tel. +49 711 4405-200
Fax +49 711 4405-220
www.hatjecantz.com
A Ganske Publishing Group company

Hatje Cantz books are available internationally at selected bookstores.
For more information about our distribution partners please visit
our website at www.hatjecantz.com.

ISBN 978-3-7757-3926-9
Printed in Germany

Cover: Monika Sosnowska, *Tower,* 2014 (detail)
Photo: Genevieve Hanson

Special thanks to Foksal Gallery Foundation,
ENDIK Andrzej Kaczmarczyk Poland Legionowo and his associates,
and the team at Hauser & Wirth New York.